OLD SCHOOL PHOTOGRAPHY

100 Things You Must Know to Take Fantastic Film Photos

BY KAI WONG

CHRONICLE CHROMA

CONTENTS

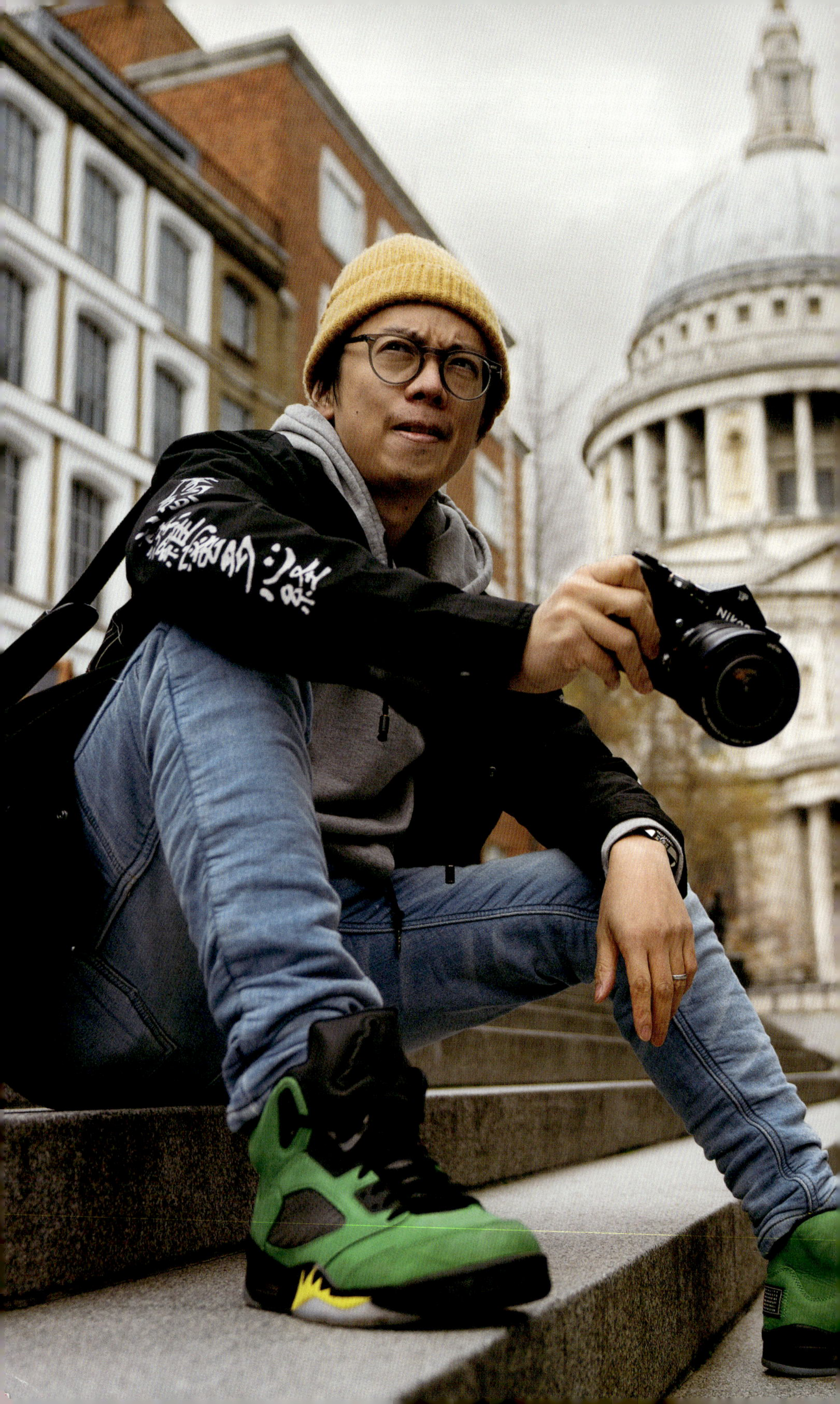

HOW TO STOP WORRYING AND LOVE FILM

For those familiar with my work, you might know me as the Asian YouTube dude with an English accent who likes to talk about the latest and greatest digital photography gear, but what you may not know is that my fondness for all things photography-related started with a 35 mm film camera.

When I was a kid, everyone shot with film cameras, because that was the only option. When I was a big kid learning photography in university, digital was an option but beyond my means as a penny-pinching student. It wasn't just the money (or lack thereof) that made me choose film, though, because, to me, film was the very essence of photography. The unique process of shooting film felt like such an essential part of the creation of the image and what made photography fun, engaging, challenging, and rewarding—that's what made me gravitate toward film.

Now that I'm a fully-fledged grown-up, people can take photos, upload them, and receive glowing praise from someone across the planet, all on the same device. In the age of Instagram, film photography seems somewhat antiquated. Surely there is no place for film in photography today? Well, you'd be wrong to think so, because the future of film is looking quite bright.

Kodak has reintroduced its beloved Ektachrome film, and on top of that, Fujifilm started producing monochrome black-and-white film again, a year after stopping production of it. Film is going through a sort of renaissance right now, and the reason for bringing film back from the dead isn't because of a handful of old-school film users buying a few rolls of film to scratch a nostalgic itch. Rather, a whole new generation of photographers is flocking to film.

I still love film photography, which is why I love the fact that film is being appreciated and explored by an entirely new crowd of photography enthusiasts. That is why I'm making this book: to share my passion for analog; to help anyone eager to get started with film photography; and most importantly, to develop your curiosity into a full-blown obsession.

These pages are a collection of one hundred tips that I've picked up and learnt over the years from taking photos, studying the works of some fantastic photographers, and meeting many amazing people in the community—all translated into a language that I would want to read. This is not your typical, technical, how-to photography manual. It is a book that will help you figure out how to use the gear, and to get you thinking about how to get creative and take fantastic photos—with all the usual, dull, geeky bits edited out. Learning photography shouldn't be so rigid and uptight; it should be about getting out there, taking photos, and enjoying the process.

Modern film photography should also be about bringing together a global community of like-minded individuals who share that same passion for film. So I want to take this fantastic opportunity to celebrate and share some of the inspiring images, photographers, and knowledgable experts that make being part of this film-photography family so enjoyable.

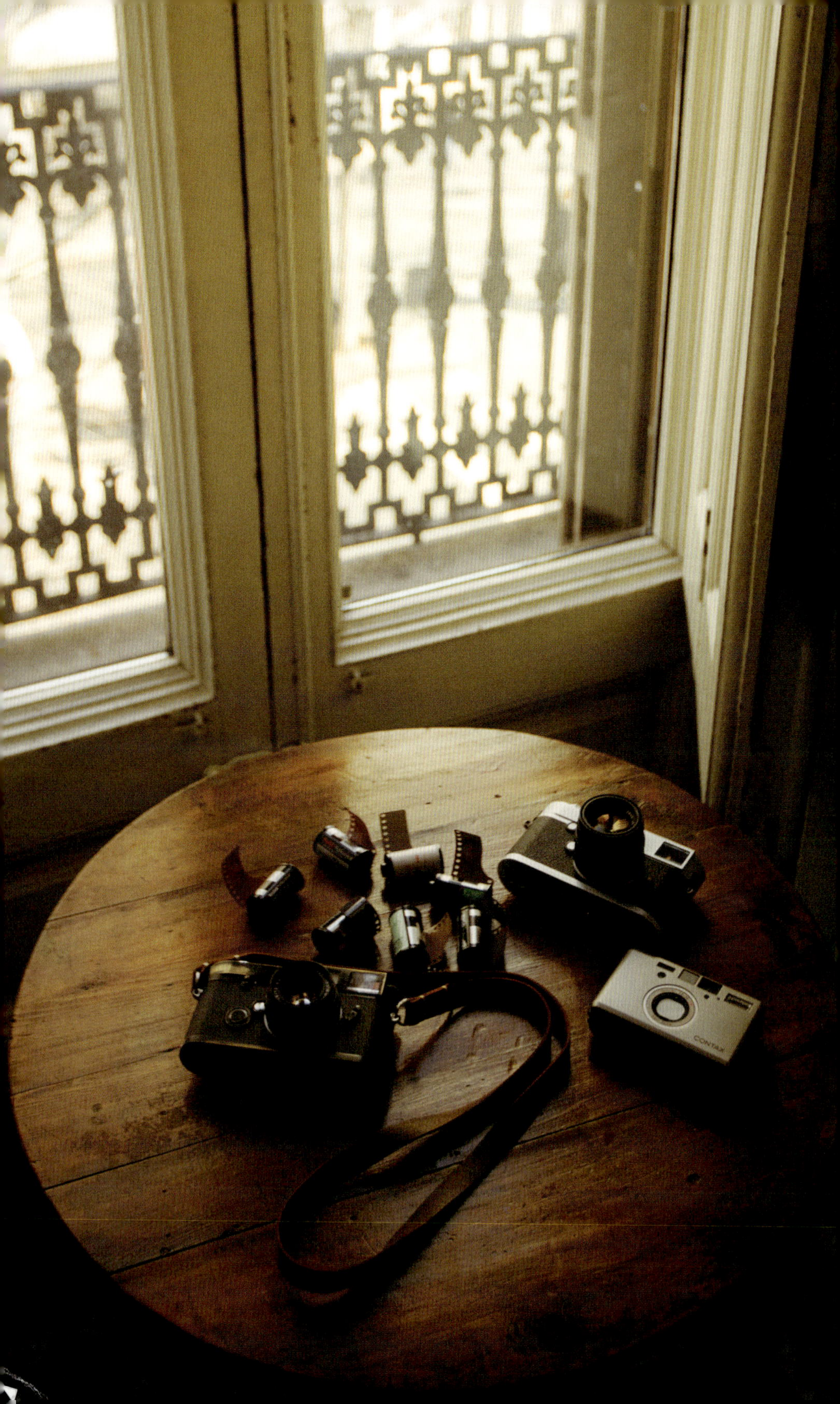
CONTAX

#1

35 MM: THE EASIEST WAY TO GET STARTED

A 35 mm film camera is the perfect place to start because it gives you that desirable pairing of providing top-notch image quality in a perfectly formed camera body.

The film itself is neatly tucked inside a compact, light-tight metal canister. One roll of 35 mm film will give you thirty-six shots (some cameras will even eke out an extra one to three shots), which is more than adequate. It's certainly enough to allow you to go through a whole day of shooting without having to change film, and not so many that you'll start taking photos of random crap just to get that roll of film finished.

There are film formats smaller than 35 mm, and there are larger film formats. Smaller film is mostly pointless, rarer than rocking-horse poo, and nobody will bother developing it for you. Larger film will give you greater detail, but the cameras and lenses are larger, heavier, and clunkier. Thirty-five millimetre film is simply the best way to start shooting film, and here's why:

Perfect-Size Camera

A 35 mm film camera fits perfectly in most hands: the size hits that sweet spot of being not too small that you don't know how to hold it properly, and not too large that it feels like you're using a toaster to take photos. Most people will be happy to carry a 35 mm camera around their neck all day, but only a sadist would enjoy punishing their neck with the weight of a film camera larger than 35 mm format, like a Pentax 67 or Mamiya RZ67.

Photography becomes a tedious task when your camera is weighing you down like a ball and chain. Ideally, you need a camera light enough to allow you to do more, to see more things, and to ultimately take more photos.

Take Your Pick

The only problem with choosing a 35 mm film camera is that there's so much to choose from: you can get plastic toy cameras that take "artistic" lo-fi photos; professional cameras made for photojournalists; underwater cameras; disposable cameras; panoramic cameras; and cameras that will fit in your jeans pockets. There are 35 mm cameras suited for practically every genre of photography, and there's something for every kind of budget, too. You can get one for as little as thirty dollars, or you can empty your life-savings accounts to get a three-million-dollar Leica 0 if that tickles your fancy.

Ease of Use

It's not like medium-format cameras are complex devices; after all, they have pretty much the same basic buttons and knobs you'd find on any other camera. It's just that using a 35 mm camera is a much smoother process, from taking photos to loading the film.

You can remove the film from its packaging, load it in the camera, and have it ready to shoot using just one hand—blindfolded. With medium format, it's definitely a two-handed process.

Cheaper and More Convenient to Develop

Once you've finished a roll of 35 mm film, you can take it to a supermarket or drug store to process. Try doing that with medium format and you might get some funny looks.

Thirty-five millimetre negative film is the cheapest and quickest way of turning your undeveloped film into prints or scans. Not only will every film lab worth calling a film lab develop it without any issues, they might even offer a one-hour service.

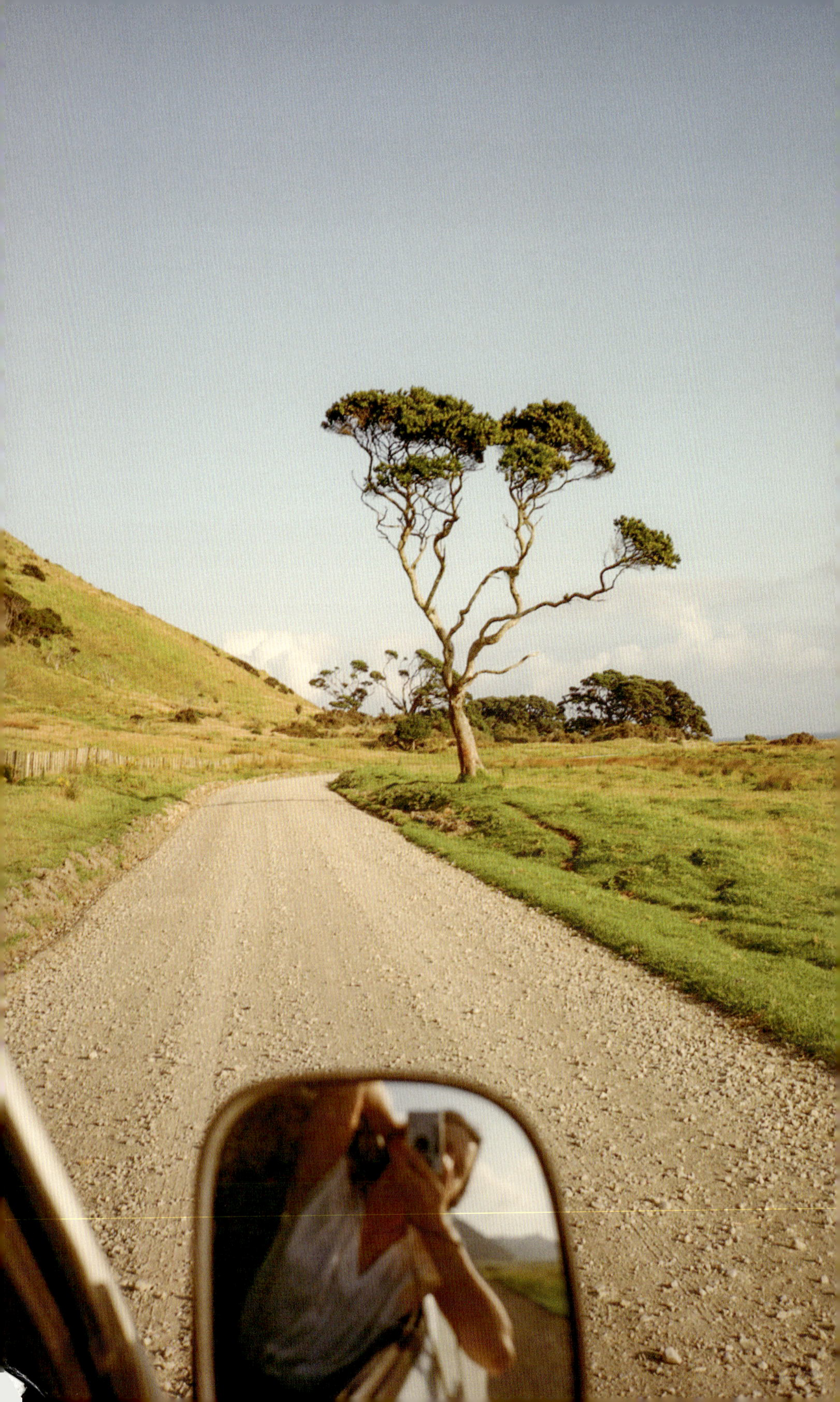

#2
COMPACT CAMERAS: IT'S WHAT YOU DO WITH IT THAT COUNTS

In order to take some flippin' fantastic film photos, you'll need a capable camera. But capable doesn't necessarily mean the beefiest, most feature-laden camera, and compact cameras are proof that the best things really do come in small packages.

You'll most likely want to get out there and start taking photos, not stay cooped up indoors figuring out how to use your fancy-pants camera. With a compact camera, you're doing away with the unnecessary bells and whistles of a more sophisticated camera that would add more fuss and faff to the photo-taking process.

Compact cameras are characterised by their small shape and fixed lens; in operation they are quick and convenient to switch on and get the shot. A lot of them have some form of automation, whether it be autofocus and/or auto-exposure, so they aren't best suited for those who love tinkering around with settings. But that does make them fabulous cameras for simplifying the process of capturing that fleeting moment.

Legendary photographer Daido Moriyama was known for favouring a 35 mm film compact (Ricoh GR1) for his gritty, black-and-white, street photos in Tokyo. With street photography, less is more; it's more important to have a discreet little camera that will get the shot quickly and stealthily.

The svelte size of a compact is not only a blessing for your bag (and back) but its diminutive size allows you to palm it, fingers on the buttons, ready to switch on and snap. They're quick, they're slick, and even if you don't want to use a compact as your primary camera, you should consider buying one just to have a camera to take with you all the time. After all, any time you don't have your camera, you're potentially missing out on a number of amazing photos.

The good news is that there's plenty to choose from. The bad news is that due to the popularity of some models, prices remain pretty firm—to the point that it might seem unreasonable to pay that much for something merely for its small size.

You can also get manual-focus, manual-exposure, compact cameras, but you'd be better off going fully automatic to experience the true benefits of shooting with a compact camera.

A really good camera doesn't always mean the one that has the most impressive specs.

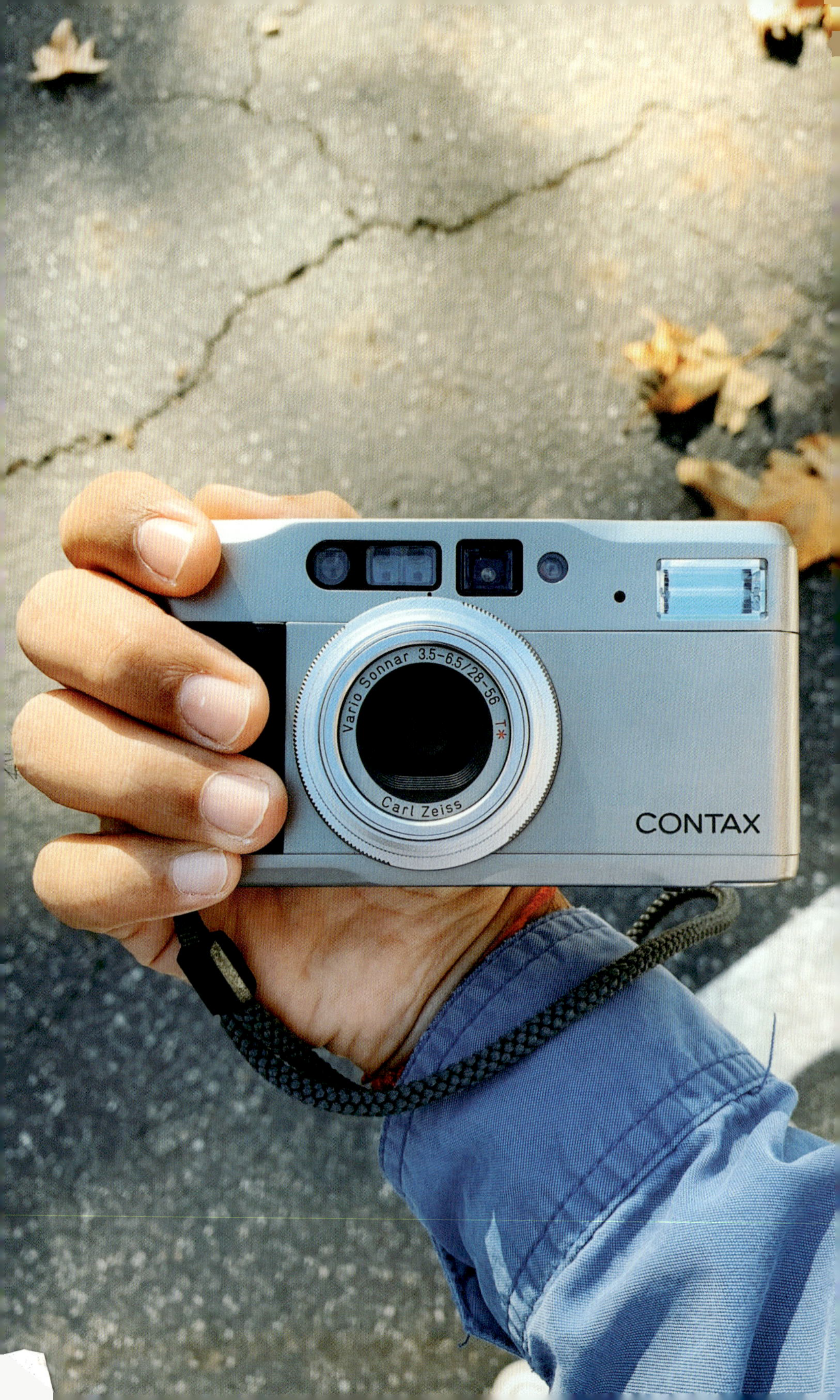
Vario Sonnar 3.5-6.5/28-56 T*
Carl Zeiss
CONTAX

#3 GREATEST COMPACT CAMERAS EVER MADE

If I could spend your money, I'd splash the cash on one (or all) of these superb compacts:

Yashica T2-T5

It looks crap; takes sweet photos. The T2-T5 series of compacts are a stonking set of compact cameras suited for those on a shoestring budget—or even for those who can afford a cupboard full of shoestrings. After all, the cost of gear has no correlation to the quality of the images a camera can produce.

Save those pennies and savour the tiny little Zeiss 35 mm Tessar T* f/3.5 lens that's tucked away neatly into the body of the camera, because it's a classy bit of glass that produces pleasingly sharp photos. The T3 is a little different in that it cheekily packs a slightly faster 35 mm f/2.8 lens (handy for low-light shooting) and is a tad more solidly built, so that is the one I'd recommend. But you can't go far wrong with any of them.

Olympus XA

The XA has some unique qualities that make this a must-have: although it's a compact camera, it uses a rangefinder system for manual focusing, and the aperture value can be set by you, too, allowing you to feel like you have some creative control. Even better, they're filthy cheap.

Alternatively, if you want a manual-focusing compact, then you could also check out the German-designed, Singaporean-made Rollei 35—even if it's just to see what a German-designed, Singaporean-made thing looks like.

Ricoh GR1

If you want compact, then this thing is properly compact: with a depth of just 26.5 mm (34 mm including grip), it makes many other compacts feel brick-like. Although the electronics aren't all that robust—the LCD screen is one of the first things that will go kaput—if you can find one in good nick, then it'll probably last you a while before it electronically pops its clogs.

The Ricoh has a slightly wider 28 mm lens, meaning you'll be able to capture more in the frame than a 35 mm lens. Optically it's a bit of a beast, even though it's the cutest little lens that retracts back into the camera body every time you switch it off. Try one; I think you'll like it.

Contax T2/T3

If you want a bit of glitz and glam in a cam, then these are for you. Whereas the GR1 is a stealthy-looking (i.e. dull) thing, the T2 and T3 are all show with plenty of go. The bodies are made out of titanium, and the T2 came in a variety of different finishes: champagne, gold, two different shades of black, and a platinum version with an ostrich skin grip that pushes the boundaries of good taste.

The T3 has a 35 mm f/2.8 lens and the T2 a 38 mm f/2.8. Both produce very sharp, contrasted images. The T2 has a simpler interface but, really, you can't go wrong with either.

Prices are sky high, so if you want a bit of premium without paying premium, check out the Nikon 28Ti and 35Ti. They will set you back much less, but are made out of titanium with the extra benefit of some Seiko-made, gorgeous, analog dials.

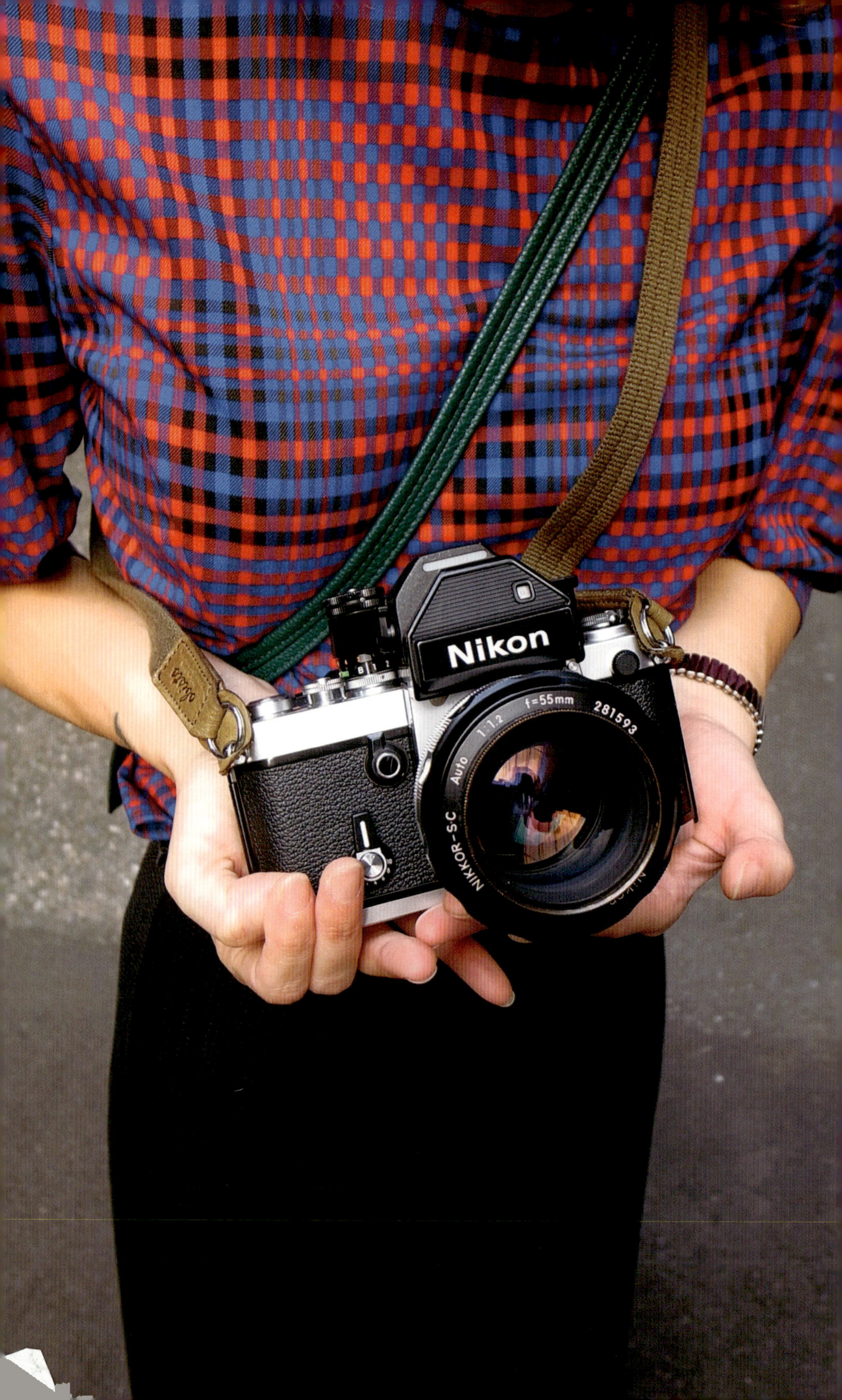
Nikon
f=55mm
281593
Auto
1:1.2
NIKKOR-S·C

#4 WHEN YOU NEED AN SLR

If you want to change your photographs, you need to change cameras. Changing cameras means that your photographs will change. A really good camera has something I suppose you might describe as its own distinctive aura.

—Nobuyoshi Araki

If you're going to get serious about your photography, you'll want to use an SLR. A single-lens reflex viewfinder lets you see precisely the image you will get through the lens. When you press the shutter button, a big, fat mirror flips up out of the way and the shutter opens, allowing the image that you've just seen through the lens to be recorded onto the film.

They are more technical than compact cameras; those extra buttons and dials give you more control, letting you change settings like shutter speed or aperture for creative effect. But if all that extra knob-twiddling sounds a bit too much to handle, too soon, a modern SLR—with automatic exposure modes—can help turn you from a knob noob to a knob know-it-all.

Another reason to love SLRs is that they are system cameras—meaning you're not just buying a camera but also choosing a whole ecosystem of camera bodies, lenses, and accessories. Most SLRs let you change lenses, which may lead to a potentially financially damaging obsession of collecting expensive bits of glass. Still, even if your bank balance is in the red, you'll have a supremely versatile camera setup—every cloud has a silver lining, eh?

You can get tele-focal lenses to take photos of things far away, or a wide lens to get lots more things in your frame—and any kind of lens in between. The through-the-lens viewing makes the SLR the most accurate way of framing and focusing your shots, whatever lens you use.

Inside the big hump that gives SLRs their unique silhouette is where all the magic happens; it uses a neat array of mirrored surfaces and glass to beam that image from the lens and into the viewfinder. A lot of them are fixed, but some professional SLRs allow you to change finders.

When it comes to finders, I wouldn't worry about interchangeability of it, but these are some things worth considering:

Viewfinder Coverage and Magnification

Not all viewfinders are built equal. Some are built bigger, brighter, and more accurate.

The bigger the projected image you see in the viewfinder, the easier it is for you to study the details in your frame. The higher the magnification number, the bigger the viewfinder image will appear.

One hundred percent accuracy/coverage finders will show you exactly what you are getting, but if you're a specs wearer like myself, you might find it hard to see the whole frame with a high-magnification, 100 percent accuracy finder. If you're a fellow four-eyes, a high-eyepoint finder is the answer.

Pentaprism vs. Pentamirror

Viewfinders can be dark, dingy peepholes, but pentaprisms are the panacea to your viewfinder woes. Pentaprisms transmit light much more effectively than a pentamirror.

Pentamirrors are usually seen in lower-end SLRs because they are cheaper to manufacture than pentaprisms. One benefit of a camera with a pentamirror is that the camera will be lighter in weight than one with a pentaprism, because it uses mirrored surfaces instead of one big, fat block of glass.

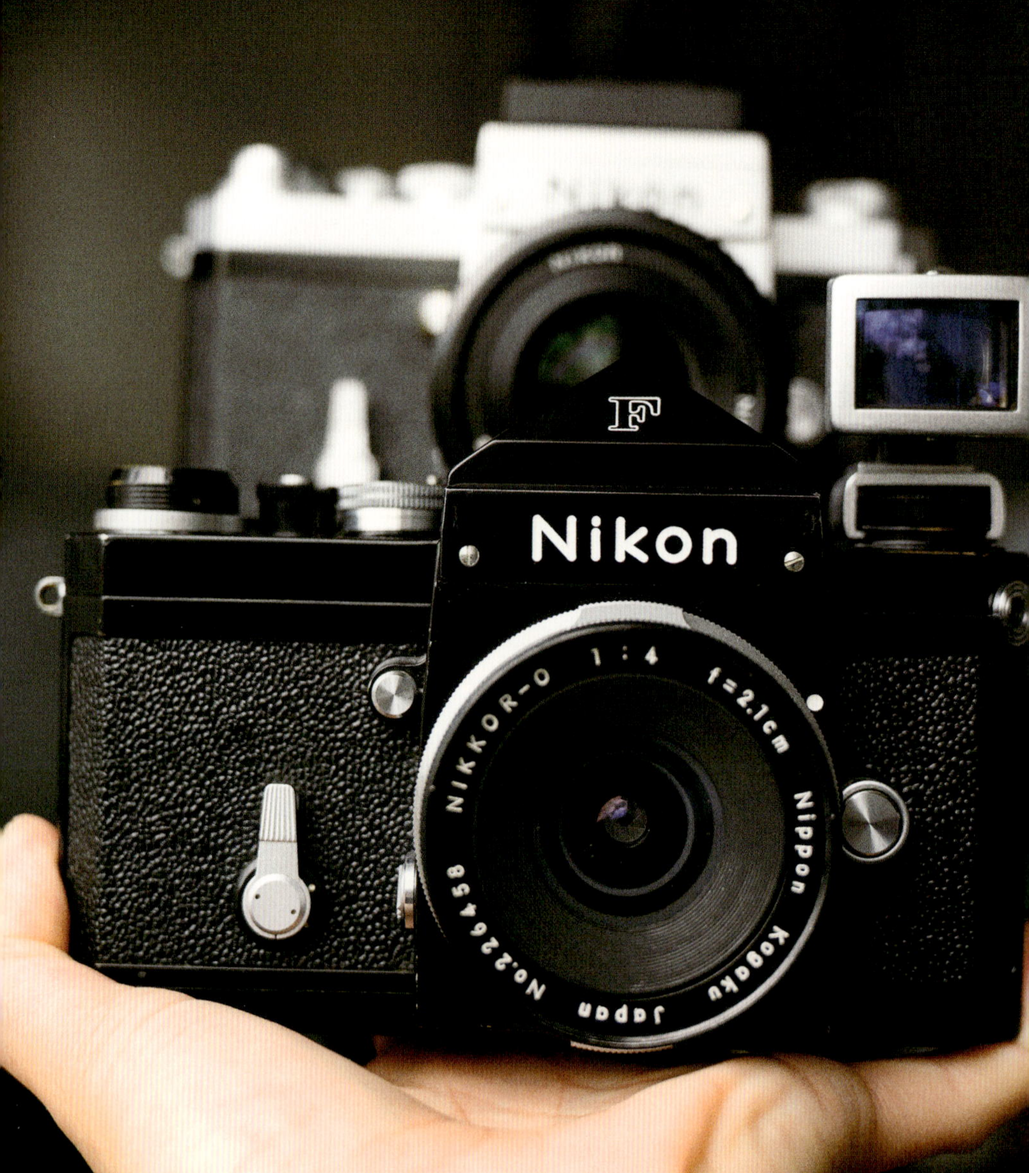
F
Nikon
NIKKOR-O 1:4 f=2.1cm
Nippon Kogaku Japan No.226458

#5

FIVE SUPERB SLRS TO GET YOU GOING

Nikon F (any)

If you want to own a legend, look no further. The Nikon F might not have been the first SLR ever made, but it was the most important SLR ever made. The single digit Fs are bulletproof—photographer Don McCullin's life was spared when his Nikon F stopped a stray AK-47 round—tested by time to be one of the most durable cameras ever built.

The F and F2 are classics in their own right, but if you're looking to get your first SLR, then I'd suggest the F3; it is a manual-focus-only camera but has autoexposure, making it convenient and quick to get decent exposures.

If you want a camera that can do the focusing for you, take a look at the F6, F5 and F100 (in that order).

What's more, as Nikon hasn't changed the lens mount since they introduced the F in 1959, you now have more than four hundred different lenses to choose from.

Canon EOS-1V

Nikon was dominant in the pro-level market until Canon introduced the EOS system in 1987. Their decision to ditch the fantastic FD-mount, manual-focus-only system cameras to move to a new autofocusing, electronic lens mount system worked out well for them because professional photographers flocked to the EOS system, and Canon has been a dominant force ever since.

The EOS-1V was the pinnacle of EOS-system cameras, with the standard version taking three-and-a-half film frames per second, and the high-speed version allowing you to shoot ten frames per second. By all means go for the high-speed one if you have money to burn, but for everyone else, 3.5 fps should suffice. With forty-five autofocus points, at least you have plenty of dots to choose from to make sure your focus is on point (excuse the pun).

Minolta Maxxum 7000

If you think the 1980s were cool, then you'll think this camera from Minolta is awesome. For everyone else, it looks like a calculator and a camera had a baby together.

This camera was a vision of the future (not in terms of design) because it was the first autofocusing SLR. It uses A-mount lenses, which can be adapted onto Sony Alpha digital cameras, too.

Pentax Spotmatic

Pentax might've fallen out of favour in the digital era, but they made pretty cool film cameras and quality lenses. The Spotmatic F and SP SLRs are every bit as classy-looking as the Nikon F but can be had for much less.

Instead of using a bayonet mount where you twist the lens and it clicks into place, they are screw mount, which involves a lot of screwing (obviously) to get the lens in place. The M42 mount was used by a number of different brands, including Zeiss, Praktica, and Zenit; so there are lots of lenses to choose from, and most of them can be had for bargain-basement prices.

Leica

You wouldn't usually associate Leica with bargain-basement prices, but their SLRs are relative bargains when compared to their iconic rangefinders.

My pick would be the R5, which offers an autoexposure mode and fixed many of the electronics problems that plagued the R3 and R4.

The greatest thing about getting an R is that you can buy some excellent Leica lenses for far less than you would pay if you bought the M (rangefinder) versions.

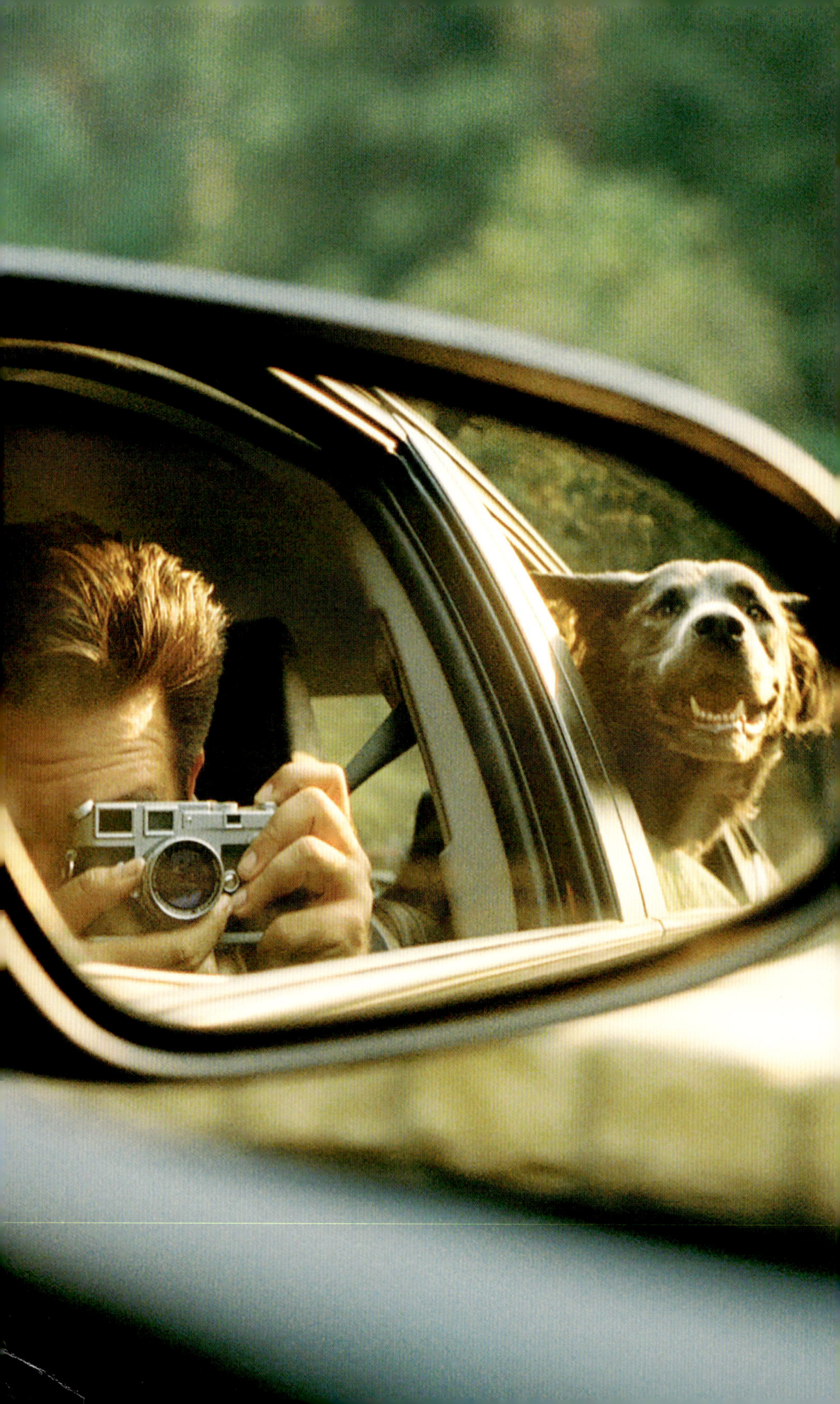

#6 WHY RANGEFINDER CAMERAS ROCK

Once you've bought a compact camera, because it's small, and an SLR, because you're seriously serious about photography, you will absolutely need to experience shooting with a rangefinder.

The Nikon F almost killed off rangefinders by offering up a more advanced, technical camera that allowed for through-the-lens viewing, but the loyal following of photographers that still favour the way of the rangefinder has kept it alive and relevant into the modern day.

Whereas an SLR lets you look through the lens for accurate framing, a rangefinder camera uses a viewfinder window, slightly above and to the side of the lens, with frame lines representing what you will expect to capture in your frame. As you are not looking through the lens, there is a slight margin of error (parallax error) when it comes to framing, which becomes more prevalent when the subject is up close.

Although it sounds like an outdated way of composing photos, there are plenty of benefits to using a rangefinder camera:

Discreet and Discrete

Many street photographers choose to shoot with rangefinder cameras because they make less noise and look less intimidating than a loud and proud SLR. It doesn't have a flappy mirror that clacks every time you take a photo; some rangefinders have a cloth-curtained shutter that makes less noise than you do opening the curtains in the morning.

If you want to take a candid photo without distracting your subject, a rangefinder camera is a less intimidating sight than an SLR, as it's smaller and doesn't hide half your face and eyes. You'll look less like a private detective.

Rangefinder lenses tend to be built smaller than SLR lenses, too, meaning you can pack more lenses in your camera bag, or even slip them in your pocket if you don't mind drawing attention to your pocket bulges.

Bright Viewfinder

With an SLR, you have mirrors and a prism to reflect the image into the viewfinder. With a rangefinder, the viewfinder is just a window—a couple of surfaces of glass that separate the scene in front of you from your eyes—so the result is a viewfinder that doesn't feel as much like a peephole as an SLR's finder.

Also, the viewfinder won't black out when you take a shot, because there isn't a mirror that needs to flip up and out of the way like you get with an SLR. No viewfinder blackout means while the exposure is happening you can still look through the viewfinder and tee up the next shot. It's also a nice feeling to be able to look at the scene during the exposure.

No Mirror Slap

Not only is the sound of a mirror in an SLR louder than the subtle shutter click in a rangefinder, but the movement of the mirror and the vibrations it makes can potentially ruin your shots.

If you're taking a long exposure, or even using a slower shutter speed like 1/15 sec., those mirror-slap vibrations in an SLR would most likely make your photo a bit shaky, thus less sharp-looking. A rangefinder has less intense vibrations, so you can quite easily get some stable shots.

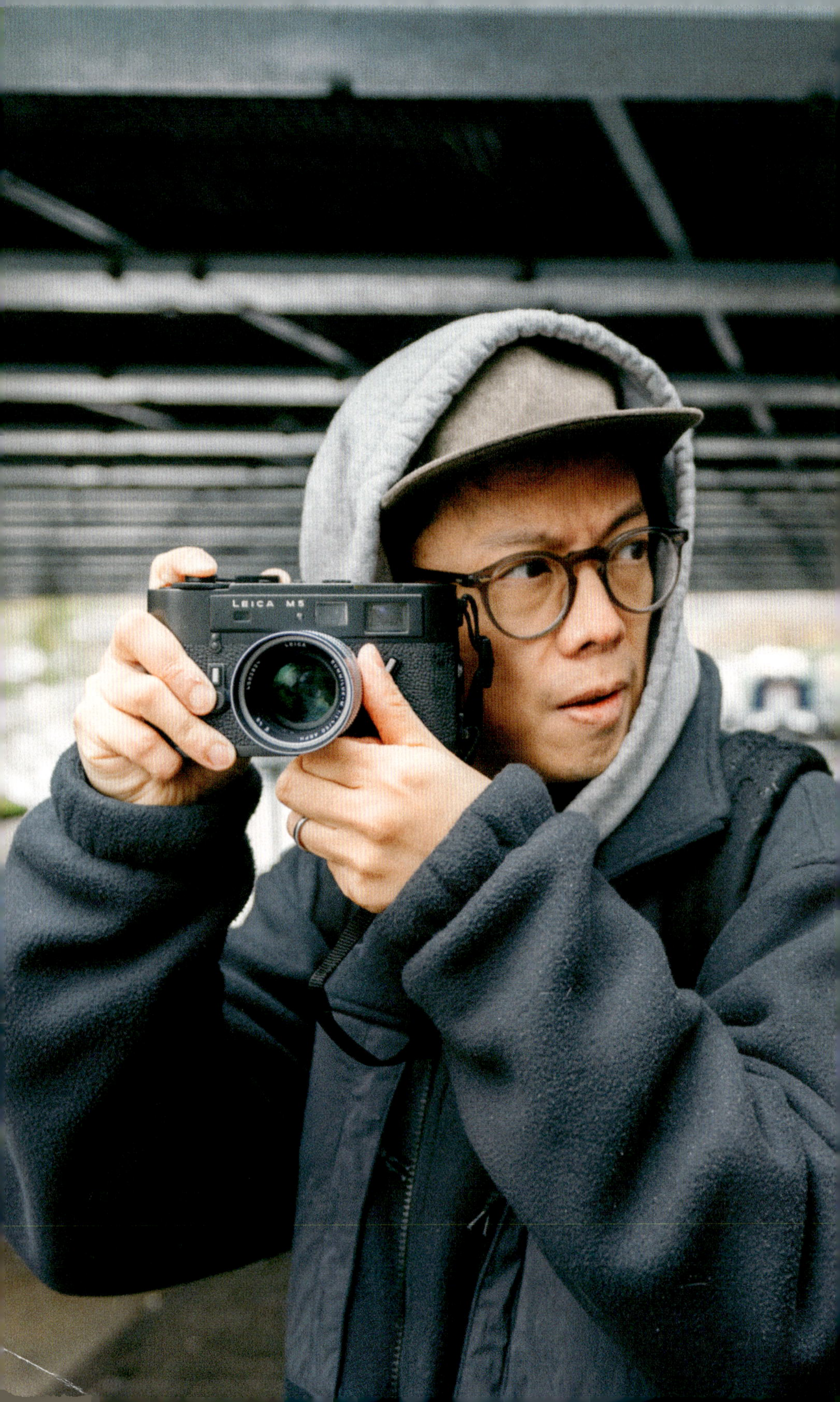
LEICA M5

#7 RANGEFINDERS TO TRY BEFORE YOU DIE

Leica M

You can't talk about rangefinders and not mention the iconic Leica M in the same breath. It would be a crime not to. To many camera-loving peeps, the M is the quintessential camera. It may not be the cheapest way to dip your toe in the world of rangefinders, but the fact of the matter is that nothing really compares.

Introduced in 1954, the M3 is the granddaddy of them all and still considered to be the ultimate M by many Leica aficionados. It has the highest magnification viewfinder in any M, making it easier to focus, and has the least cluttered viewfinder of all Ms, with 50, 90, and 135 mm frame lines.

I'm not sure what family member the M2 would be, but it offered a wider 35 mm frame line instead of the M3's 50 mm. The M4 had both and, to some Leica fans, was the last of true classic Leicas.

Later Ms came with light metering, but all of them look more or less the same—apart from the marvellous M5, which was considered the ugly duckling of the Leica M lineup because it dared to look different. That means the 5 can be had for cheaper prices than some of the more classic-looking Ms, along with the Canadian-German M4-2 and M4-P, which are also not as popular amongst collectors because they represented a tight-sphinctered time in Leica's manufacturing process.

Voigtlander Bessa R

We can't all be exuberant with our spending, though, so if your purse doesn't stretch far enough to secure yourself a Leica, the Bessa R cameras from Voigtlander are a great alternative—they take Leica M-mount lenses (they even made their own super set of M-mount lenses), with a much more accessible price.

Konica Hexar

With the Hexar, you could get the RF, which is an M-mount rangefinder, but there aren't too many reasons to get an RF over a Leica M or Voigtlander Bessa R, other than the looks. If you're getting a Hexar, I'd recommend the AF because it comes with a fixed lens, which is available for a very reasonable price.

Contax G

You need a shiny rangefinder to match your Contax T2? Look no further than this shiny shooter. The G1 will be available for quite a bit less than the G2 because the autofocus wasn't as reliable. The wise purchase would be to get a G2.

I did say autofocus, so some might say that they're not true rangefinders, but I can happily suppress the pedantry because the Contax G is awesome. They benefit from having a higher-tech (for its time) viewfinder that would zoom in and out depending on what lens you choose to mount on it, which you won't get with your conventional rangefinder viewfinder. The compact Contax G lenses are stunningly sharp, and they're just pretty-looking cameras.

Also Worth Mentioning

A Nikon S rangefinder is a must for any camera collector, although it doesn't incite the same level of fanatical gushing praise as a Leica does. That's what makes it great for collecting and using the S-series of cameras. A lot less cool but a little more useful is the Canon 7; it's more useful because it takes Leica M39 thread-mount lenses. If you're on a budget and don't need to change lenses, have a look at the Canonet G-III QL17, Olympus 35SP, and Yashica Electro 35 GSN.

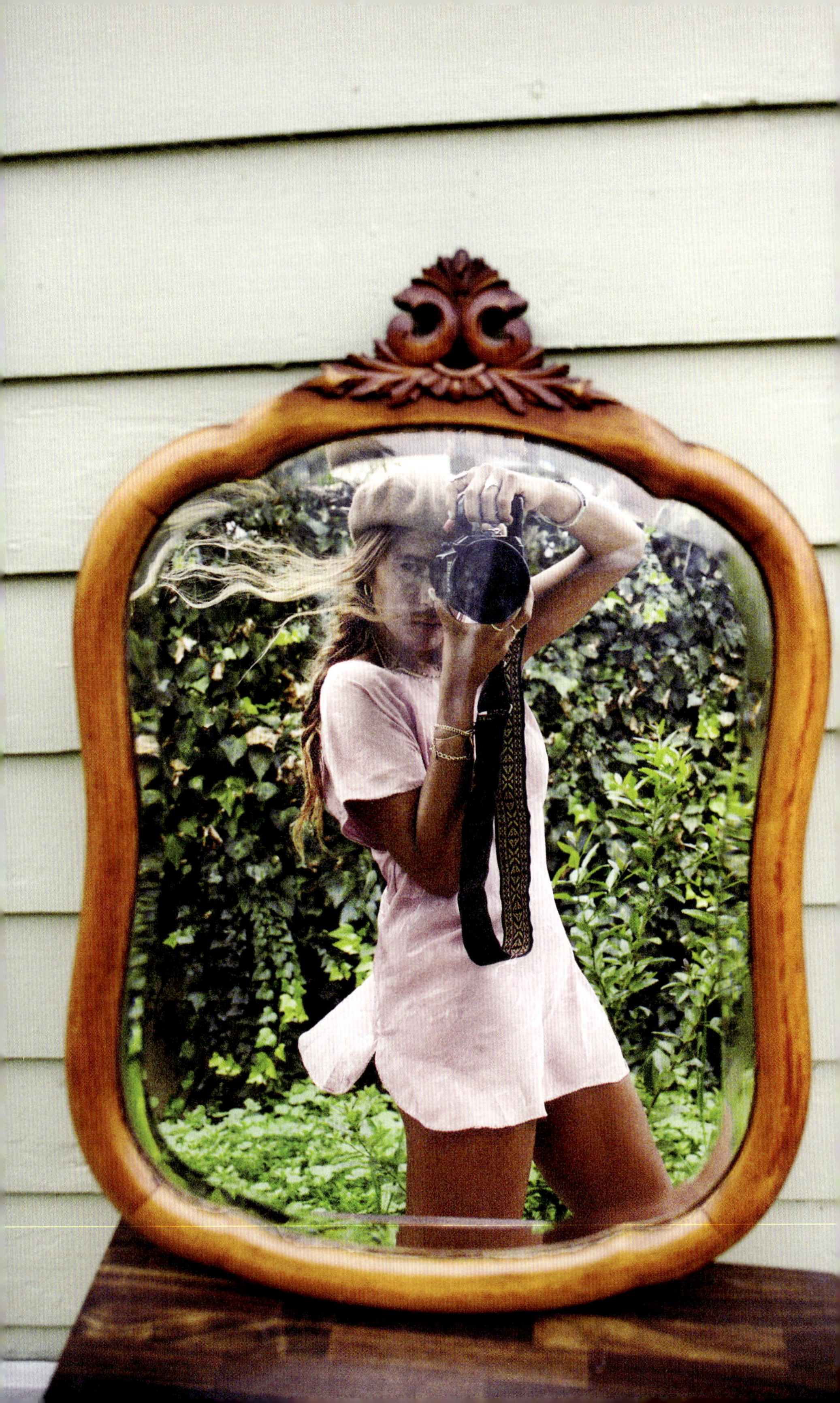

#8 MEDIUM FORMAT: TAKING THE NEXT STEP UP

Mostly, I'm going to be focusing on 35 mm film photography in this book, but there will certainly be a point in the near future when you feel the need to take your film obsession further by taking a step up, format-wise.

120/220

120 and 220 are medium-format films (220 is just a longer version of 120), and the film itself is stuck to a bit of backing paper and wound around a spool. It's a bit fiddlier to load than your drop-in 35 mm film, but once you see the impressive size of that film, you'll forgive it for being a bit fussy.

The surface of film that is exposed is much larger than 35 mm, giving you gorgeous, gigantic negatives filled with detail. With 35 mm film cameras you'll find that they mostly expose a 36-by-24-millimetre portion of film, whereas medium-format cameras will expose a minimum 56-by-41.5-millimetre area of film (different medium-format cameras shoot in different aspect ratios, thus using varying sizes of film section).

Resolution

If you're worrying whether 35 mm film can compete with high-resolution digital sensors, get a medium-format camera.

Using a portion of film at least two times larger than 35 mm film (even larger depending on aspect ratio) will certainly provide you with incredibly detailed, sharp images—perfect for photos that could do with that extra-crispy resolution.

Next Step up from 35 mm Film

Although in use medium-format cameras tend to be a bit slower and clunkier, if you're already familiar with using 35 mm film cameras, then taking the next step up won't be too taxing on the brain. Think of it as an oversized 35 mm camera, and you'll be fine.

Modular

Some medium-format cameras have detachable backs so you can change to a different roll of film without having to remove the film from the camera. This is convenient if you're shooting in bright sunlight and then suddenly need to take a photo indoors or in low light.

There are also different backs for different aspect ratios, so you can choose one to suit your subject or framing.

Shallow Depth of Field

With a format larger than 35 mm film, you get a jump up in terms of juicy, shallow depth of field. (Depth of field will be covered in more depth later.) The drop-off from the in-focus parts to blurry, out-of-focus is more distinct than with 35 mm film, making images pop.

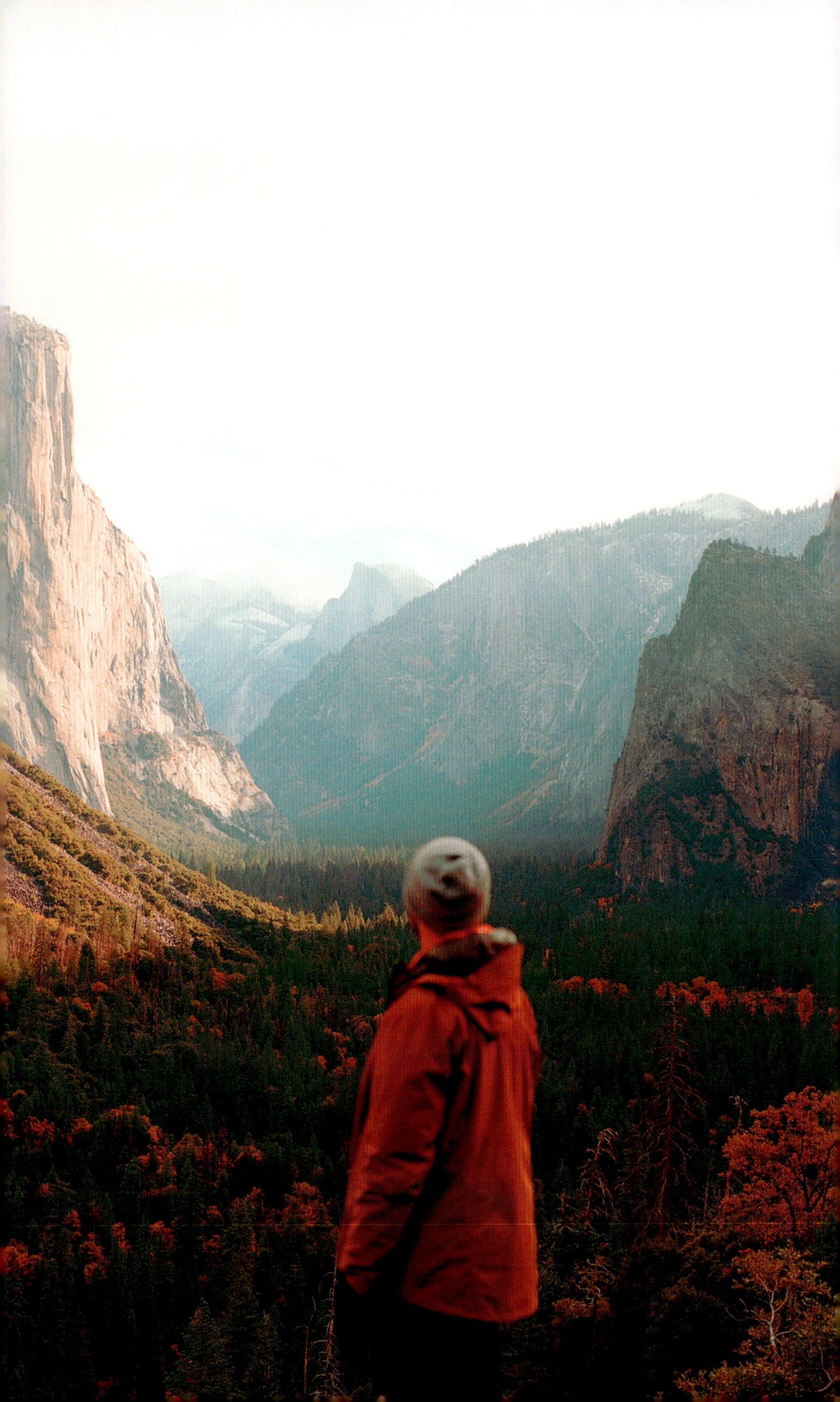

#9
FIVE FANTASTIC, MEDIUM-FORMAT CAMERAS

Hasselblad 500 Series

A Hassie 500 series is arguably the most iconic medium-format camera of all time, with a supremely chic combination of highly polished chrome framing those black, leatherette-clad, slab-sided surfaces. It's almost too pretty to be a camera.

You'll be glad to hear that it's not just a thin veneer of fanciness, though—what lies beneath are top-notch mechanics, time-proven by years of hard use and abuse in countless photographer's studios. Hasselblad's reputation for making rock-solid cameras was set in stone with the use of modified Hasselblads in the Apollo 11 mission—Buzz Aldrin and Neil Armstrong used them to take photos of their moonwalk (not of the Michael Jackson variety).

Rolleiflex 2.8 F

It almost reaches the same iconic levels of the 'blad, but it never went to the moon, so it's not nearly as cool. Still, if you think of twin-lens reflex cameras (TLR), the Rolleiflex is the epitome of that unique, two-lens look. Instead of the one lens of a single-lens reflex, where you look through the lens to compose your photo, a TLR has one lens you look through for composing the shot. The photo-taking lens is below it, which is where the shutter opens to make the exposure on the film.

The Rolleiflex 2.8 F and 3.5 F are the ones you should check out, but you can also check out the Rolleicords, which came in at a much cheaper price point due to the slightly cheaper build.

Mamiya 7

When I think of Mamiya, I instantly think of the 6-by-7-centimetre format. The RB and RZ67 were popular as studio cameras, because they're built like a brick outhouse and weigh just as much as one.

The coolest Mamiya medium-format camera, though, is the 7, which offers the lightweight versatility of a rangefinder camera with the monster size of medium-format film.

The 6-by-7-centimetre format ekes out as much crispy detail as you can get from medium format (without going panorama).

Bronica ETR/ETRS/ETRSi

The smart money would go on buying a Bronica ETR—a camera made to do everything well apart from looking interesting. It's not ugly, just dull. But, really, you can't turn your nose up at the prices and the excellent Zenzanon lenses. It takes photos in a 645 format (6 by 4.5 cm), which is quite an easy aspect ratio to work with.

Pentax 67

There There is something strangely alluring about the savage-looking Pentax 67. It's just so beefy. If it was a burger, it would be a rare beef patty sandwiched between two rare beef patties. It's meaty and unapologetically so.

If you like your cameras tank-like, and shoot massive 6-by-7 film negatives, this might just be the one for you.

Also Worth Mentioning

Like the Mamiya, the Plaubel Makina also shoots in the 6-by-7-centimetre format, but it has a collapsible lens, which makes the camera incredibly compact to slip into a (reasonably-sized) bag.

For 6-by-4.5-centimetre format, I'd thoroughly recommend looking at the Contax 645 Pro and Pentax 645, too.

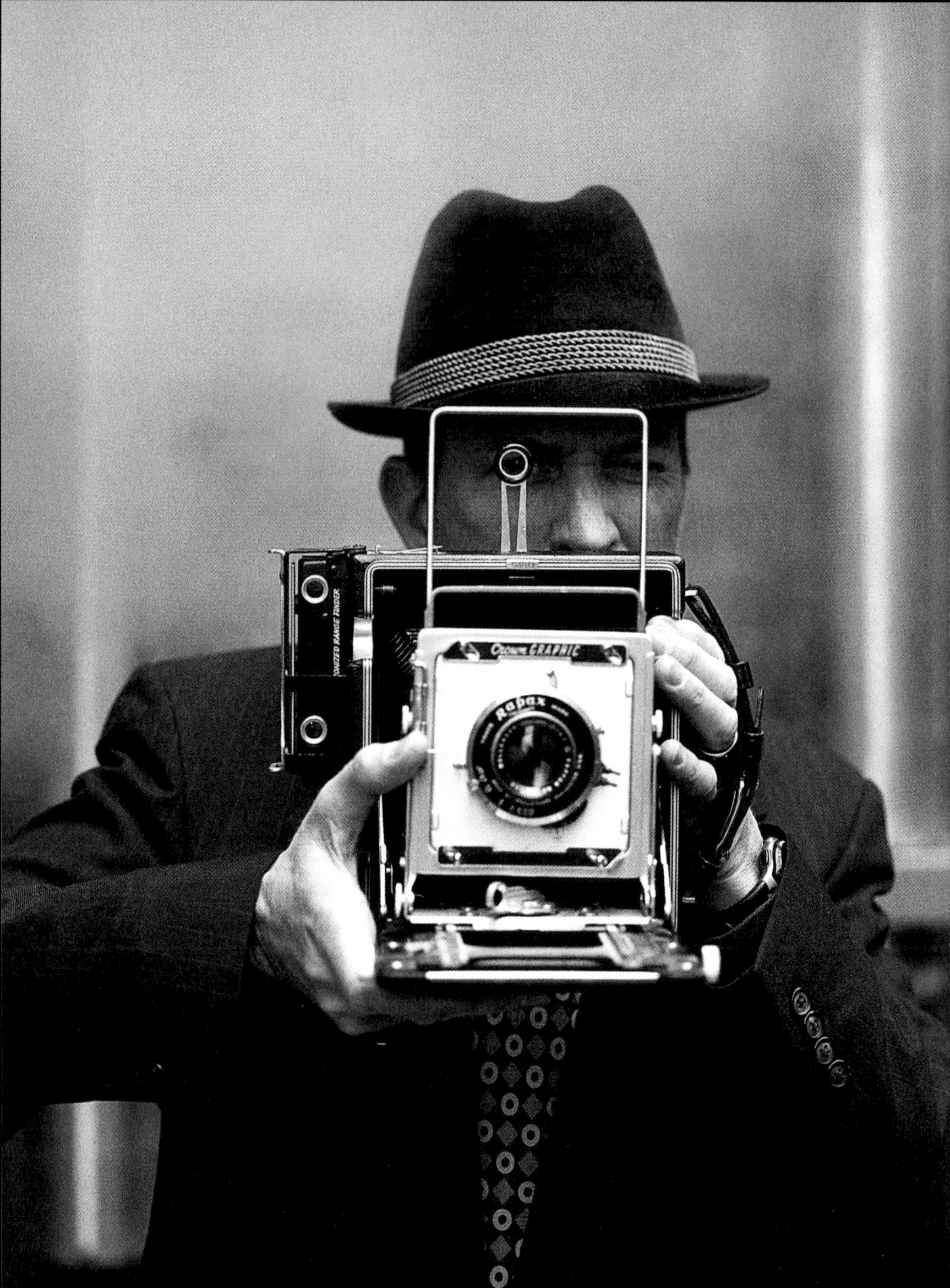
Crown GRAPHIC
Rapax

#10

LARGE AND NICHE FORMATS: WHEN YOUR OBSESSION HAS GONE TOO FAR

You've taken your photography obsession to level eleven when you find yourself yearning for a bit of large-format photography. If you were thinking of using a camera that you could carry around in your little satchel, then you'll want to stop thinking about large format (legendary landscape photographer Ansel Adams had a mule to carry his large-format camera around), because it might just end up bursting through the bottom of your satchel and end up on the floor.

Large format is an imaging format of 4 by 5 inches, giving you sumptuously detailed, monster-size negatives. If for some reason you find yourself looking at a medium-format scan or print and thinking that it's lacking a bit of that sparkle, large format will give you the magic you crave by the bucketload.

A little word of warning, though: large-format cameras don't come with a mule or any animals that can't crawl into the camera, so do find your own if you plan on lugging one up a mountain.

Other Formats You Should Know of (but Not Use)

There are many other film formats that are not worth mentioning simply because they are not in use anymore.

APS

APS is one of those crap films that met its demise but just about deserves a quick mention because it still lends its name to a digital sensor size: APS-C imaging sensors are so-called because they're approximately the same size as APS film in the C or Classic setting.

APS film pointlessly offered three different formats in one, all of them smaller and more inferior in quality to 35 mm. You can still get them developed if you want to buy a camera that takes a film they don't make anymore.

110

Some childhood memories aren't so great, and god-awful 110 film cameras are one such example. I remember these cheaply made, compact, rectangular boxes that held the cartridge-based 110 film inside. I imagine someone must've invented it thinking that they could feel like a spy, using these small cameras, but in reality the film sucks at making sharp prints.

Strangely enough, you can still get them developed if you want to bother buying a 110 camera. Otherwise, shooting with 110 now is more for a novelty than anything else.

127

Here's another film that you can still buy and get developed but, in my opinion, is not worth playing with. In terms of size, it comes in somewhere between 35 mm and medium format at 4 centimetres wide, but if you ever want to sell your 127 camera on eBay, you'll find that there will be fewer people wanting to buy a 127 camera than a 35 mm or medium-format camera.

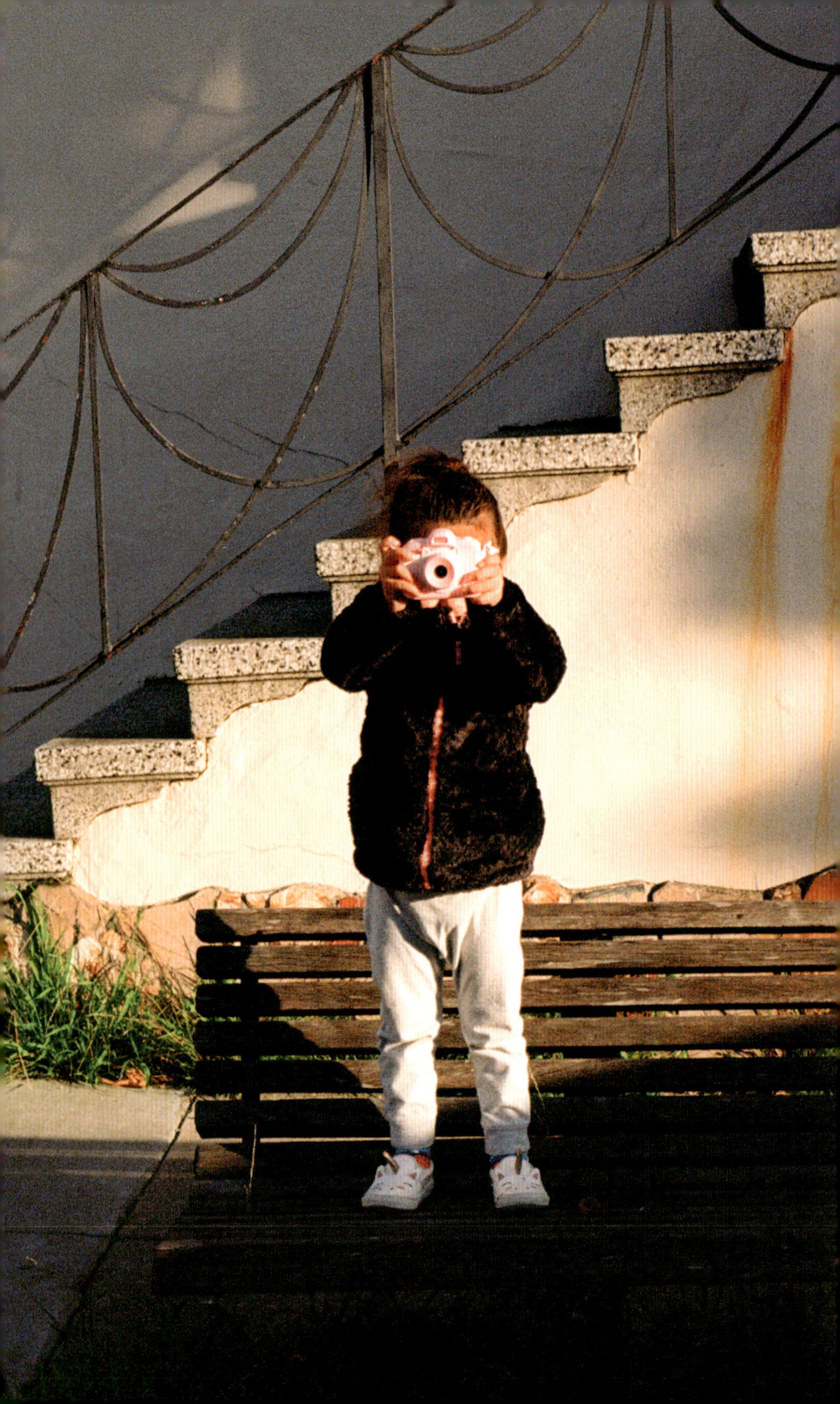

#11

TOY CAMERAS: WHY THEY'RE STUPID BUT FUN

Toy cameras are a bit of an acquired taste—they're plastic and not always fantastic.

Lomography was responsible for injecting a little fun into photography, but also for injecting a big, fat markup on that fun. A lot of their cameras are made out of piss-poor plastic, so don't be surprised if you only get to run a few rolls through one before it goes the way of the crapper.

Having said that, I've had stupid amounts of fun with toy cameras—you just need to be comfortable with:

1. Paying for the marketing and graphics folks to make a nice packaging for it. But that describes a lot of the crap we buy these days.
2. The fun lasts only until the camera breaks.
3. Knowing that you could get a proper camera for less than the cost of a toy camera.

If that hasn't put you off, then these are the three toy cameras that I'd check out:

Holga GN

The original Holgas were built to offer a cheap way into medium-format photography. I have a lot of love for the unpretentious look and the rather basic features: one single shutter speed, very rough method of focusing, and only two aperture settings. Pre-2009, the two aperture settings—cloudy and sunny—were said to do the same thing, but they now offer up f/13 and f/20 apertures, which might as well be the same thing.

Let's not forget the light leaks that can leave little streaks on your film, and the crazy vignetting and softness that might (every camera is a bit different) blight your photos, thanks to that lens. But that's why people love it.

You can find cheap ones on eBay that come without all the shiny Lomography packaging for less.

Diana

Don't expect it to be a hugely different camera to the Holga. It's still the same crappy plastic construction, and in terms of features, you'll get just a mere one-aperture setting more than the Holga.

In terms of looks, it does have a more colourful livery, making it a funkier-looking crappy bit of overpriced plastic. But its redeeming quality is that you can accessorise the hell out of it—with other useful bits of shoddy plastic parts—including adding an instant film back that uses Fujifilm Instax film, for instant film fun.

Lomo LC-A

The camera that started it all is a Russian-made compact camera that looks a bit like the Japanese-made Cosina CX but takes photos that look less like those of the CX and more like the ones you'd expect from a Russian-made compact camera.

For a toy camera, it takes quite decent-looking photos, but then again it's not really a toy camera. If you compare it to regular cameras, it does fall a bit short of the mark—image quality is not great—but that's part of the charm. You'll get photos that are a little soft but contrasted with some savage vignetting (dark corners).

Sidestep Lomography's Lomo LC-A+ because, with this version, they somehow thought it would be cool to remake a Russian design in China—using more plastic in the construction, yet still charging a hefty fee. Search for one of the original Russian-made LC-As on eBay for a fraction of Lomography's remake, and enjoy the charms of the original cheapo design for an appropriately cheapo price.

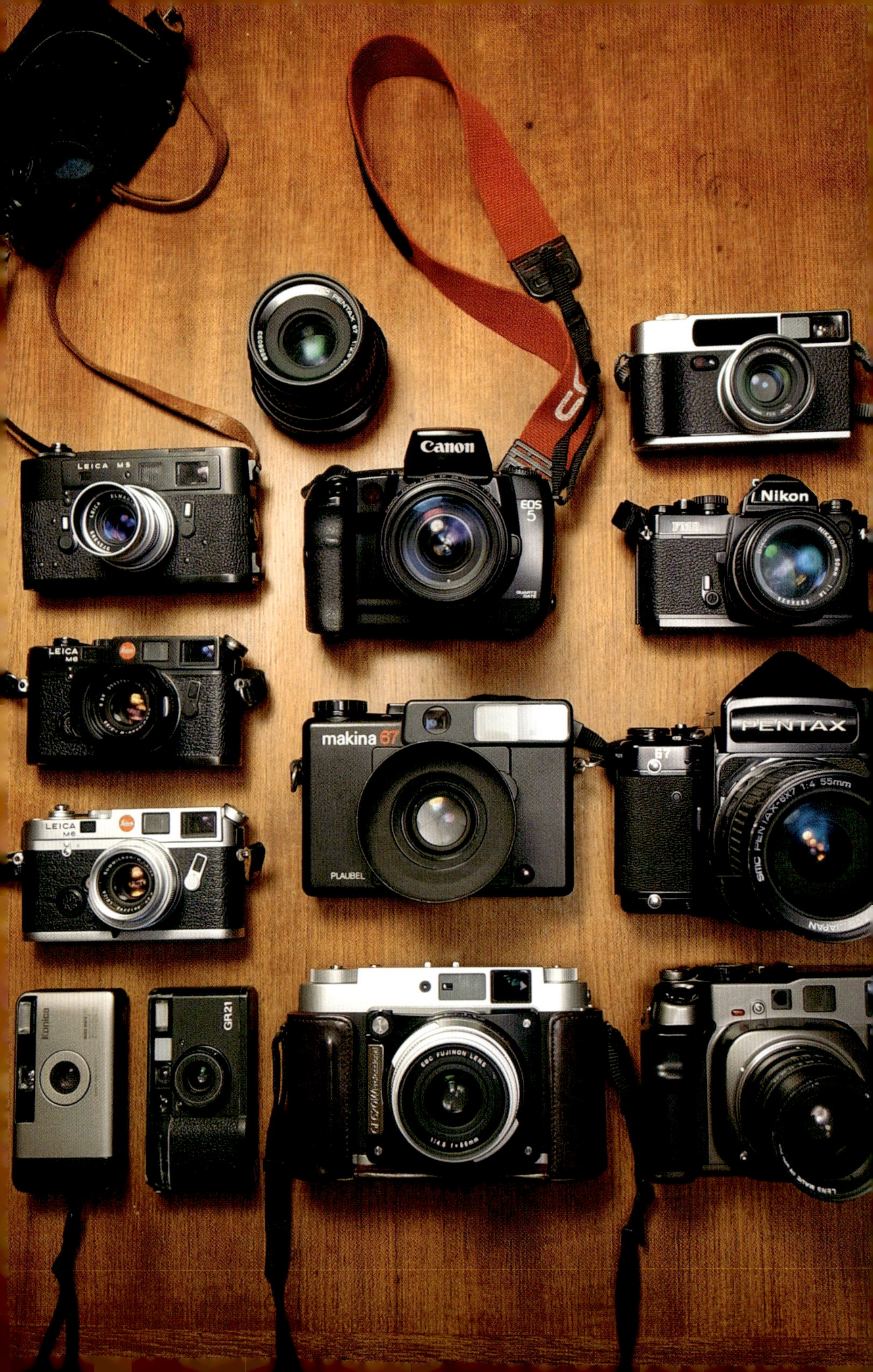

LEICA M5
Canon
EOS 5
Nikon
LEICA M6
makina 67
PLAUBEL
PENTAX
67
LEICA M6
Konica
GR21

#12
HOW TO CHOOSE THE PERFECT CAMERA FOR YOU

Now it's time to throw down a fat chunk of cash to sort yourself out with a brilliant little photo-taking machine. But just how do you guarantee sheer, bloody brilliance?

If you're looking for perfection, you'll be forever chasing—the best camera is the one that works best for you, not what someone else says is best. You're the one that uses it, so it is important that you buy a camera that is right for you.

My first camera was a birthday present from my sister, a Pentax MZ-M, which has all the basics covered: takes film, has a shutter-speed dial, and includes aperture control. It's a manual-exposure, manual-focus camera, with no frills or fancy features—nothing to distract you from learning the fundamentals of making an exposure.

Find a camera that is comfortable in your hands and won't weigh you down—you want a camera that you're happy to lug around on your neck or shoulder for a whole day of shooting. And let your photographic needs dictate your camera choice. If you're shooting stuff that doesn't move, like landscapes or architecture, you don't need a camera with fast autofocus that takes ten photos per second. Or if you plan to do a lot of travel photography, you might want a lightweight setup, like a rangefinder or a compact camera, if you feel like you don't need to change lenses.

Things to Look out for

- Shutter Speeds: A lot of older cameras are all mechanical, which means that you don't need a battery to take a photo—but that also means the shutter speeds will be less accurate over time. Usually it's the fast and slow shutter speeds that are off; budget for a camera service to ensure more accurate shutter speeds.
- Curtain Condition: Some camera shutters had a cloth curtain instead of metal, which, like your pants, can become worn out (unless you wear metal pants).
- Viewfinder: Look out for finders filled with gunky grime—you need a good, clear view through the viewfinder. For SLRs, check to see if there's any mirror separation; for rangefinders, ensure that the focusing patch lines up.
- Knobs and Twiddly Bits: Make sure all the buttons and dials function properly. You want to have a functioning film-advance lever and rewind knob.
- Mechanical vs. Electric: The great thing about mechanical cameras is that you can find a camera-repair shop to fix them or service them easily. With cameras that have electronic components, if something goes wrong, you'll be stuck with a very cool-looking paperweight.

Where to Buy

These are your two best options:

1. Ye Olde Traditional Camera Shop:It's always nicer to deal with an actual human being face-to-face, especially when you've got a load of gear-related questions to ask. You'll pay a little extra for the benefit of being able to harass the shop assistant with all of your boring questions, but the good thing is that you can come back to harass them if something goes wrong with the gear you buy from them.
2. Online: More often that not, I end up buying on eBay because of the vast amount of cameras and lenses to choose from. Buying from evilBay does throw up the possibility of being absolutely shafted for a sizeable sum of money, but all the best things in life have the potential to properly screw you over.

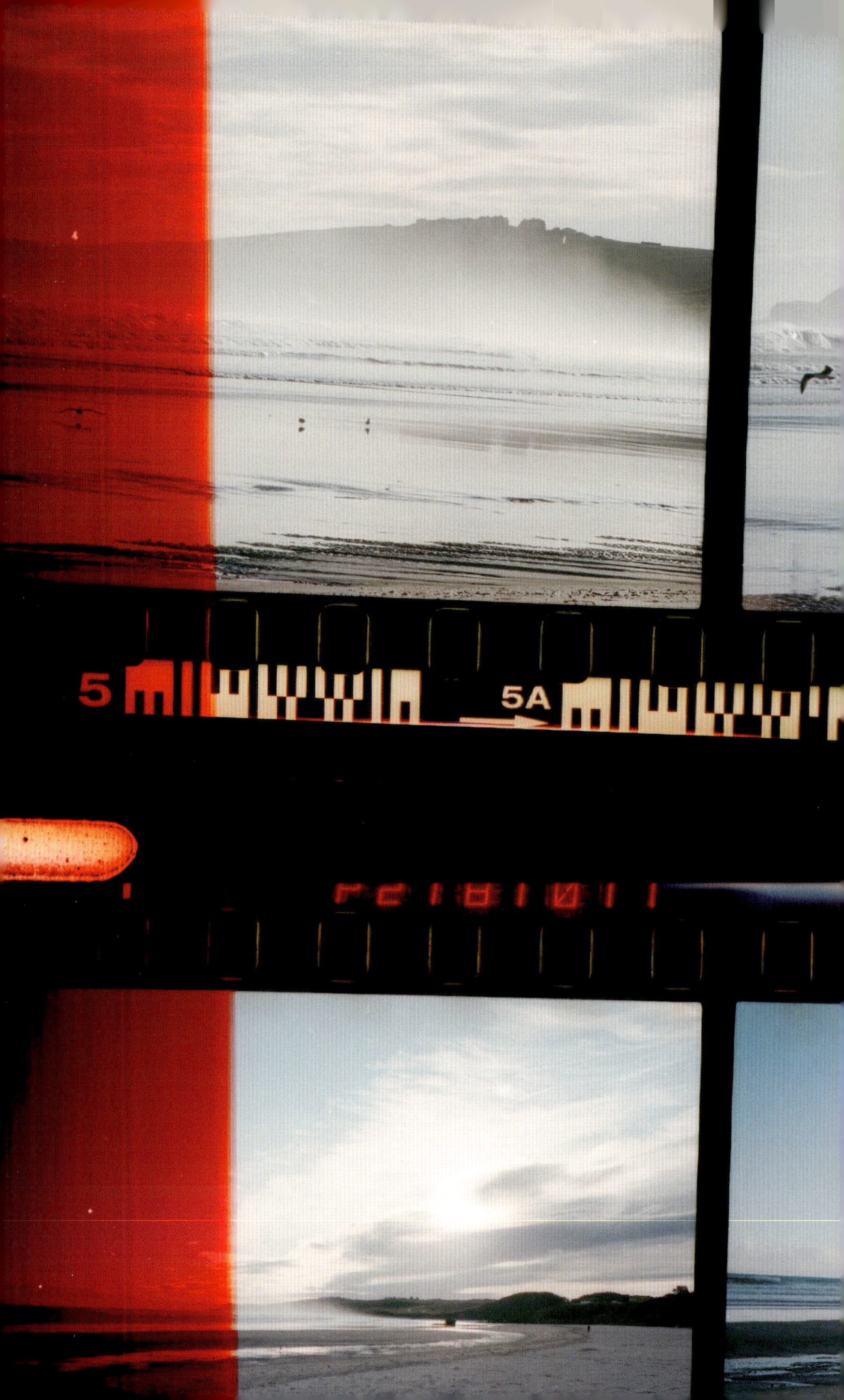
5
5A

#13
WHY YOU SHOULD SHOOT FILM, NOT MEGAPIXELS

I am not committed to film out of nostalgia. I am in favour of any kind of technical innovation, but it needs to exceed what has gone before, and so far nothing has exceeded anything that's come before.

—Christopher Nolan

It might smell like death, but film is most definitely not dead.

Film has survived and thrived not because it is better than digital for taking photos but because it has some unique characteristics and qualities that make it appealing.

The Film Look

You could spend time in Photoshop to modify your clinically sharp digital file into something that may give it a film-like quality, but let's face it: only film looks like film.

The beautiful thing with film is that there is not one standard film look, because each film stock will produce its own unique look. Different films react differently to the light, with different colour renditions, contrast, and graininess. No software required, no post processing, just a straight-out camera aesthetic that looks so very delightful.

Makes You Concentrate on the Things That Matter

When you take a photo with your digital camera, the first thing you do is review the shot you've just taken on the LCD screen. You'll check the framing, the exposure, how your subject's hair looks, how your hair looks, and then figure out how to improve the shot—and repeat the process until you're happy with the result.

There's nothing wrong with wanting to improve your photography or wanting to strive for perfection—or better hair even—but you don't want to become the person that's more interested in your camera than your surroundings.

Not being able to review your shot immediately after you've taken it allows you to concentrate on more important things: the process before you take the shot; ensuring your framing is on point and exposure is correct before you bash that shutter button; not standing there afterwards, looking at a screen, wishing you would have taken a better shot.

Good Things Come to Those Who Wait

Every time you get your film back from the lab it feels like a little bit of Christmas in an envelope: you'll be overjoyed when you find out that you've pulled off the shot(s), and that is probably the best gift you could ever get delivered in an envelope. If it didn't work out, take it as a little lump of coal to encourage you to do better for the next time.

Kai's Tips

- Enjoy the process and appreciate the results. Don't waste your time comparing film with digital. Know what you like; like what you shoot. That's all that matters.
- You get a limited amount of frames per roll of film. You pay to develop the frames you shoot. Use this to force you into thinking about how you spend those frames wisely, on subjects and shots that really deserve a photo being taken.

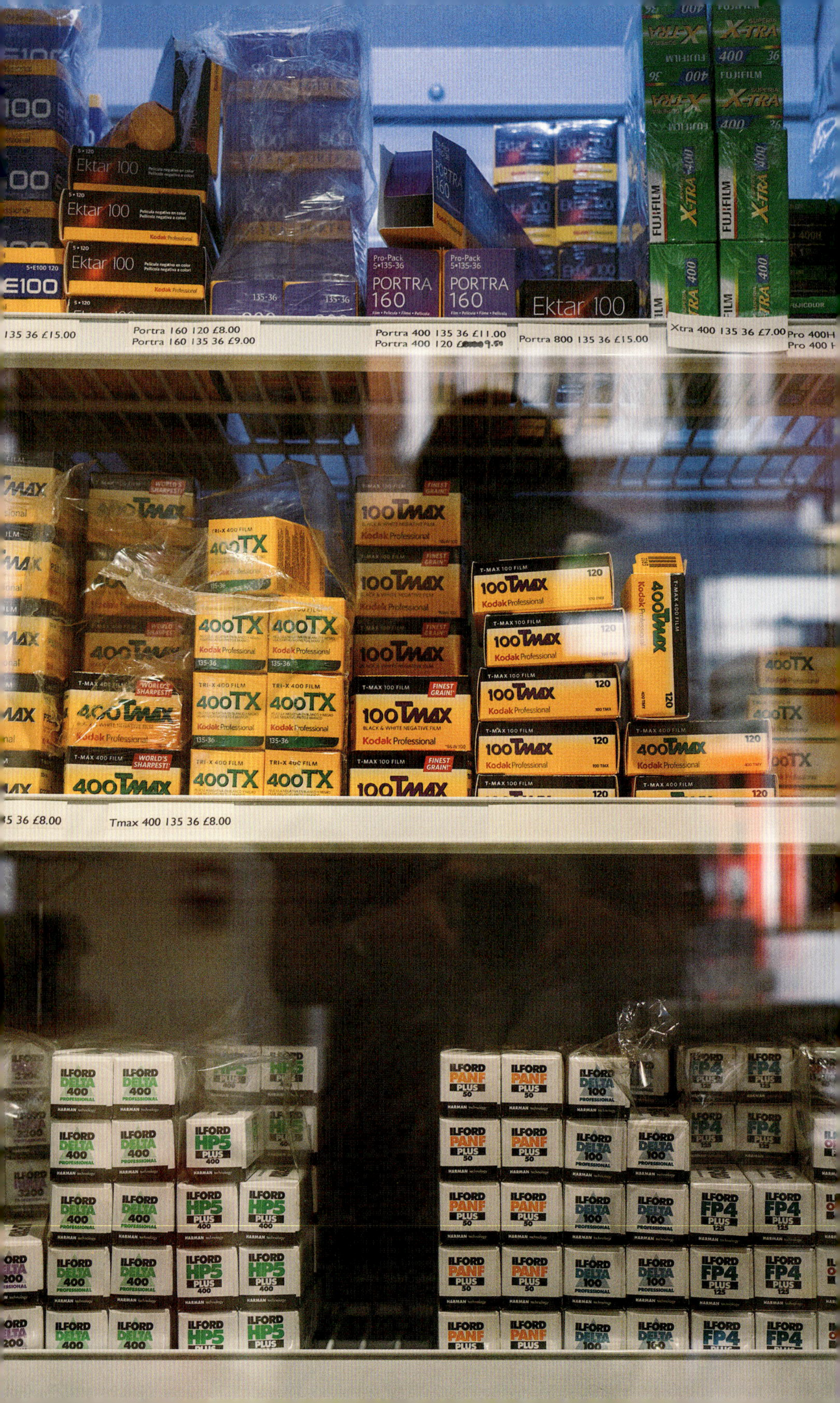

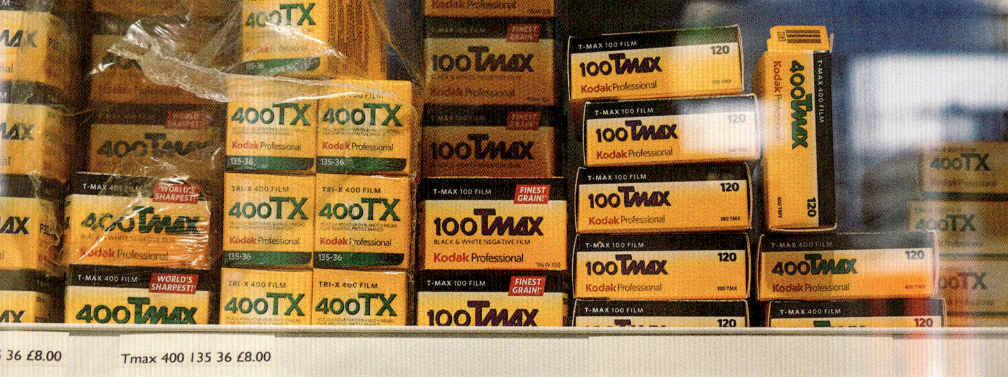
100 TMAX
Kodak Professional
400TX
400 TMAX
T-MAX 100 FILM
TRI-X 400 FILM
T-MAX 400 FILM
FINEST GRAIN!
WORLD'S SHARPEST!
5 36 £8.00
Tmax 400 135 36 £8.00

#14 WHAT TYPE OF FILM SHOULD YOU SHOOT?

There is no shortage of film and no lack of variety, with numerous emulsions that produce very unique looks, colours, and grain for you to choose from. But before we get to that, let's look at the two types of film you can purchase:

Negatives/Print Film

This is the most readily available kind of film, named because the colours and light/dark bits are inverted. It's made to be used for printing on photographic paper and developed using the C41 process, which can be done cheaply and quickly (how about one-hour quick?).

Negatives have a higher exposure latitude, which is photo-geek speak for: even if the photo is a little overexposed or underexposed (too bright or too dark), you have more control of correcting that in the printing process.

Slide/Colour Reversal Film

Slides look cool. But the price you pay for that sub-zero slickness is, well, the price of developing it. It's done using the E-6 process, which is a more complicated process than C-41, so you'll pay more for the lengthier process and, of course, wait longer before you can get your film back.

Another kick in the trousers is that it has a lower exposure latitude: if you overexpose your photo, the highlights (the bright parts of the photo) might become overblown, and the details in the photo will be lost. If you underexpose, the shadows (the dark bits) will lose some of the detail, which also cannot be recovered so easily. With slide film, you need to get the perfect exposure, whereas negatives are more forgiving.

It makes slide film sound like a right royal pain in the bum, but the big fat but is that the colours on slide film are so rich and scrumptious-looking in a way that negative film doesn't quite provide. And the grain is finer, too, which is great for making your images clean and crisp—perfect if you want to make some big-ass landscape photography prints.

Sure, it might be a fussier film to handle, but if you can nail that exposure, then it's worth the extra hassle.

An added bonus is that your processed slides can be used with a projector to beam your photos onto your wall. Or someone else's wall (if you get the permission).

Kai's Tips

- Negative film is the best type of film to start off with as a beginner, as it will ease you in to understanding how to nail your exposures.
- When you start shooting with slide film, try it on subjects that don't move too fast, or at all, to get those exposures correct.

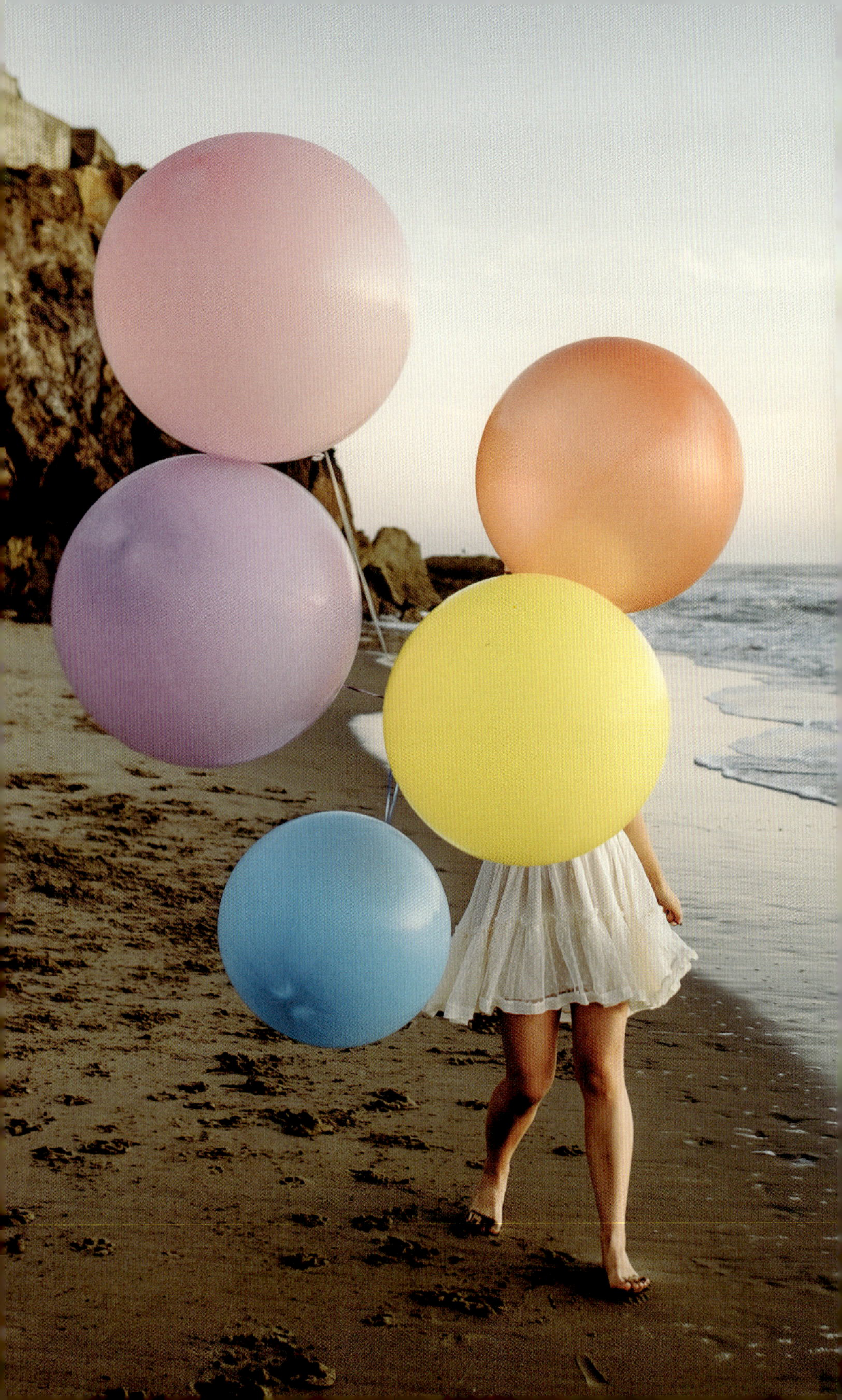

#15 KICK THINGS OFF WITH THESE COLOUR FILMS

Landscapes

If you want to shoot some sweet landscapes or nature photos, then stock up on some Fujifilm Velvia 50. This slide film is the stuff that landscape photographers swear by because it renders the world in a vibrant, saturated colour palette that always makes the grass greener on the side of Velvia.

In broad daylight, or when the sun is playing hide-and-seek on the horizon, this fine-grain (fine-grain is great for rendering those details crisply) film produces gorgeous, rich shadows, pleasing highlight roll-offs, and a load of scrumptiously warm tones. It sounds like the perfect film, but what it doesn't do well is skin colours. For fair skin, you'll find that it might make your subjects look like grinning tomatoes, pumping a load of reds onto any fleshy bits in the photos.

Velvia 100F deals with skin colours better but has less of the rich Velvia appeal for landscapes; Velvia 100 has a good balance of keeping the Velvia vibes while rendering skin tones a bit more pleasingly. The 100 label means that the film is more sensitive to light than a 50 film.

If you don't want to deal with shooting slide film, Ektar 100 is a solid choice because it also produces vibrant, highly saturated colours. It has the benefit of better dynamic range, so you won't have the problem of overblowing your highlights that you might face with slide film.

Fujifilm 160 NS would be another good negative film recommendation, but unfortunately it's harder to find now, as it's mostly available in Japan only. Kodak Portra 160 is another fine-grain negative film worth checking out for landscapes, but the tones are a little more subdued, which makes it less of a must-have landscape film—although it does make it a bit more versatile.

People and Other Stuff

Skin colours are everything when it comes to people photos. You don't want to make them look sunburnt, jaundiced, or like they've just had a bad, spray-on tan.

Kodak Portra might not be the first choice for landscape photography, but it is a mighty fine choice for portraits. Portra 400 has slightly more saturated colours than Portra 160, and less so than the 800 variant, giving the perfect balance for making those skin tones look just right.

When I can't make up my mind what film to use, I'll probably just grab a roll of Kodak Portra 400 and forget about it. It's just a versatile, good-looking film that doesn't look unflattering with most photos shot in daylight. It's also a negative film so it's easier to work with, and keeps the details in the bright bits better than a slide film.

Fujifilm 400H is a great alternative to Portra, rendering skin tones beautifully with a pastel palette that will appeal to those who want an old-school vibe. It's got a slightly cooler look than the warmer tones of Portra 400.

If you want to try slide film, Fujichrome Astia 100F and Provia 100F are superb for portraits, with the former giving a slightly warmer look than the cooler tones of the latter. They are slower films, though, so you will need more light for your exposure.

Kodak Gold and Fujifilm Superia are worth considering, especially given the fact that not all of the aforementioned film stock can be bought in your bog-standard drug stores or supermarkets. Gold and Superia are quite common, but that's not to say they're not interesting. If you want a punchy, vivid look, go for Gold; Superia has a cooler look that brings out those blues and greens.

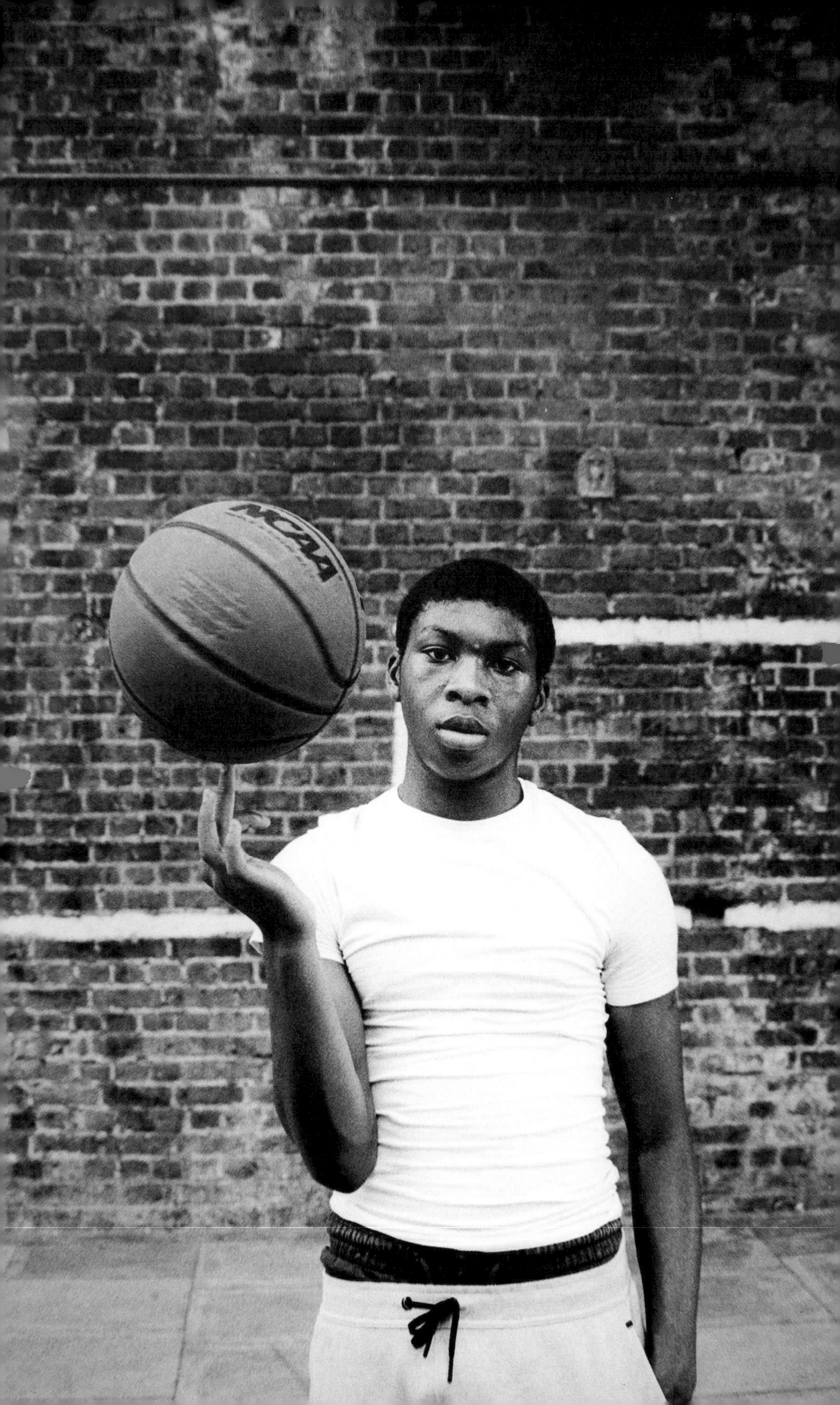
NCAA

#16 EVERYTHING MAKES SENSE IN BLACK AND WHITE

"Colour is bullshit." So said the supreme lord of street photography, Henri Cartier-Bresson, to one of the pioneers of colour photography, William Eggleston.

These days not too many would dare defecate on the use of colour in photography. Although black-and-white still has a strong association with fine-art photography, it is mostly an afterthought in the digital photographic process.

If you want to do black-and-white photography properly, you should do it with film. Luckily for you, there's an abundance of different black-and-white film available for you to try. Here are a few you might want to know about:

ISO 100

Kodak T-Max 100 is great for reproducing those sharp, crispy details with minimal grain. It's an easy-to-like film that produces buttery smooth, grayscale images.

Alternatively, Ilford Delta 100 is every bit as good as T-Max 100, if not better, if you're a sucker for richer tonality, and a sharper look.

When Fujifilm started making monochrome film again, they brought back Acros II. It is essentially the same as the original Acros, albeit with a subtle difference—it produces a more contrasted look.

Due to its lower sensitivity to light, ISO 100 black-and-white film is more suited for use in bright daylight or longer exposures, and the finer-grain structure would work well for landscapes or portraits. Otherwise, if you want something more versatile—to be used in good light or bad—then you should try some ISO 400 film stock.

ISO 400

Tri-X 400 and Ilford HP5 Plus are the two classics of black-and-white photography. If you want an idea of why that grainy black-and-white look is so appealing, give Kodak Tri-X 400 a go to appreciate those moody shadows and gritty, grainy textures. If you're not looking for such a stark look in an ISO 400 film, Ilford's HP5 Plus is a great alternative, with no less of the granular goodness but with a softer tonality and lower contrast that will open up the details in the shadows and retain them in the highlights, too.

Alternatively, try JCH StreetPan 400 if you want to go maxi on the moodiness; it'll create super contrasty images, with deep, dark shadows, for a dramatic look.

Ilford XP2 Super and Fujifilm Neopan 400CN are also worth a mention for those who want the convenience of quick and easy processing. They both can be developed using the C41 process, meaning they can be dealt with in any good film labs (and bad ones, too) quickly, cheaply, and easily. It's just that the images don't look as cool as traditional black-and-white films.

ISO 3200

With higher-speed film you'd expect more prominent grain, and unsurprisingly you do get more, but it's not as intrusive as you might think.

For ISO 3200 film, you have the choice between Kodak T-Max P3200 and Ilford Delta 3200. Although their box speed is 3200, T-Max P3200 is actually an ISO 800 film designed to be pushed to 3200, and the Delta 3200 is a 1600 film pushed to 3200 (we'll cover push and pull processing later). T-Max P3200 is slightly sharper, less grainy, and more contrasted than Delta 3200. The look of Delta 3200 has a more vintage vibe to it, with the grainy, softer, low-contrast image.

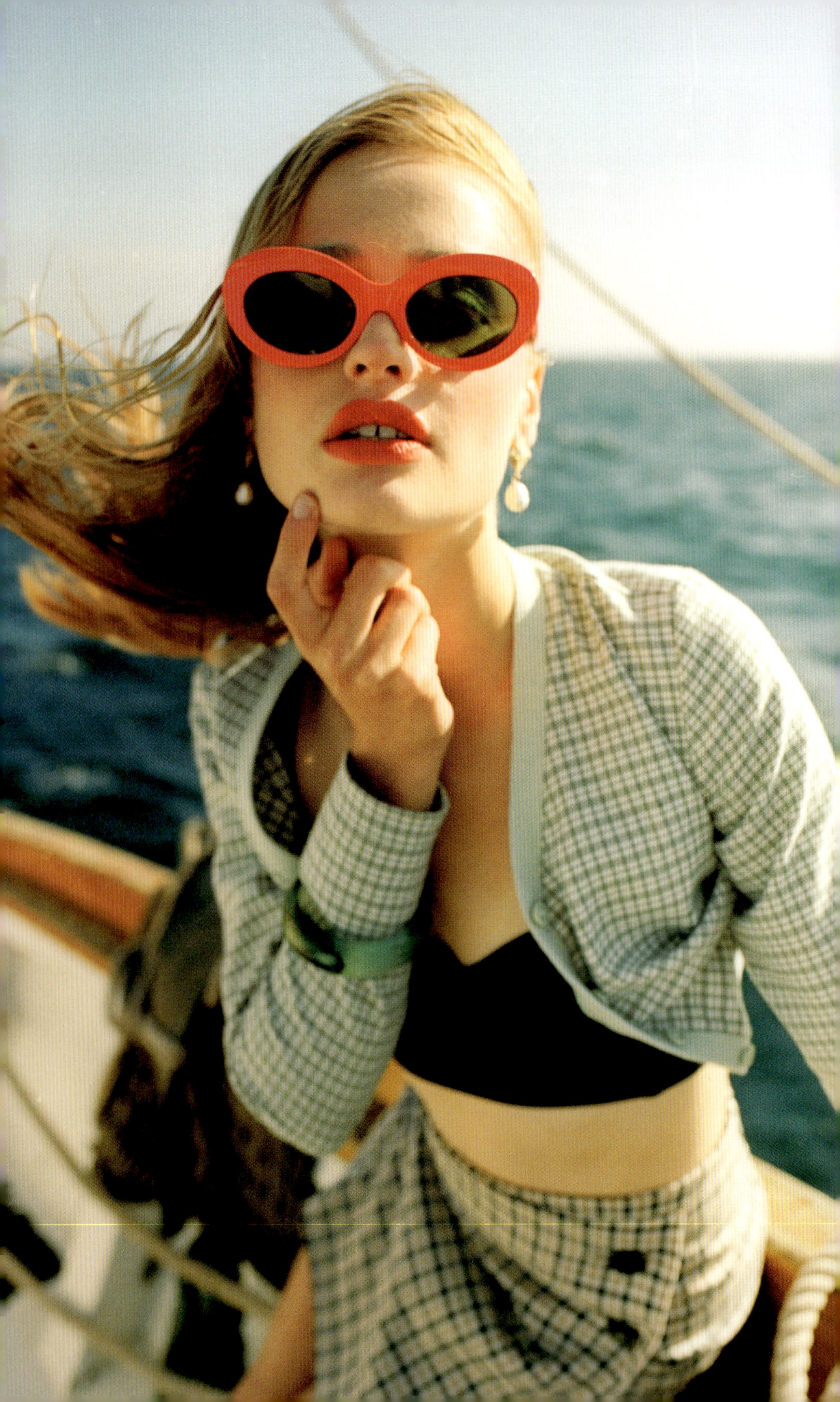

#17
HOW TO BUY YOUR "PERFECT" LENS

Don't underestimate the importance of investing in good glass. Whereas a camera is just a branded, light-tight box with a mechanism that opens and closes a trapdoor to let light through, the lens is that hunky chunk of exotic glass on the front of the camera that injects a bit of a pizazz in your photo.

In an ideal world, you'll want the perfect lens. In the actual world we're living in, you'll have to make do with whatever you can afford. So don't let some internet dude with a load of subscribers tell you which lens to buy with your hard-earned cash. A review will only take you so far; your eyes have to make the decision for you. Figure out what it is that you want in a lens, and then look at sample photos to find out if what you see is what you like.

Focal Length

First, you will need to figure out what lens focal length you require. A focal length is usually indicated in millimetres (or centimetres on your granddad's lenses). The smaller the number, the wider it is, and the more things you will get in your frame. A bigger number means a longer lens, a telelens, which is good for photographing things far away, or getting a tighter crop on a subject.

Maximum Aperture

The next thing you should consider is what maximum aperture you would like. An aperture opens up to let more light in, and closes to let less light in. The maximum aperture—that is, how large it will open—is rated with an f/ number that is almost always printed on the front of the lens. The lower the number, the larger the aperture can be opened and the faster the lens is. A fast lens lets in more light, which sounds good, but often a lens will perform at its crummiest when shot with the lens aperture at its largest setting.

Bokeh

When a lens is set to its largest aperture, you will get some gorgeous subject isolation, where the subject is in focus and the background is thrown out of focus. It makes your subject pop, drawing the attention toward the subject, so the last thing you want is some distracting out-of-focus elements in the background.

When photo geeks talk about bokeh, they're referring to the attractiveness of those blurry elements in the photo. A good lens will make those blurry backgrounds melt away, whereas a not-so-good lens will make those blurry bits distracting.

Sharpness

Some people only consider lens sharpness when evaluating a lens, but there is a lot more to a lens than just how sharp it is. Still, most modern lenses perform to a decent level, as a lot use aspherical elements in their design, which produce very sharp, clean results and are made to correct a lot of optical imperfections.

Modern lenses will produce crisper results, but you will have to figure out if you prefer a sharper image or a more retro vibe that you might get with older lenses.

Kai's Tips

- The perfect lens is what looks good to you and what fits your needs—not the popular opinion or what someone else says about a lens.
- You will hear about things like chromatic aberration, astigmatism, and coma. Reading all about it will probably put you in a coma, and to be honest, you shouldn't get too hung up about lens imperfections.

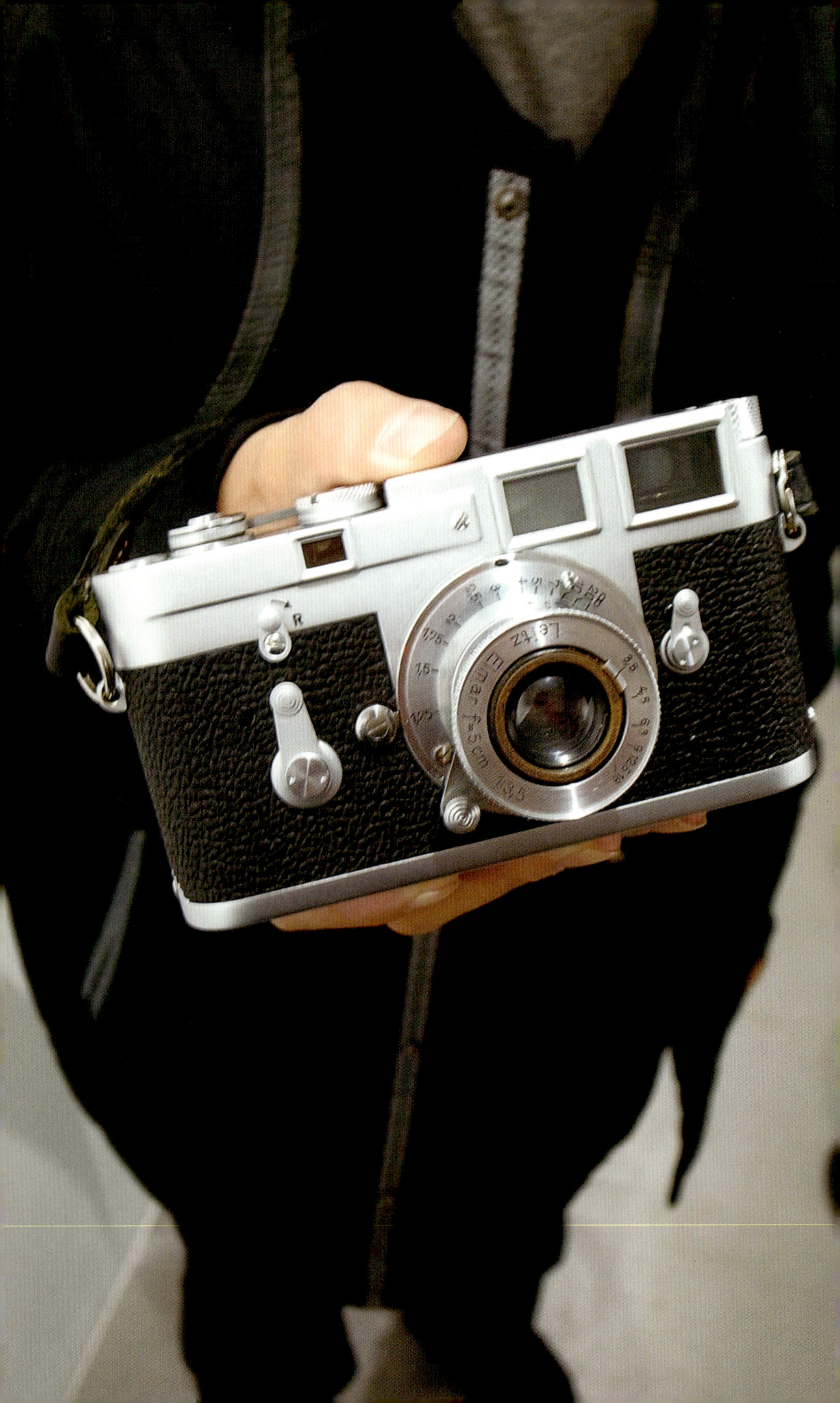
Leitz
Elmar
R

#18

FIVE THINGS TO LOOK OUT FOR WHEN BUYING A VINTAGE LENS

Scratches

Unless someone etched a drawing of some genitalia on the front lens element, a few fine scratches shouldn't be problematic; if it's not a deep scratch, it won't detrimentally affect your image. The only thing that it might damage is the resale value, but that's fine if you bought it for a fair price.

Dust

I've not seen any amount of dust inside a lens severe enough to become problematic to your image. Dust getting inside your lens is an inevitability: a lens has parts that move in and out, sucking air in and out of the lens; so it's no wonder that bits of dead skin end up inside your lens.

Fungus and Haze

Both of these are down to keeping lenses in hot and humid conditions. Haze is formed when the lubricants used within the lenses become vaporised and trapped within the lens; fungus is mould, and both can be seen by shining a flashlight straight into a lens. Both fungus and haze will lower the contrast of your photos and make it look softer.

Make sure the used lens that you're buying is free from fungus and haze, because even though you might be able to get the lens serviced, the damage to the glass may be irreversible.

Grungy Focusing Ring

Make sure the focusing ring is buttery smooth. Vintage lenses might have decades of some greasy guy's finger grunge trapped underneath the focus ring, making it harder to rotate, which is not a good thing if you need to manually focus. Check that the aperture ring clicks succinctly, without any gunky resistance.

Aperture Blades

Aperture blades can get oily, which causes problems with the movement of the blades. And if the oil gets onto the lens elements, it will be super sucky for your images. Do check on the movement of the blades: that they open up in a uniform way and don't have anything obvious, like blades swinging loose.

Kai's Tips

- Do the flashlight test when buying a lens. Bring a torch or use the flashlight feature on your iPhone.
- If you're buying a lens on the internet, ask about all the things mentioned above.
- The lens doesn't have to be in perfect condition unless you're a collector. Gear was made to be used.

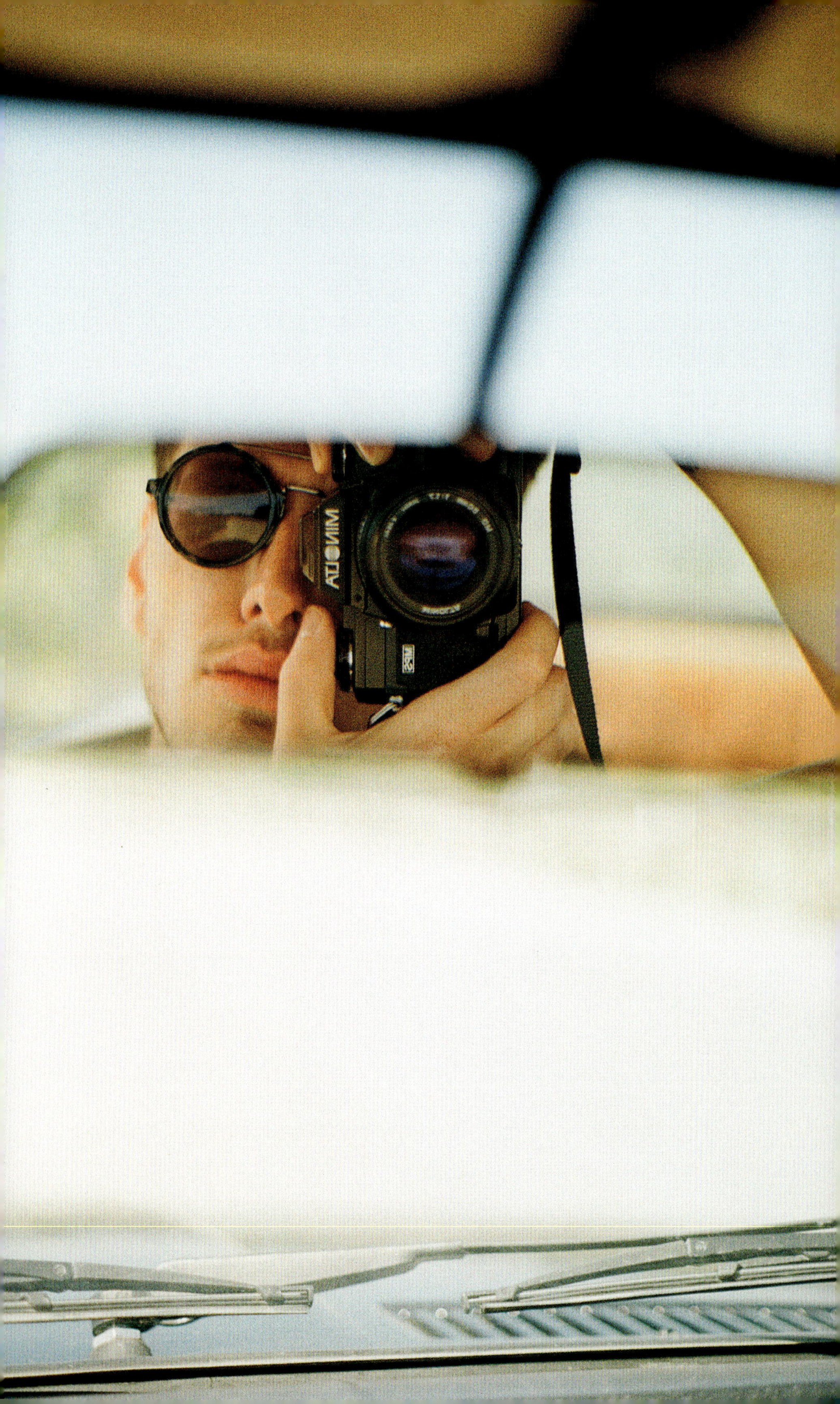

#19 WHY A "STANDARD" LENS IS YOUR BEST FRIEND

A standard lens doesn't sound particularly thrilling, but not only will it be your most useful lens, it could also quite easily be the most fun you can have with a bit of metal and glass.

In 35 mm film camera terms, 50 mm is the standard lens focal length (although pedants might point out that it should actually be 43 mm). If you're using a medium-format camera, the standard lens will be longer.

Everything Looks Good with a Standard

Photos taken with a standard lens just look correct because they are closest to what the human eye sees. That's what they say anyway. Although those magnificent little balls nestled in your skull actually pick up an angle of view far wider than a 50 mm standard—it's more like 20 or 24 mm—a lot of that is peripheral vision. What you can actually focus on visually, your point of fixation at any one time, is more akin to that of a standard lens.

That is perhaps why a photo taken with a 50 mm lens looks so pleasing to the eye—because our brains can relate to it: the angle of view, the perspective, the magnification; it feels like you're looking at a scene through someone else's eyes. Or maybe there's no need to explain it, and we can just accept that it looks better.

Fast Fifty

If a fast maximum aperture and creamy bokeh is what you're after, you're going to love a fast fifty. Some of the largest-apertured lenses in the world are 50 mm lenses, with lenses such as the Leica's naughty Noctilux 50mm f/1.0, even naughtier Noctilux f/0.95, Canon 50mm f/1.0L, and slower-but-by-no-means-slow f/1.2L stretching the f-stop ratings to levels lower than other focal lengths can stoop to.

Even if a fast fifty isn't your bag or not for your wallet, there are plenty of other options to choose from.

Nifty Fifty

The thrifty photographer's choice of lens has always been the affectionately named Nifty Fifty, which has nothing to do with the stock market and everything to do with offering excellent levels of optical quality for a minimal amount of money.

Most brands made a 50 mm f/1.8 (or f/2.0) as a low-cost option to their faster offerings, and the 1.8 is still the sensible choice today. Sometimes the slower lens actually gives better image quality than the more expensive, larger-apertured options, too.

For Everything and Everywhere

With 50 mm lenses, there isn't just a cheap option and an expensive, fast one. There are 50 mm macro lenses for extreme close-up shots of things like flowers and creepy insect photos that will make your skin crawl, and 50 mm tilt-shift lenses for photographers who like keeping their straight lines straight when taking photos of buildings and the like.

The focal length is not too tight that you won't see much other than a tight crop of your subject's nostril hairs, and not too wide that you'll have some inadvertent photo-bombing aunties creeping into your frame. You won't need to move too far backward to get all of your subject in the frame, and you won't have a problem having too much detail in your shots. The 50 mm keeps things tidy by including just the right amount of bits in your frame.

That means you can use the 50 mm lens for different types of photography, from portraits to landscapes, street photography to macro shots. And to top that off, 50s are some of the neatest, most-compact lenses around; these are the reasons why this could be your number one lens, or your only lens.

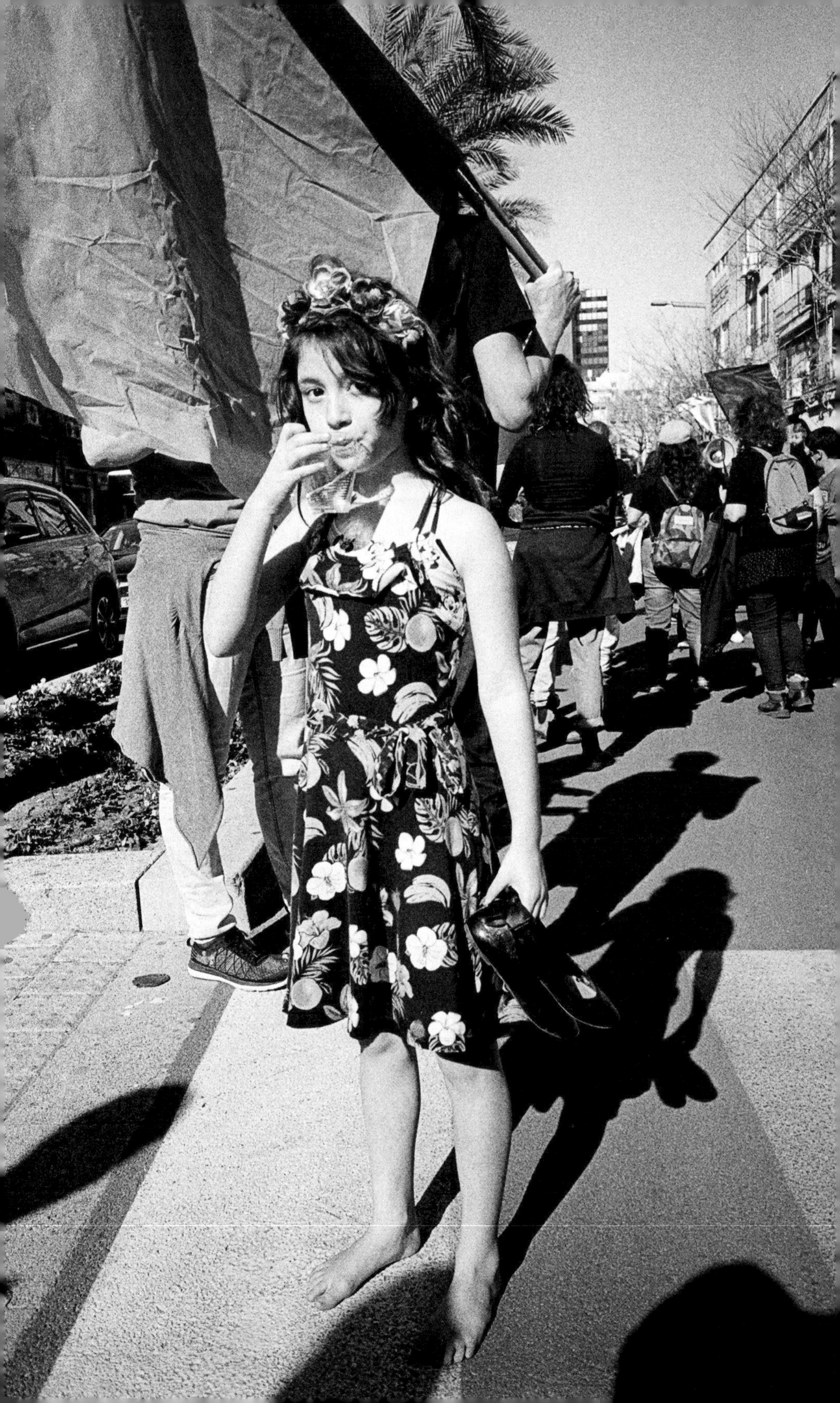

#20 WIDE ANGLES: THE LENSES THAT KEEP ON GIVING

If you ever find that with a 50 mm your back is to the wall, desperately trying to fit everything in the frame, then you'll need a wide-angle lens to give you the space you need to play with. However, once you've gone wide, you will inevitably want to go wider. And wider. It is a heck of a lot of fun playing with lenses that let you fill a frame with so much more detail.

35 mm

A 35 mm lens on a 35 mm film camera is often classed as a wide-angle, but it functions more like a wide-standard. It just doesn't look vastly different than a 50 mm—essentially giving a little more room around the edges. So if you've bought a 50 mm already, it doesn't make too much sense to get a 35 mm lens to introduce you to the wonderful world of wideness.

28 mm

A few millimetres less makes a lot of difference. At this focal length you'll start to get a taste of what wide-angle can offer: things appear to be pushed a little farther away than they actually are, and you'll find that you are given a significant amount more room to play with without looking too different from what you're seeing with your own eyes.

24 mm

If the 28 mm doesn't seem roomy enough, then you might as well shave 4 mm off the focal length and go for a 24 mm. It's still moderate enough to show you the ways of the wide without making it difficult to relate to what you're seeing through the viewfinder.

The wide-angle reality distortion becomes more apparent—things in the background appear noticeably smaller than they do with just your own eyes, and shapes and lines appear elongated, more exaggerated.

21 mm/20 mm

At this focal length, you suddenly see everything in the wild way of an ultrawide-angle. It has this dramatic effect of making anything you put closer to the lens appear as if it has been sucked in, making limbs look Mr. Tickle-like, and pushing anything away from the lens even farther away. It might make your human subjects look like the headline act of a freak show, so it is best advised not to use an ultrawide for portraits unless you don't like the person you're photographing.

10–16 mm

Anything in this range could still be called ultrawide, but it doesn't do these lenses justice to be given the same label, because the angle of view goes from 107 degrees (16 mm) to an extreme 130 degrees (10 mm). You have to be careful about anyone or anything to the sides of the camera, because your perfect composition might be ruined by the inclusion of a stray finger or photobombing granny.

These are special-use lenses that need very careful framing to achieve good-looking shots. Just like with the 20 or 21 mm, shapes and lines are exaggerated, but to a much higher level. Even holding the camera a couple degrees off axis can make the lines look horribly distorted in your photo. If you can spend some time learning how to work with them, you'll be rewarded with some fantastically out-of-this-world-looking photos.

Fish-eye

If you're talking about images that look unlike anything you'll see with your own eyes, then you might want to try lenses that show the world through the eyes of a fish. You have linear fish-eyes and circular fish-eyes that either fill the frame or show a circle within the frame that is characterised by heavily distorted lines and shapes.

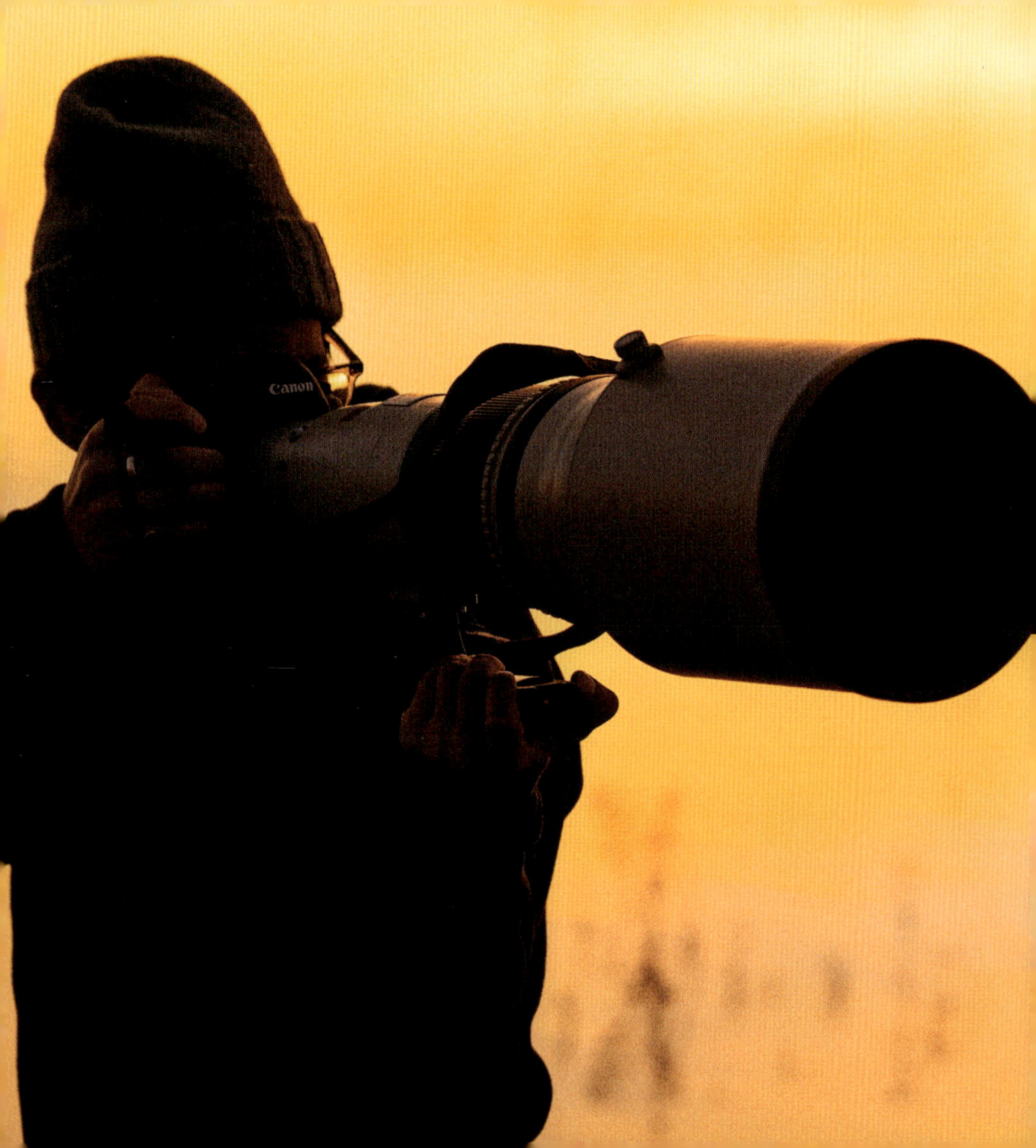
Canon

#21 TELEPHOTO LENS: MAKING THE IMPOSSIBLE POSSIBLE

Telephoto lenses need little introduction. Even if you've never used one before, you probably already associate those long-ass lenses with sports photographers, fishing-vest-wearing bird-watchers, and dodgy people who wear trench coats with nothing underneath. Perhaps.

Longer, focal-length lenses give you more reach, allowing you to take photos that would be otherwise difficult or impossible because of the distance between you and the subject. But although this is one of the main reasons to use one, a telephoto is useful for other things.

Blow Those Backgrounds Away

A telephoto lens can help to separate the subject from the background, minimizing the number of distractions and directing the attention straight toward the subject by making those background bits melt away like a gooey, cheesy fondue, while keeping the subject tack sharp.

Longer focal lengths have a higher magnification, which enlarges the subject as well as everything else in the frame, including the out-of-focus elements. Contrary to what some might say, it's not that you get shallower depth of field with a telephoto compared to a standard or wider lens per se—you do if you're shooting the same subject from the same distance, but not if you step backwards to make the subject the same size in the frame. Ignore that stuff about perspective compression because that's all boring crap, and just think of telephoto lenses as magnifiers of mushiness for blowing away those backgrounds into oblivion.

Short Telephoto

Anything from 75 mm to 135 mm is classified as a short tele, which are ideal focal lengths for portraits. These allow you to create some gorgeous, blurry backgrounds and put the focus squarely on what matters most—that thing with a face in front of you—without being so far away from your fleshy subject that you'll need a walkie-talkie to give them directions.

In use, they won't feel too wildly different from your trusty standard lens because they are just a little bit longer, in terms of focal length, but that inevitably means they don't offer the kind of magnification that would be useful for photographing anything much farther away.

Medium Telephoto

If you want to take sports photos, focal lengths up to 300 mm are your most useful (depending on the sport), giving you the ability to get close to the action without becoming an obstacle on the field of play.

Whereas short telephotos are easier to get stable shots handheld, you will need to be careful with a medium tele. Use a fast-enough shutter speed to make the shakes less apparent, and/or get a tele with image stabilisation that works to even out your shakiness. The longer the lens, the more difficult it becomes to get a stable, handheld shot.

Super Telephoto

Anything above 300 mm is for the hardcore enthusiasts. If you're going to spend that amount of money on a glass-filled tube, and lug around the equivalent weight of a newborn baby on one shoulder all day, then you must be very serious about your craft. In my opinion, these lenses aren't your typical film photography lenses; but if you want to carry around a suitcase or rent a mule for the day, then so be it.

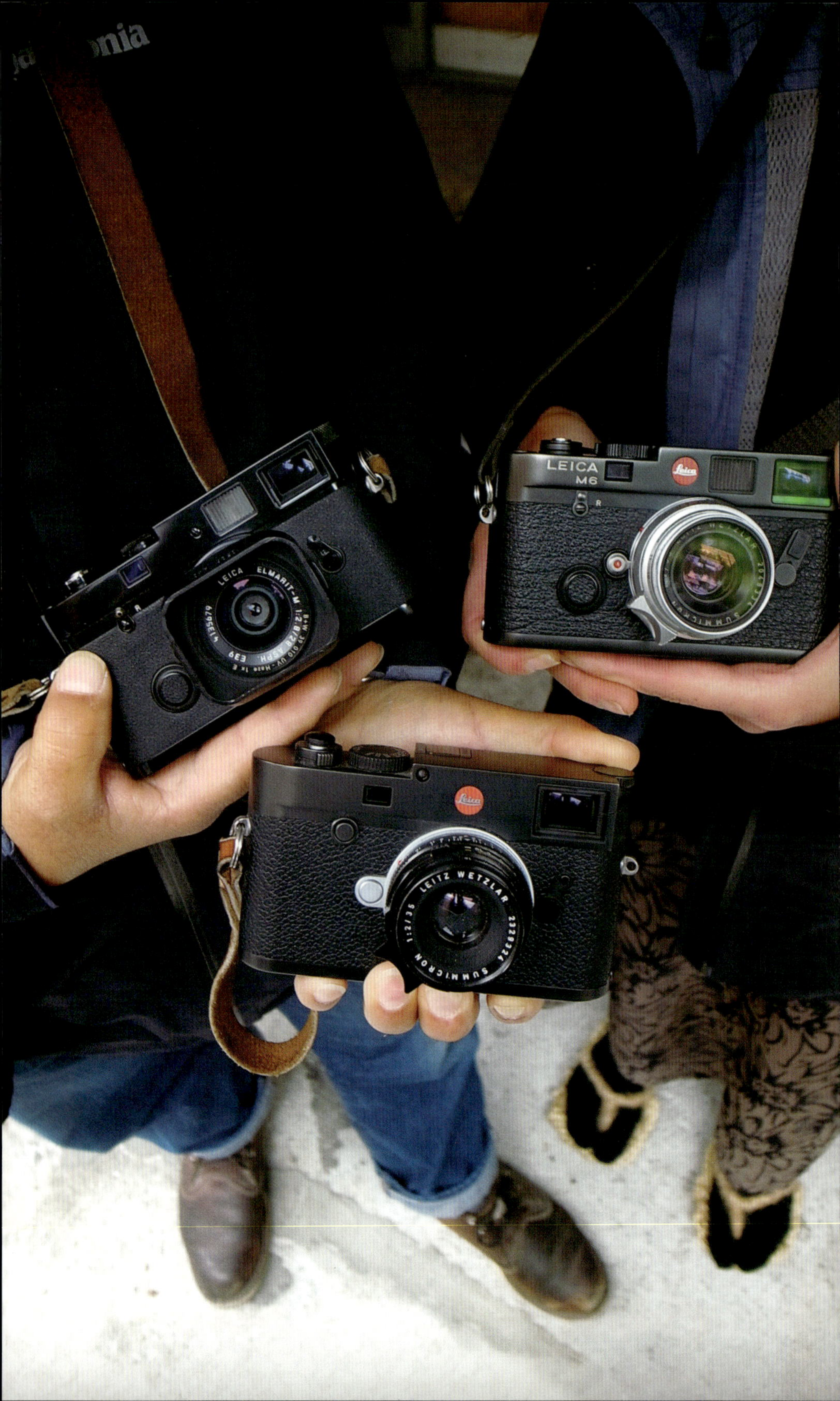
LEICA
M6
Leica
LEICA ELMARIT-M
Leica
LEITZ WETZLAR
1:2/35
SUMMICRON

#22 WHY THREE LENSES ARE ALL YOU NEED

Three is the magic number—nobody needs to carry more than three lenses when out taking photos. If you know what you want to photograph, then you'll come prepared with just the right tools for the job, instead of lugging your whole toolbox around with you.

Only you can decide what lenses you need, but restricting it to three keeps things simple, so you won't faff about contemplating which lens to use and waste time swapping lenses around.

To give you some ideas on how to compile the perfect set of optics, here are a couple of three-lens setups that I might use:

28-50-85: The Travel Setup

This trio is a tidy little setup to take on your travels because it covers pretty much anything that you'd want to take pics of, from landscapes and scenery to street scenes and portraits.

At night you can switch to a fast 50 mm to ensure that you won't have any problems getting enough light for your photo—although an 85 mm lens can do the low-light stuff too, as a lot of them have quite large maximum apertures (f/2 or below, usually). Bear in mind, the 85 mm will probably be the chunkiest bit of glass out of the three and, being a short telephoto, won't be as helpful to get stable, handheld shots.

You can always make this a 24-35-85 setup if you prefer something a little wider as your standard. If it's for travel, or you're just out and about in town, this is a nice set of focal lengths to be packing that will have you prepared for most eventualities without overcomplicating things.

16-24-35: The Landscape Setup

Landscape photographers don't strictly use wide-angle lenses, but I find that most landscapes that I shoot fall in this focal range.

As landscape subjects tend to be static, having 16 mm, 24 mm, and 35 mm gives me three different focal lengths that still cover the range I usually work within without leaving too many gaps in between. The camera would be mounted on a tripod, and I'd spend some time moving the camera around to try different positioning and swapping lenses over if needed.

The three lenses that you carry don't have to make sense to anyone else other than yourself. Pack the focal lengths that will be useful to you and nothing else, to keep your setup as simple and uncomplicated as possible.

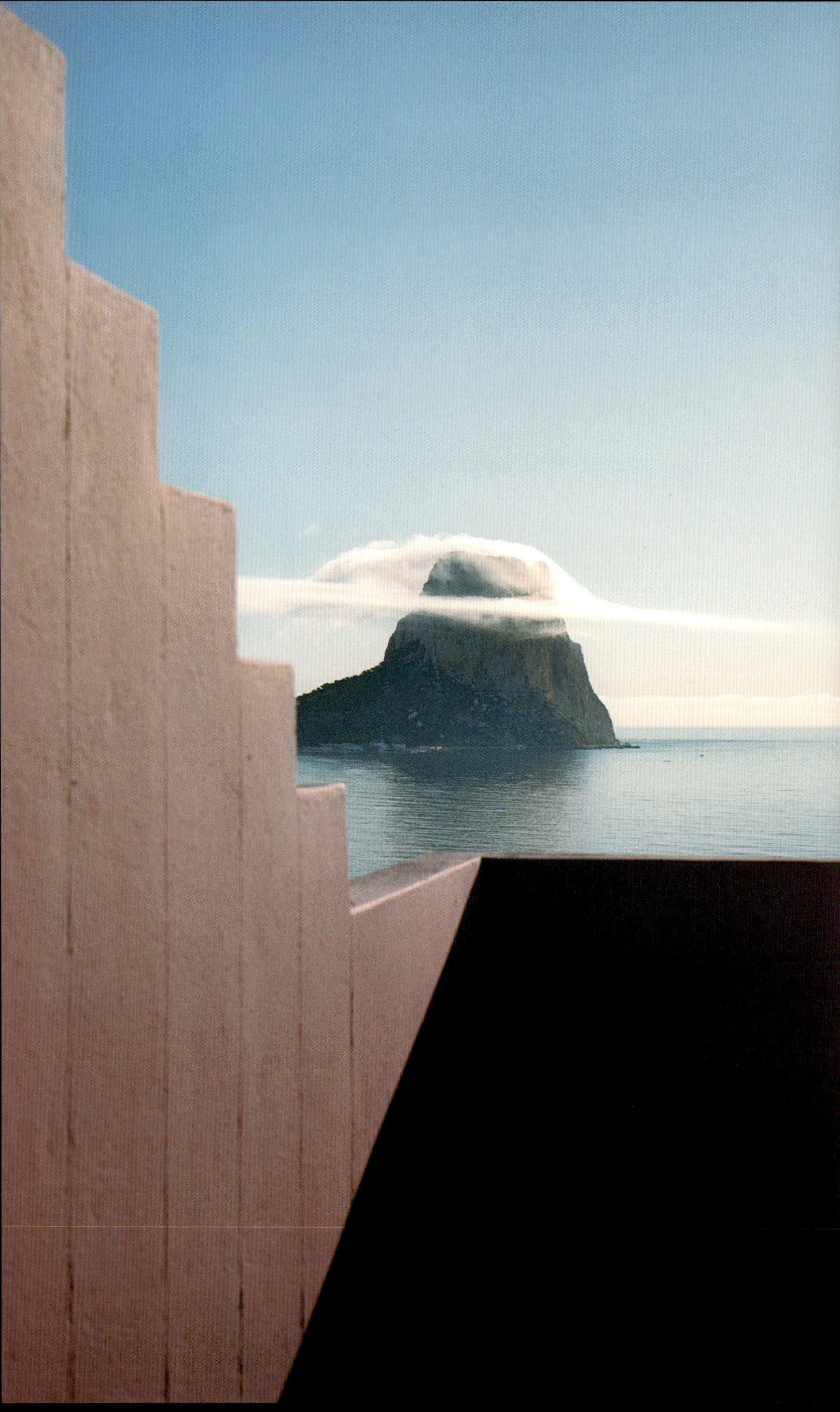

#23
ZOOMS vs. PRIME LENSES: WHICH ONE SHOULD YOU GO FOR?

Keeping things simple and limiting yourself to just three fixed, focal-length (prime) lenses seems like sensible thinking until you bring zoom lenses into the equation. If practical is what you're after, then you might want to just carry a zoom lens, because it means you can have those three focal lengths (and more!) in just one lens.

Which one should you use, though? It's as personal a decision as buying boxers or briefs. I can't tell you which one you should go for, but I can certainly help you come to that decision (with lenses, not your underpants).

What Is a Prime Lens?

A prime lens is a lens with a fixed focal length, which means that if you want to get more things in the frame, then you need to move backwards; or if you want a closer crop of your subject, then you need to walk closer.

What Is a Zoom Lens?

Your feet needn't do any of the hard work with a zoom lens. You use your fingers to rotate the zoom ring on the lens to access all the focal lengths, to either get a wider angle or a tighter crop.

You'll see the focal length and maximum aperture printed on the front of the lens body. A 24–70 mm f/2.8-4 indicates that the zoom lens covers all the focal lengths from 24 mm to 70 mm, and that the maximum aperture is f/2.8 at 24 mm and f/4 at 70 mm. More expensive zoom lenses might have a fixed aperture throughout the zoom range (e.g., 24–70 mm f/2.8), but they are usually heftier lenses because of the more complex optical designs.

To help you figure out which lens is right for you, here's a rundown of reasons why you'd go for a zoom or prime lens:

Prime Lens

- Prime lenses tend to be smaller and lighter than zoom lenses.
- You can get a faster maximum aperture with primes, making them better suited for low-light shooting.
- Image quality: although not strictly true with all primes versus zooms, a lot of primes will take top-quality images that you won't get with a zoom because of the more complex optical designs involved with a zoom.
- Prime lenses force you to move to get the shot, so you're actively thinking and concentrating on the framing instead of standing on the spot hoping that you can nail it by simply moving your fingers.
- It's easier to know what you're getting with a prime: the angle of view, the magnification, the depth of field.

Zoom Lens

- It's quicker to change focal length with a zoom than changing from one prime to another.
- One prime lens might be lighter than one zoom, but a zoom is lighter than all the focal lengths it covers.
- If you carry three zoom lenses in your bag, you can cover a huge range of focal lengths.
- A zoom is useful when you're standing in a spot where you simply can't move forward and backward to get a tighter/wider shot.
- It's beneficial if you're photographing a fast-moving subject that might sometimes move closer to you or farther away.
- If you're not photographing at the largest aperture, you won't always notice a huge difference in image quality compared to primes, as most lenses perform really well at moderate aperture settings.

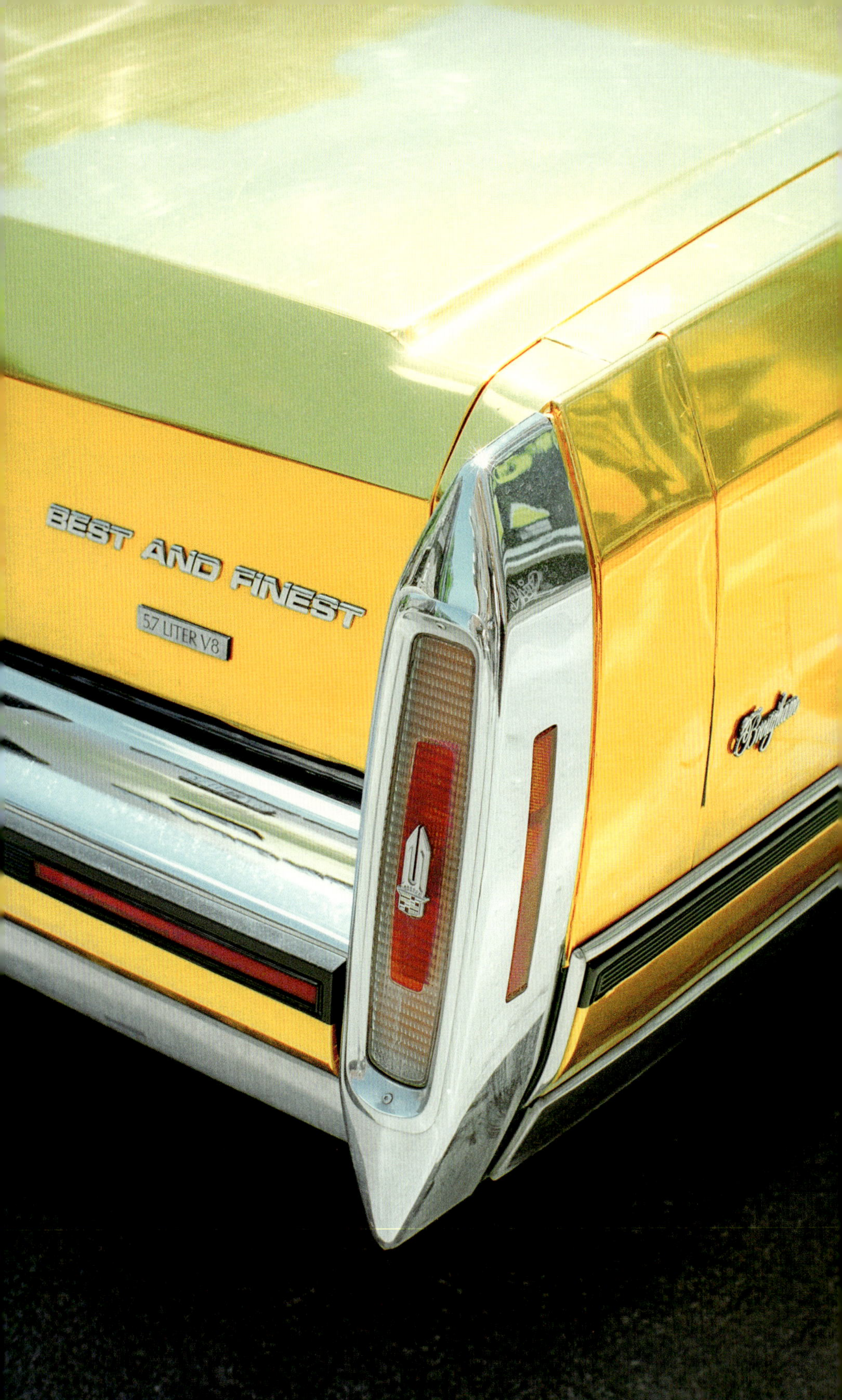
BEST AND FINEST
5.7 LITER V8

#24
AUTO vs. MANUAL: WHICH ONE SHOULD YOU USE?

Mastering manual doesn't make you a master of photography. If you feel more comfortable letting the camera decide what settings to use, don't feel like you're any less of a photographer for it.

Automated modes are designed to make life easier for you, so why would you bother messing with manual?

Autofocus vs. Manual Focus

This is all you need to do: look through the viewfinder, pick a point, and press the shutter button halfway. It's really that simple to focus your autofocusing camera.

But just so you know, if you're accustomed to the blazing autofocus speeds of modern digital cameras, then you might be a little underwhelmed by the glacial autofocusing speeds, and the lack of focusing points to choose from, on some older film cameras.

There are times when using manual focus will not only feel quicker but also might instill you with more confidence, knowing exactly where the focus is going to end up instead of waiting for the autofocus to hunt around—only for it to end up not focusing properly.

Autofocusing film cameras can be a blessing; just bear in mind that the autofocusing performance can range from spiffy to just plain iffy.

Autoexposure

These are some of the autoexposure modes that you can use (depending on the camera):

1. Full auto: Letting the camera decide what shutter speed and aperture setting to use to get a good exposure.
2. Aperture priority: You decide what aperture setting to use, and the camera will pick the best shutter speed to use to ensure you get a good exposure.
3. Shutter priority: You pick the shutter speed, and the camera will pick an aperture setting to get a good exposure.
4. When I first started learning how to take photos, I was adamant that I use an all-manual camera because I wanted that creative control—to make it feel like I was working to make that shot, to feel connected to the camera and the photographic process (or something pretentious like that).

It does feel fun to shoot all-manual, and if you're going to get into film, then shunning all of the mod cons and going all out with the old-school experience kinda makes sense. There are also times when you need to use manual exposure because it lets you have full control of exposure. Having said that, I'm 100 percent happy to use any form of automatic if it means I can get that shot easier.

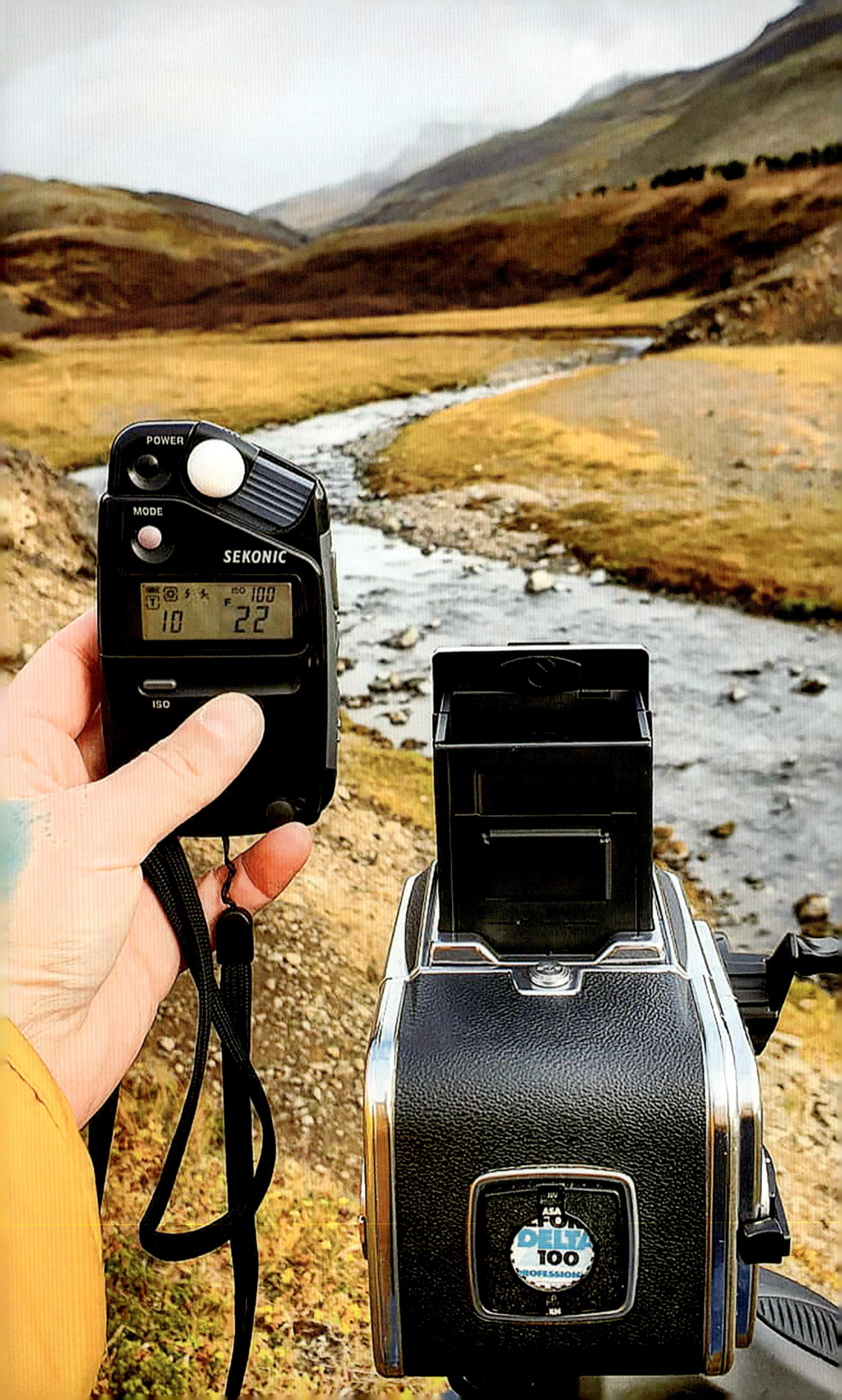
POWER
MODE
SEKONIC
100
10
F 22
ISO
DELTA
100

#25 MAKE PERFECT EXPOSURES WITH LIGHT METERS

If you're fluent in Greek or fluent in Wikipedia, you might well know that photography means drawing with light. To paint the perfect picture, you will need to use just the right amount of light, and to ensure you don't overexpose (too much light) or underexpose (not enough light), you should use some form of light meter to aid you in choosing the right settings.

Handheld Light Meter

If you want accurate readings, then a handheld light meter will give you just that. It's just that you might eventually loathe using one.

The thing is: It's a great tool, but you too will look like a bit of a tool using one—holding a device that looks like an air-con remote with half a Ping-Pong ball glued to the end of it. Then, once you've got your light reading from it, you still have to input the suggested settings from the light meter into your camera.

That's totally fine if you're in a studio where you can take your time, and not many people will see you, but otherwise it's just a clunky process that doesn't always feel conducive to the photo-taking process.

Hot Shoe Light Meter

I regularly use a Voigtlander VC II (#notanad) hot-shoe-mounted light meter on cameras that don't have built-in light meters. It's as rudimentary a device as you can get: You enter your film ISO according to the film that's inside your camera, and then you adjust the little shutter speed and aperture setting dials on the VC II until the green light shows up. Then you use those settings on your camera.

It's far less cumbersome than using a handheld meter, making this, in my opinion, a better method to meter if your camera doesn't have one built-in already. The only problem I have with it is that it might look like a bit of an eyesore, mounted atop your otherwise beautiful, classic camera.

By far the most convenient way of metering, however, is in-camera metering.

Reflective vs. Incident Light Metering

Handheld light meters can take incident meter readings: measuring the amount of light that is hitting the subject. This is a super accurate way of measuring light, but you will need to place the light meter directly next to your subject; and you won't always have the permission required for such invasion of personal space.

The hot shoe (and in-camera) light meters use reflective light measurements: light that is reflected from the subject/scene and into your camera, and assumes whatever you're photographing has a reflective value of 18 percent grey. That's great if you're photographing 18 percent grey, but if you're photographing a white scene, you should overexpose a little to ensure your whites don't end up looking grey. And if you're photographing a black scene, underexpose a little so the black bits don't look grey.

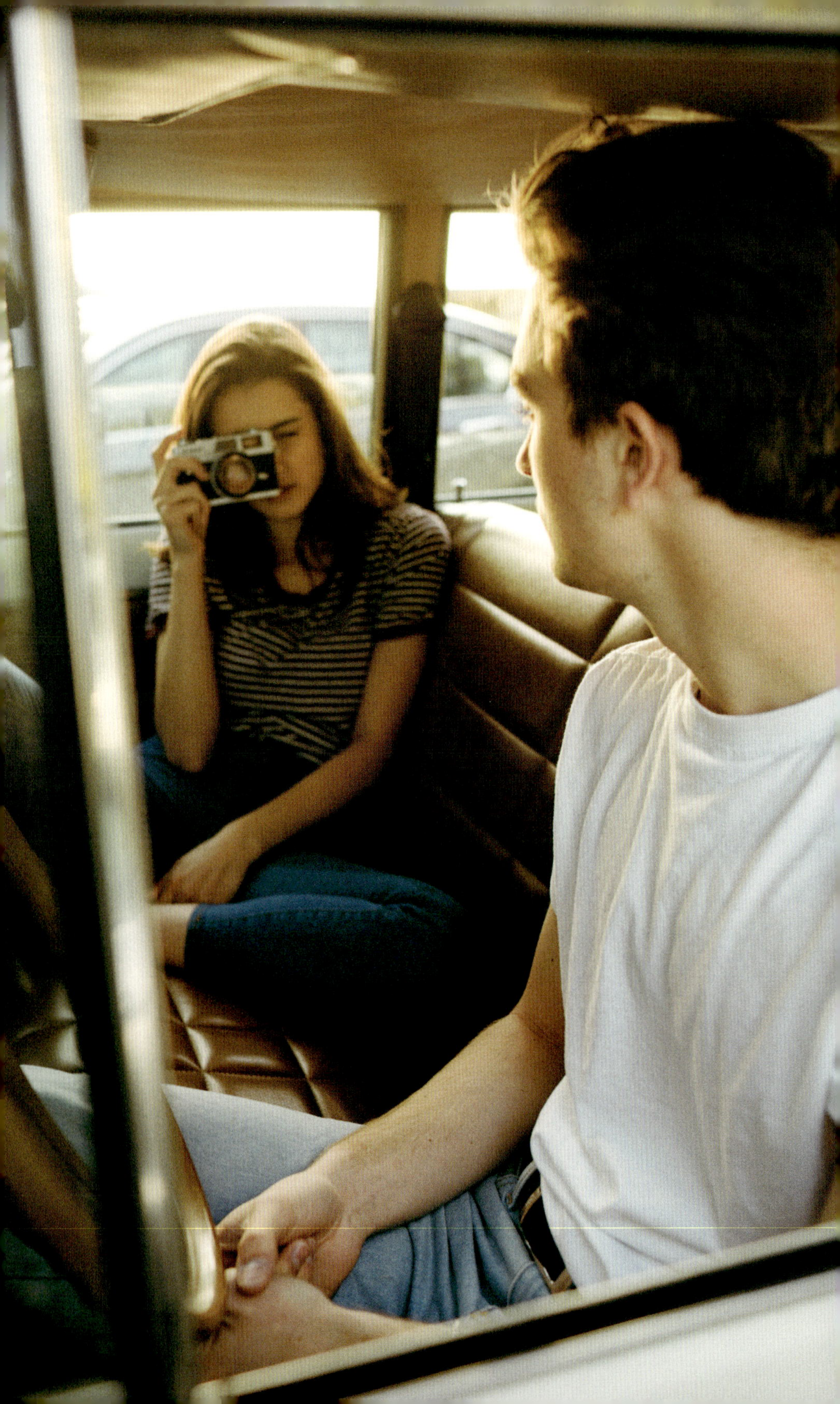

#26
THE IN-CAMERA METERING MODES THAT MATTER

This is what you need: a light meter built-in to your camera, which allows you to check your exposure without having to move your eye away from the all-important viewfinder because of the thoughtfully placed exposure indicator inside. That way you don't have to keep glancing away from your framing.

One thing you should definitely check before you buy a camera is whether it takes mercury batteries. They were once a popular source of power because they offered a stable voltage, and people of that time apparently loved danger.

To keep those mercury-powered meters working and working accurately, you'll need an MR-9 adapter. It might seem somewhat pricey when you see the piddly little thing that you get for your money, but it has some clever-but-simple circuitry that reduces the voltage of a 1.55 V SR43 battery to the 1.35 V you'd get from the mercury battery, meaning you can use the in-camera meter and rely on it.

There are a number of in-camera metering modes that you may or may not have the benefit of choosing from:

Spot/Partial

Basic is sometimes best. Spot metering uses a tiny little dot in the middle of the frame to measure the exposure. As it's just covering a small area, you'll get a pretty good exposure for your subject because it won't be influenced by any other areas of the frame. However, because it's only concerned with the exposure of whatever is under that spot, the rest of the scene might end up too dark if your subject is much brighter, or too bright if your subject is too dark. The camera will expose correctly for that tiny little dot only.

With cameras that have more than one autofocus point, the spot will move depending on where you move the focus point, which is different than:

Centre-Weighted Average Metering

Unlike spot metering, which meters from whatever focus point in the frame you choose, centre-weighted takes the reading from only the centre portion of the frame. Sounds somewhat limiting, but certain types of subjects fill up a significant amount of the centre, and some types of portraits require the subject placed slap-bang in the middle of the frame. Obviously, the problem with this method of metering is that if you suddenly decide to frame your subject to the side of the frame, you're still exposing based on the meter reading for whatever is in the centre of the frame.

Evaluative Metering

I've saved the most useful for last: evaluative metering is the easiest to begin with. This method of metering will evaluate all the elements in the frame to come up with the most balanced exposure.

Even if it sounds like the perfect metering mode, you shouldn't expect that this, or any of the metering modes, will give you the result you are envisioning every single time.

With all of the metering modes, you should familiarise yourself with how they work but also learn how to weigh up the scene and determine whether there are certain elements that can trick the light meter.

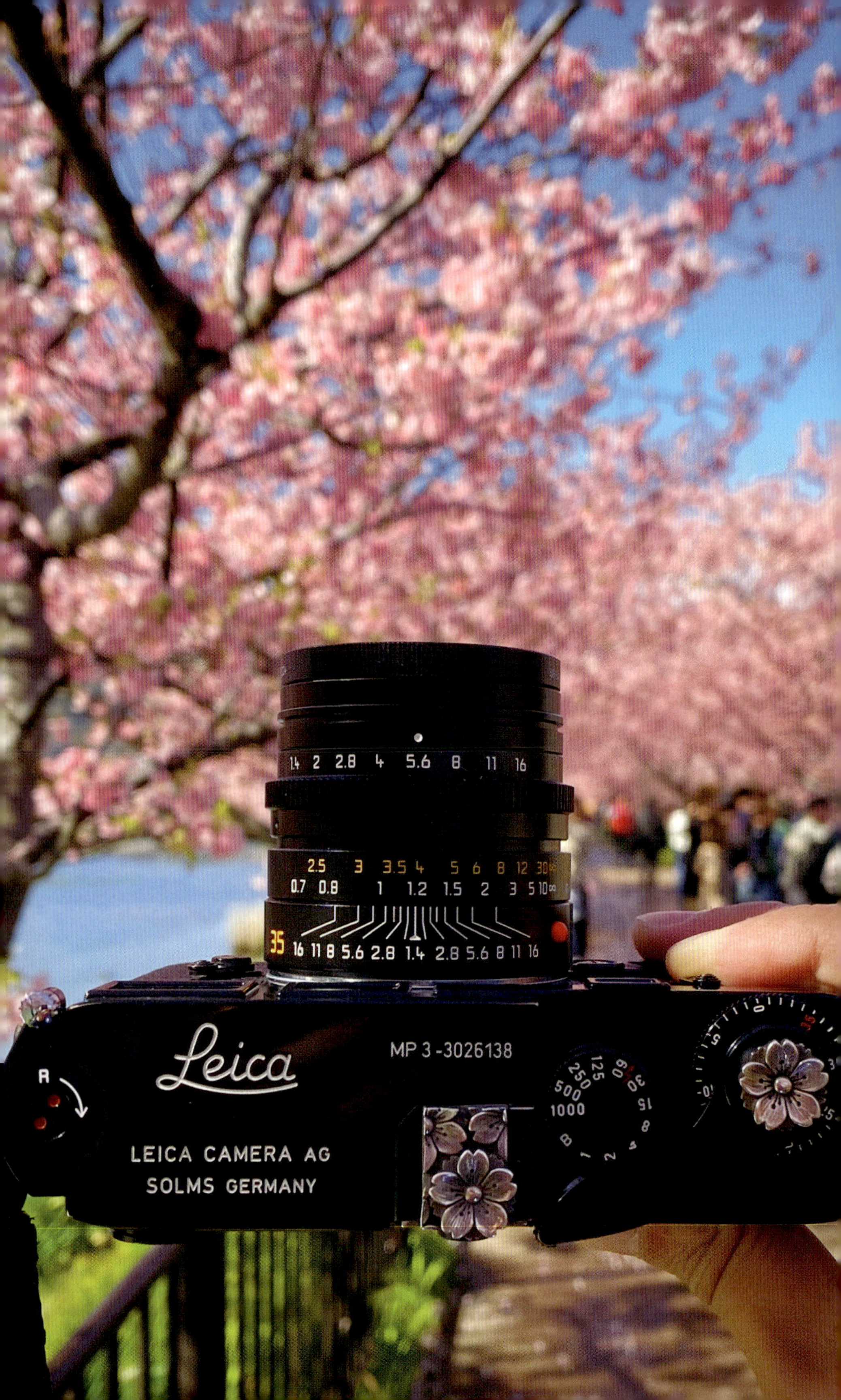
1.4 2 2.8 4 5.6 8 11 16
Leica
MP 3 -3026138
LEICA CAMERA AG
SOLMS GERMANY

#27

KNOB KNOW-HOW: BASIC CONTROLS ON A FILM CAMERA

A film camera is easier to understand than a digital camera simply because it has fewer buttons to press and no clunky menus to navigate. There might be a few rogue knobs and twiddly bits that look a tad scary if you've never handled a film camera before, so here's a quick rundown of what some of them do before talking about how to use it.

Shutter-Release Button

The fun button: press this to take your shot. On older, mechanical cameras, you'll tend to find a little thread in the centre of the button—this allows for a cable release to be screwed in.

Cable Release

Using a cable release will allow you to take a shot without using your fingers to physically depress the shutter button. Sometimes your hands are the weak link in the process, ruining an otherwise perfect shot by pressing a little too hard on the shutter button and making the camera shake. The shake becomes more noticeable if you're using a slower shutter speed. This is also a useful tool if you find yourself wanting to take an old-school-style selfie.

Film Advance Lever

Wind this to advance the film to the next frame. Some are single stroke, some double, meaning it takes either one or two tugs of the lever to move the film onto the next frame.

Exposure Counter

This shows how many shots you've taken, so you can get an indication of how many shots you have left on your current roll of film by using some simple math in your head.

Rewind Knob

When you have no more shots left to take on the roll of film in your camera, you'll need to rewind your film. Some will have a little lever that flips out; some will simply be a knob that makes the rewinding process feel laborious. You should feel some resistance when rewinding it. Keep rewinding until you suddenly hear a muted click and no longer feel that resistance. Only then is it safe to open up the back.

Self-Timer Lever

Flick this switch to activate the countdown timer. At the end of the countdown, your photo will be taken. Mechanical cameras use a little timer that sounds like—and is probably the same as—the one inside a kitchen egg timer. Watch the self-timer lever sweep its way back to the standard position; after that it will take the shot. Electronic cameras will have more accurate timers, with a choice of countdown times, and will make that countdown clear with timed beeps and flashing lights.

Viewfinder

It's your peephole into the world. This is what helps you frame the shot and focus, and it provides information on how to correctly expose your shot (if the camera has a light meter).

Aperture Ring

This feature adjusts the aperture of the lens. It usually has a thoroughly pleasing clicking action, so you can train yourself to remember what aperture setting you're choosing just by counting the number of clicks.

Shutter-Speed Dial

This dial sets the shutter speed: the amount of time the shutter is open to let light shine onto the film. "B" means that the shutter will be open for as long as you press down the shutter-release button.

Focusing Ring

Unlike the aperture ring, it doesn't have a clicking action; the ring should rotate with a nice, smooth, buttery action.

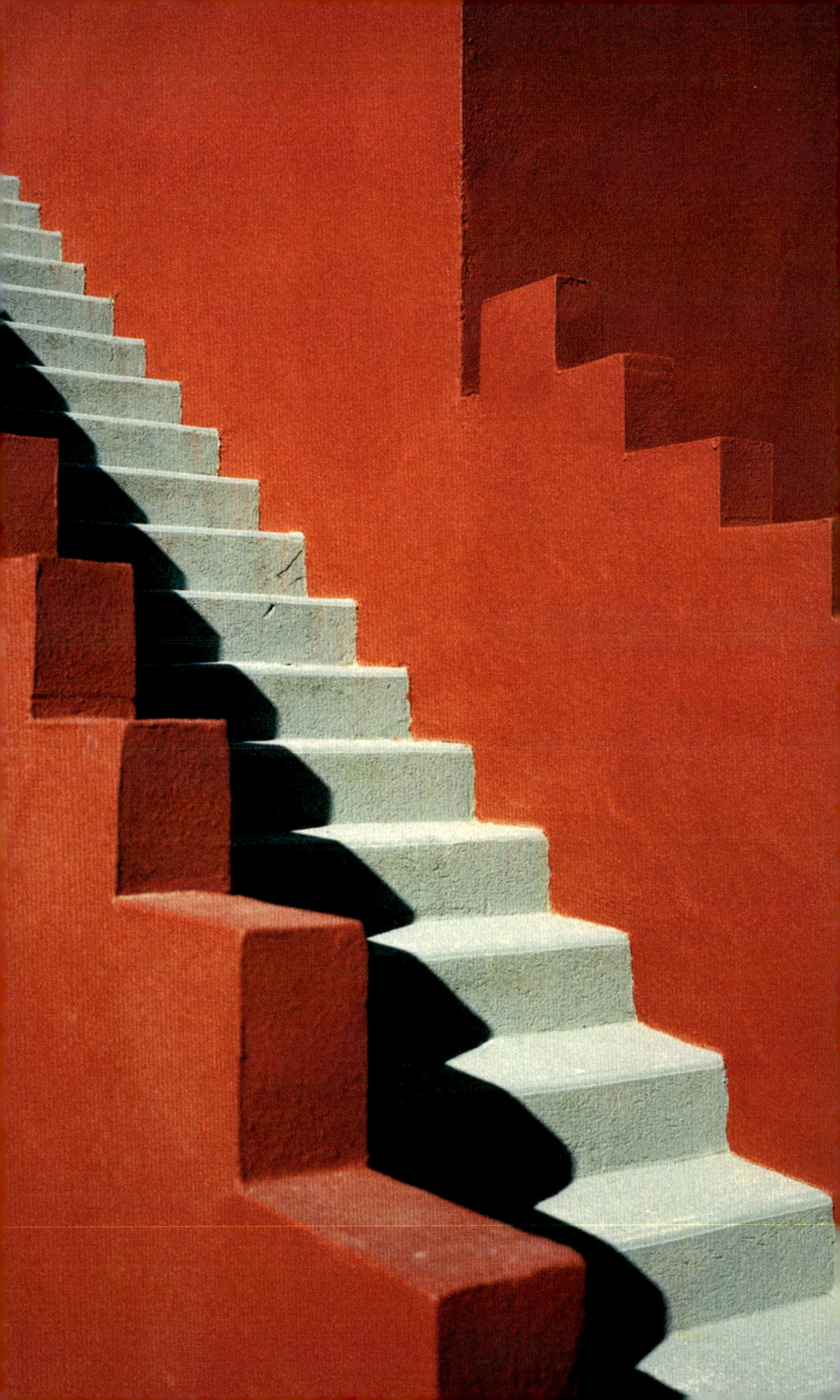

#28 SIMPLE GUIDE TO THE EXPOSURE TRIANGLE

There have been many attempts to make the exposure triangle more exciting by presenting the three-sided shape in a new light (Google image search: exposure triangle), but there's no escaping the fact that it's just a regular triangle with ISO, shutter speed, and aperture slapped onto each side. Its sole purpose is to provide a simple visual representation of how those three key values work together harmoniously to make the perfect exposure.

Mind you, it's not the triangle that needs spicing up but rather the text, explaining in great length how the exposure triangle works, that usually accompanies it. It really doesn't need to be that complex and long-winded.

Exposure Triangle

You need enough light to make a photo. All three of these things impact how much light your photo gets:

1. ISO

- ISO is your film speed rating.
- Once you've put film in your camera, you're stuck with that ISO until you finish the roll of film.
- Higher ISO film is more sensitive to light, but you get more film grain.
- Lower ISO film has finer grain, but it's less sensitive to light, so you'll need to get more light from adjusting the shutter speed and/or aperture accordingly.

2. Shutter Speed

- The shutter speed is how long your shutter is open when you press the shutter button.
- The slower the shutter speed, the more light you get, but the more prone you are to motion blur and shaking hands ruining your image.
- Faster shutter speed will better freeze the motion. It's less prone to shakes, but the shutter is open for a shorter duration of time, so you'll need higher ISO film and/or a larger aperture to ensure there is enough light for your exposure.

3. Aperture

- Inside a lens there's an aperture that opens and closes.
- It opens up to a larger aperture to let in more light.
- It closes to a smaller aperture to let in less light.
- The larger aperture gives a shallower depth of field.
- A smaller aperture gives greater depth of field.
- You need to use ISO and shutter speed to balance the exposure.

If you look on the aperture dial, the shutter-speed dial, or look at all the different ISO of film you can get, the difference between one number to the next number up/down is one stop.

Examples of Increasing Light Exposure by One Stop:

Shutter Speed: 1/30s -> 1/15s

Aperture: f/5.6 -> f/4

ISO: 200 -> 400

Examples of Decreasing Light Exposure by One Stop:

Shutter Speed: 1/60s -> 1/30s

Aperture: f/1.4 -> f/2

ISO: 800 -> 400

The whole idea of the exposure triangle is that if you change a setting by one stop, you will need to adjust one of the other two settings to ensure you keep the same exposure. For example, if you increase the exposure by one stop with a slower shutter speed, you can balance that out with a smaller aperture (one-stop decrease).

Kai's Tips

Take a pen and notebook out with you. Take note of the settings used (aperture and shutter speed) for each frame. This is your best way of understanding how the settings affect your exposure and create the desired effect.

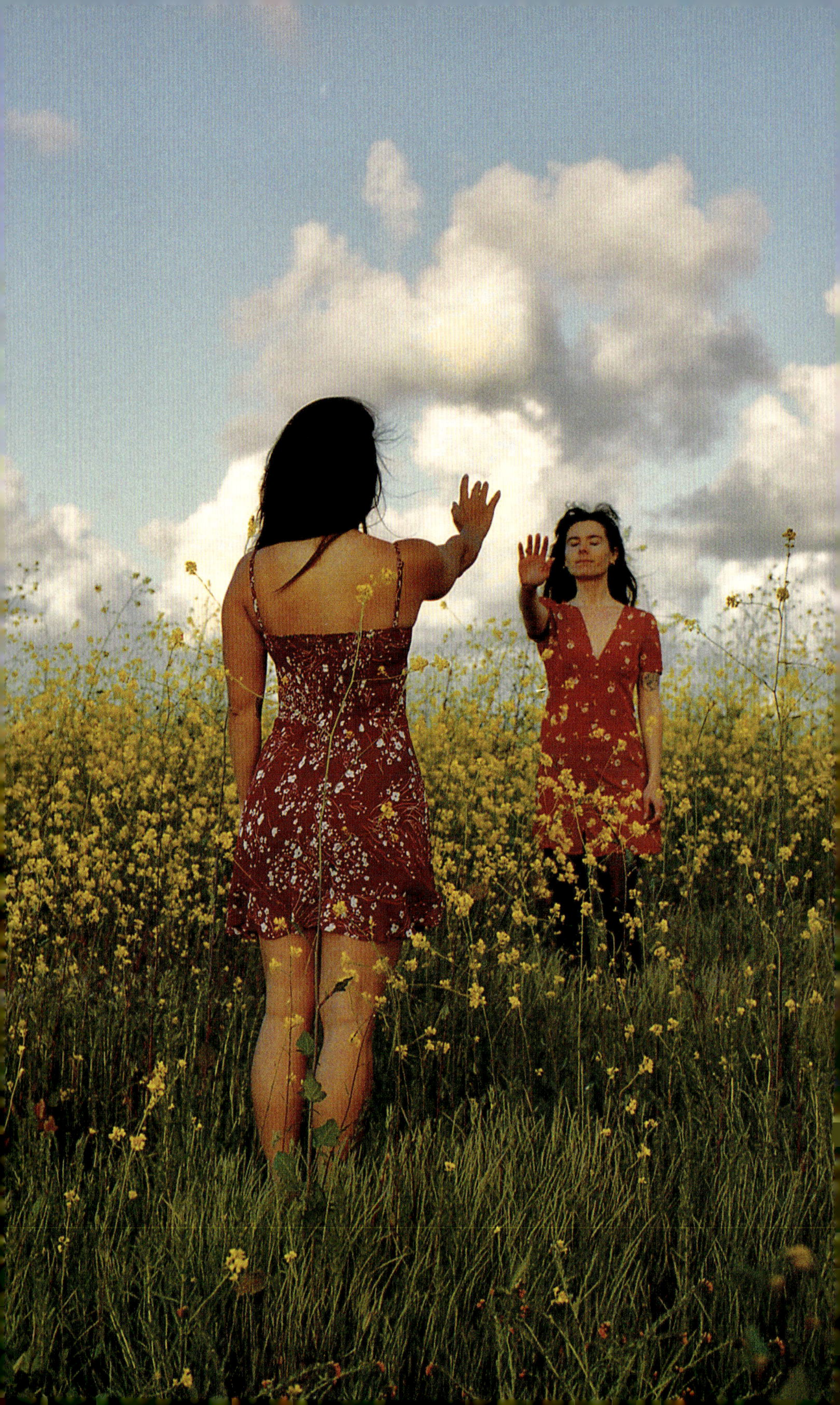

#29
WHAT THE f IS DEPTH OF FIELD?

Knowing why an f-stop is called an f-stop is not important (and it's kinda boring, too)—understanding what it means for your photography, and how to apply it creatively, is all you really need to know.

Inside a lens there are a number of blades that form an aperture; it can be opened up (larger aperture) to let more light in, or closed down (smaller aperture) to let less light in.

The f-number (you'll see it written on a dial on your lens) correlates to the size of the aperture but, weirdly, a smaller f-number equals a larger aperture, and a larger f-number is a smaller aperture. Again, it's not worth looking into why—that's time out of your life that could be used for something more interesting—and just accept it as it is.

Changing aperture doesn't just change the amount of light coming through the lens but also the depth of field.

Small f-Number/Large Aperture = Shallow Depth of Field

- The point of focus will be sharp and in focus, and everything in front of it or behind it will be out of focus.
- One of the reasons to use a shallow depth of field is to make it blatantly obvious what the point of interest is. By blurring everything other than just the point of focus, you're smudging out all those other possible distractions.
- If you use too shallow a depth of field, you might have too little in focus. A portrait won't look great when it's just the tip of your subject's nose in focus.
- Shooting wide open (at the lens's largest aperture) usually shows off lenses' inadequacies—softness, vignetting, and aberrations.

Large f-Number/Small Aperture = Deep Depth of Field

- The point of focus will be in focus, but everything in front and behind will be in focus, too.
- There are times when you don't just want the attention to be drawn to one specific point of interest in the image. If you want to give context to your subject by making all the surrounding details visible (e.g., a photo of someone in a street scene), or if the main interest takes up a huge part of the frame (e.g., architecture), then you need deeper depth of field.
- Shooting at the smallest aperture is never a good idea either, as it will make your image softer due to diffraction. The optimal aperture for sharpness is usually around f/8–f/11.

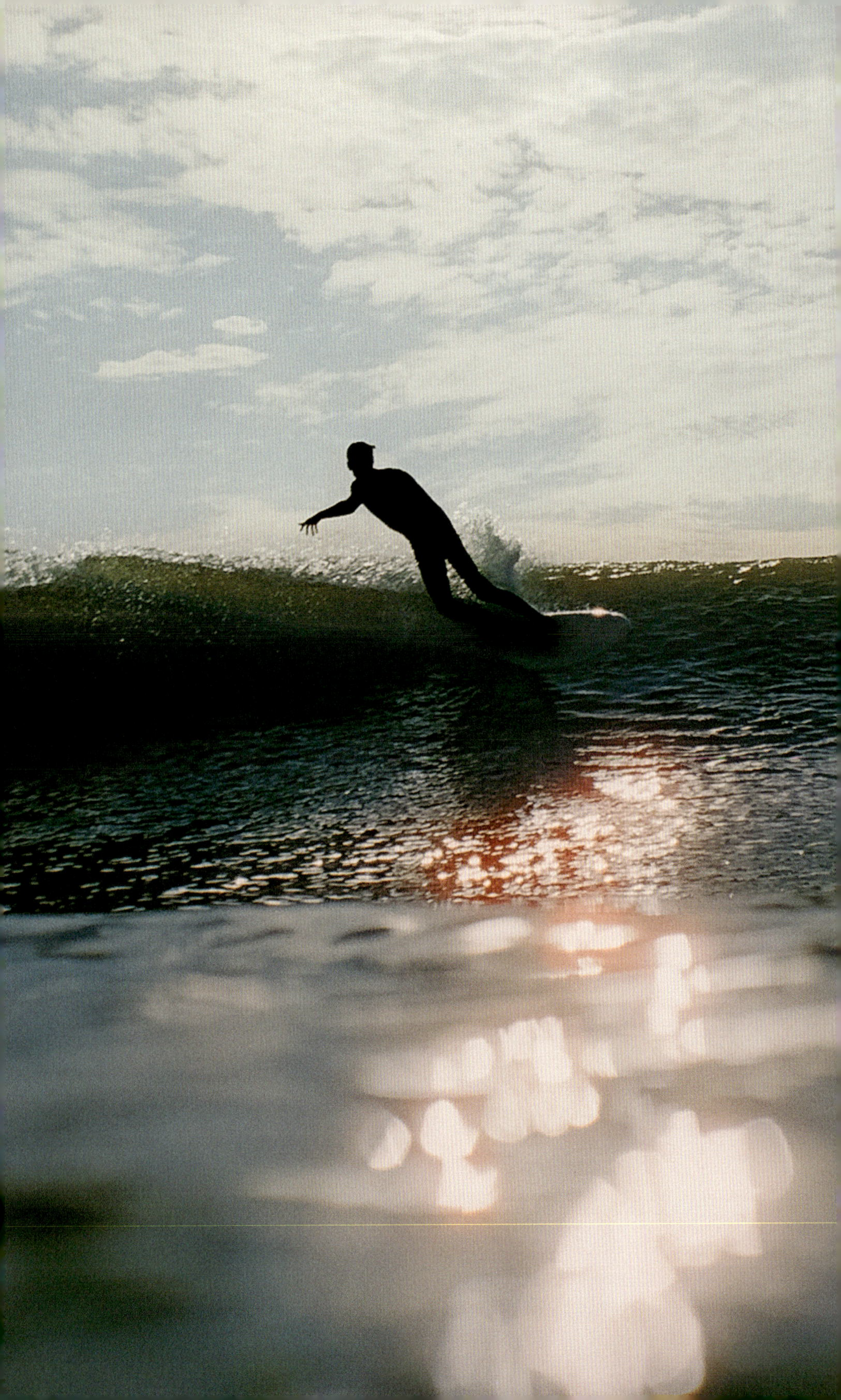

#30 SHUTTER SPEED: FAST vs. SLOW

There are two types of shutter: focal plane and leaf. The most common is focal-plane shutter, which you'll see is like a little curtain right in the centre of the camera, near where the film is loaded. You're more likely to find leaf shutters in 35 mm compact cameras, and instead of being in front of where the film goes, they are inside the lens itself.

Whereas a focal plane shutter is noisier than a leaf shutter, they tend to be able to achieve faster shutter speeds.

Fast

If you want to freeze the action, you use a faster shutter speed. You can also ensure that your shots aren't ruined by any slight hand movements while you're taking the photo with a faster shutter speed.

You could just use the fastest shutter speed there is, but then you're letting in the least light at the fastest shutter speed. The best approach is to pick a shutter speed that is just fast enough—or rather, the slowest speed you can get away with—so you're not losing too much light.

How fast a shutter speed do you need to use, though? They say that to get shake-free images you should take the focal length of the lens you're using and add 1/ in front of it, e.g., 50 mm = 1/50s. But that's not taking into account moving subjects.

If you're photographing fast-moving wildlife, you'll need 1/1000s. You don't need that for non-running human subjects—a shutter speed of 1/100–1/200s works fine for walking-pace humans.

Slow

It's not always about speed and freezing the motion, though. There are times when you want to emphasise the motion, and you can do that by using a slower shutter speed. But if you're shooting handheld, you're prone to picking up those very slight movements that happen when you're holding a camera in your hands.

Find something steadier than your two hands. Put the camera on a solid surface—floor, wall, bin—or you can put your camera bag down and then put your camera onto that. Alternatively, you can find a more dedicated solution, like a tripod, but you should definitely consider getting a cable release or remote, too. Even on a solid surface, pressing down on the shutter button can still move the camera ever so slightly.

As you'll be getting lots more light coming through to the film due to the slower shutter speeds, you need to balance it up with your aperture (refer to the exposure triangle). Bear in mind that you can only make your aperture so small before it starts softening your image, so you might want to use neutral density filters (see #34) to reduce the amount of light coming through.

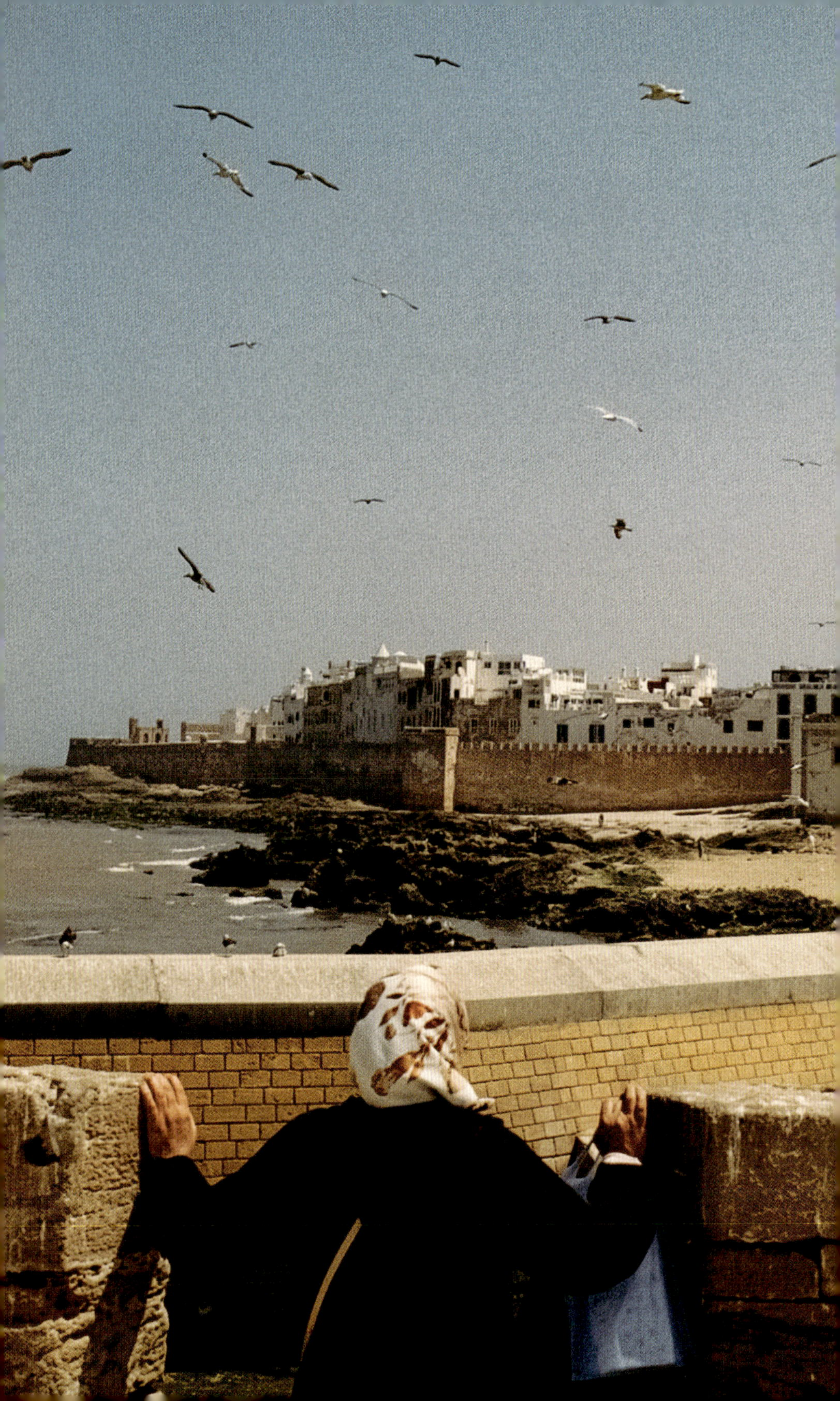

#31

ISO: WHAT FILM SPEED SHOULD YOU USE?

ISO is the international standard of measuring film speed: how sensitive it is to light. Slow-speed film is less sensitive to light, so it needs more light to get a decent exposure; high-speed film is more sensitive to light, which requires less light for the exposure.

With a digital camera, you can change your ISO anytime you like. With film, you're stuck with whatever ISO film you put in your camera until you've finished the roll, so make sure you've thought carefully about what ISO you really need to use before going out on a shoot.

Slow-Speed Film

If you're taking photos on a nice, sunny day (a rare sight in the UK), ISO 100 and 200 offer fine grain and low sensitivity, which allow you to use moderate aperture settings and a fast-enough shutter speed without resorting to filters to darken the exposure.

As there's less grain with slow-speed film, go for ISO 200, 100, or even 50 film for photos that require that extra-clean, crispy detail you'll get with a film low on visible grain.

You might need to plan ahead and consider how long you're going to carry on shooting in the day, especially if you're only doing handheld shooting. Even with a lens with an extremely large maximum aperture, like a Leica Noctilux f/0.95, you're still going to struggle to get a decent exposure in a really dimly lit environment with slow-speed films.

Medium-Speed Film

If there is a chance that you might shoot through the day and into the night, you're better off loading up on some ISO 400 film. This is the most versatile film to put in your camera, although it won't provide the finest grain; even if the light conditions change during the day, you're pretty much covered with an ISO 400 film.

On a sunny day, you might still wish you had a slower film to allow you to use a larger aperture, or you might have an old camera with a mechanical shutter with shutter speeds that don't go fast enough. Conversely, in really dark environments, you're still going to find that ISO 400 just isn't fast enough.

Still, it's always useful to stock up on a load of ISO 400 film like Portra, for colour, or black-and-white classics like Tri-X and HP5 Plus for those days when you need that flexibility.

High-Speed Film

For fast-moving subjects, you might need to bump up the ISO to allow you to use the fastest shutter speed possible to freeze the motion—think sports and wildlife—but of course you'll need high-speed film when you're going out to take low-light shots.

When you're just taking photos at night, handheld, it makes sense to be loaded up on a high-speed film of at least ISO 800. ISO 1600 would be ideal, but then you need to figure out whether you want the extra grainy look you'll get once you start upping the ISO.

As mentioned earlier (in the black-and-white chapter), you have ISO 3200 films like T-Max P3200 and Delta 3200, but they are essentially ISO 800 and 1600 films designed to be pushed to 3200.

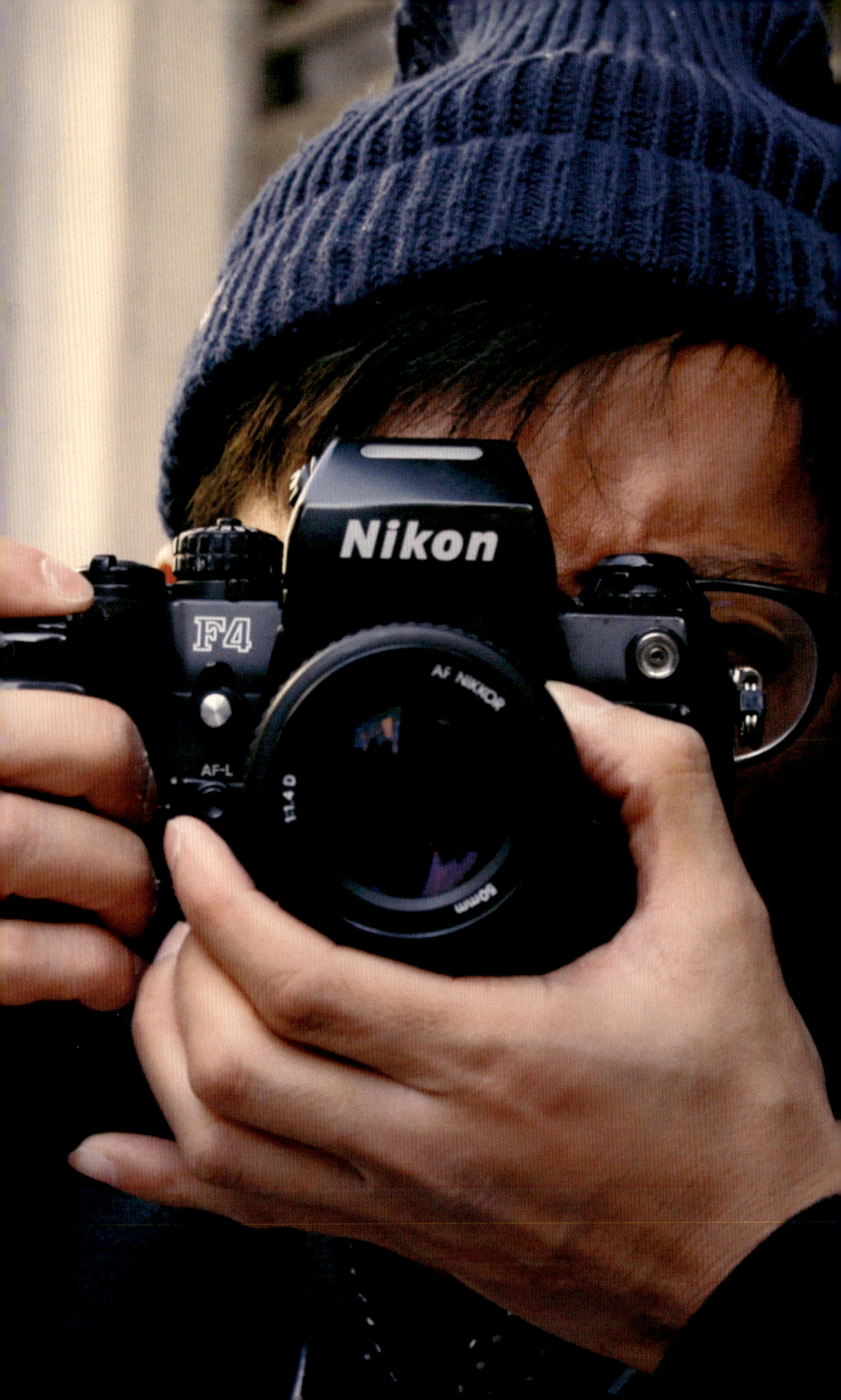
Nikon
F4
AF-L
AF NIKKOR
50mm

#32 MASTERING THAT MODE DIAL

The mode dial is a useful little thing—so little, in fact, that there's no room to fit big words on it, just a few letters to represent the four key exposure modes you will need to use on your camera.

M Mode

This is a completely manual exposure mode, which means you need to adjust the aperture and shutter-speed setting yourself. It might be a daunting task at first, but just keep checking the light meter while you're rotating those dials; and once you get that green confirmation light, leave the dials alone and the settings are locked in.

If you want complete control, then this is the mode you want to be in. But it's not going to be the quickest, most convenient mode to use for faster-moving subjects—they probably won't stand around to wait for you to fiddle about with those two dials.

A/Av Mode

Less fiddling always makes life easier, and with this mode there's certainly less fumbling around to get your perfect exposure. This is Aperture Priority mode, which allows you to still choose the aperture setting—giving you control over the depth of field while letting the camera pick a shutter speed for you.

It does make the process quicker, but you should bear in mind that the camera doesn't always pick the shutter speed you'd hope it would. If you're shooting in lower light, it might go for a slower shutter speed, which could result in a shaky, blurry shot because the shutter is open for too long.

S/Tv Mode

A bit like the above but you get to choose the shutter speed, and the camera picks an aperture setting to get the best exposure. This mode allows you to ensure you have the right shutter speed for the subject that you're photographing.

Not being able to have control over the aperture setting doesn't seem too detrimental—your shot won't be ruined—it's just that you won't be allowed control over how much depth of field you get.

P Mode

Program mode is as good as full auto, as the camera will pick both the aperture and shutter speed for you. If you want the least amount of fuss, then this is for you.

Some cameras will still let you override the aperture or shutter-speed setting, but this mode is great for quick snapshot photos. If it's more important to get the shot rather than having the creative control over depth of field, or what shutter speed you use, then P mode will work a treat.

B/Bulb Mode

This mode is like a manual mode without a shutter speed—instead of setting your shutter speed, the shutter will stay open as long as you have your finger pressed on the shutter button.

Your camera's shutter speeds only go so slow—depending on the camera, from one second down to thirty seconds—so if you need anything slower than that, you will need to use Bulb mode. A tripod is necessary, and so is a remote or cable release, which allows you to take a shot without having to touch the shutter button. Both tend to have a lock, so you don't need to have your finger pressed down on the remote or cable-release button during the whole exposure.

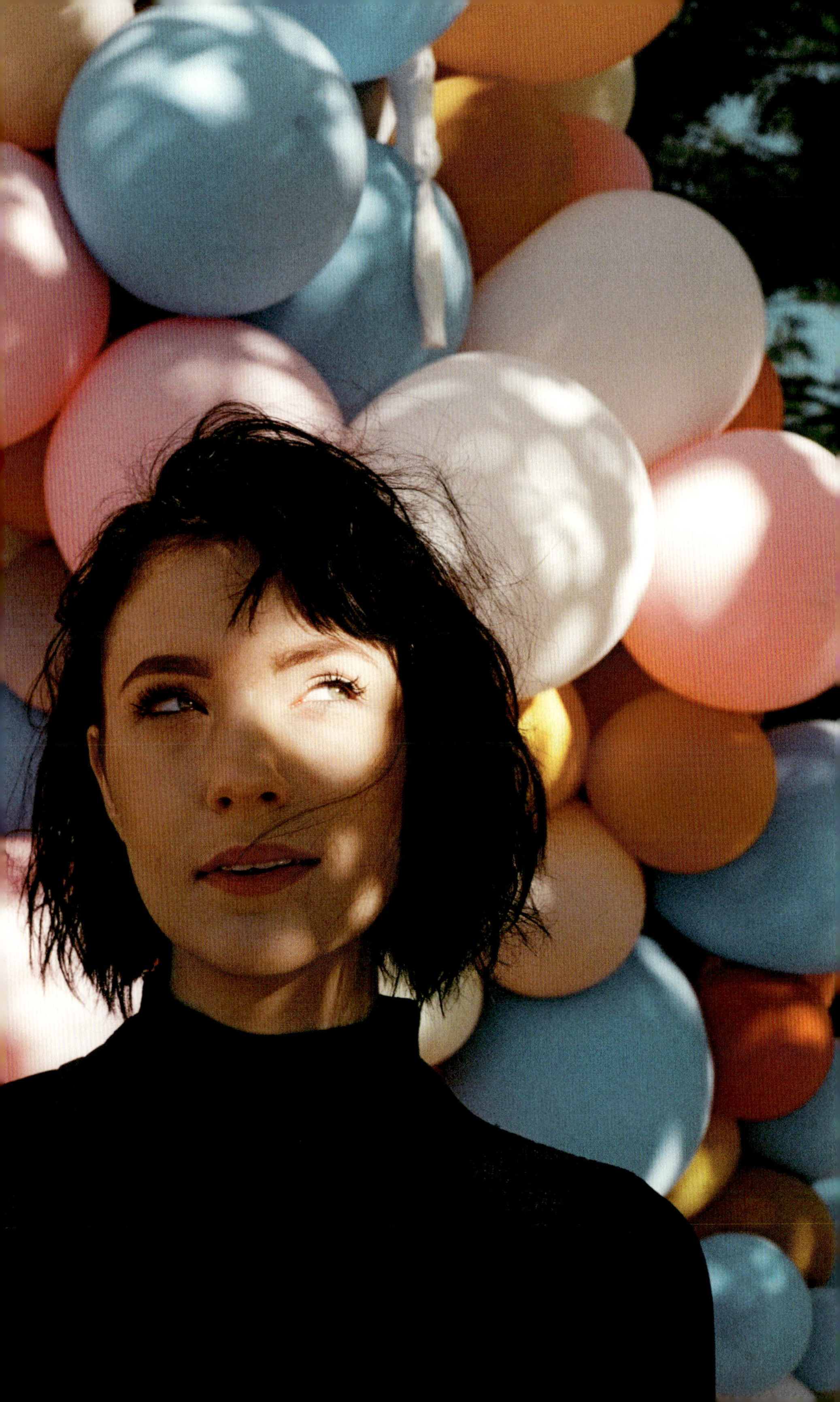

#33
SUNNY 16: OLD-SCHOOL RULES

This is going to look like such a goofy way of taking photos, because at first glance it appears that your choice of aperture setting is dictated by the weather of the day.

On some old-school cameras, you'll even find quaint little pictograms showing you the Sunny 16 Rule, with tiny graphical illustrations of different weather conditions. This was because, at one time, cameras didn't come with built-in light meters, and this was the best way to choose the right exposure settings.

Not many photographers would bother learning this seemingly antiquated method now because there is simply no need when you have light meters in everything. But if you're going to take film photos, I think you should try it out—not only will it be useful but it can make you gain a better understanding of exposure.

Mechanical cameras can still be used without a battery, because there are no electronics controlling the shutter. So even if they do have the option of using a light meter, if you run out of batteries, you can still keep shooting while having an idea of what exposure settings you should be using.

The idea is that on a sunny day you'd have your aperture set to f/16.

- With ISO 100 film, shutter speed = 1/100s or 1/125s
- With ISO 200 film, shutter speed = 1/200s or 1/250s
- With ISO 400 film, shutter speed = 1/400s or 1/500s
- You don't tend to use ISO 800 film on a sunny day.
- If the weather changes, you can change the aperture to get the right exposure.

Once you've used the Sunny 16 Rule a few times, you will get a sense of how easy it is to make slight adjustments to get a good exposure, whether it be due to changing weather or moving from the bright sunlight into the shade.

You don't even need to stick to using f/16 on a sunny day, either. Think of the exposure triangle, and make those adjustments in full stops—if you adjust from f/16 to f/8 for a sunny-day shot, then you will need to use a shutter speed that is faster than the ones suggested above, by one stop.

Even though you might never use the Sunny 16 Rule ever again, it's useful to know; and it will actually make you realise that you needn't be so uptight and precise with your exposure settings when shooting with negative film.

The Sunny 16 Rule:	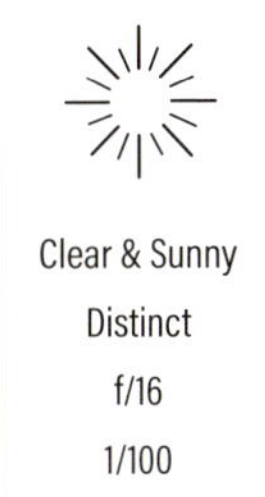	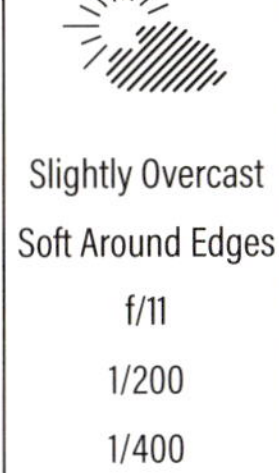	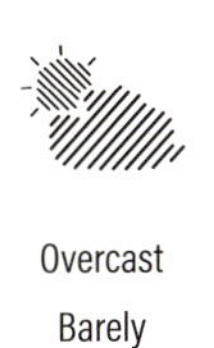		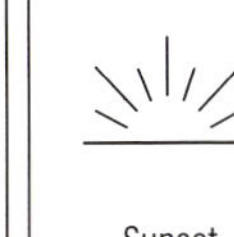
Weather Condition	Clear & Sunny	Slightly Overcast	Overcast	Heavy Overcast	Sunset
Shadow Details	Distinct	Soft Around Edges	Barely	No Shadows	No Shadows
Aperture	f/16	f/11	f/8	f/5.6	f/4
Shutter Speed at ISO 100	1/100	1/200	1/400	1/800	1/1600
Shutter Speed at ISO 200	1/200	1/400	1/800	1/1600	1/3200
Shutter Speed at ISO 400	1/400	1/800	1/1600	1/3200	1/6400

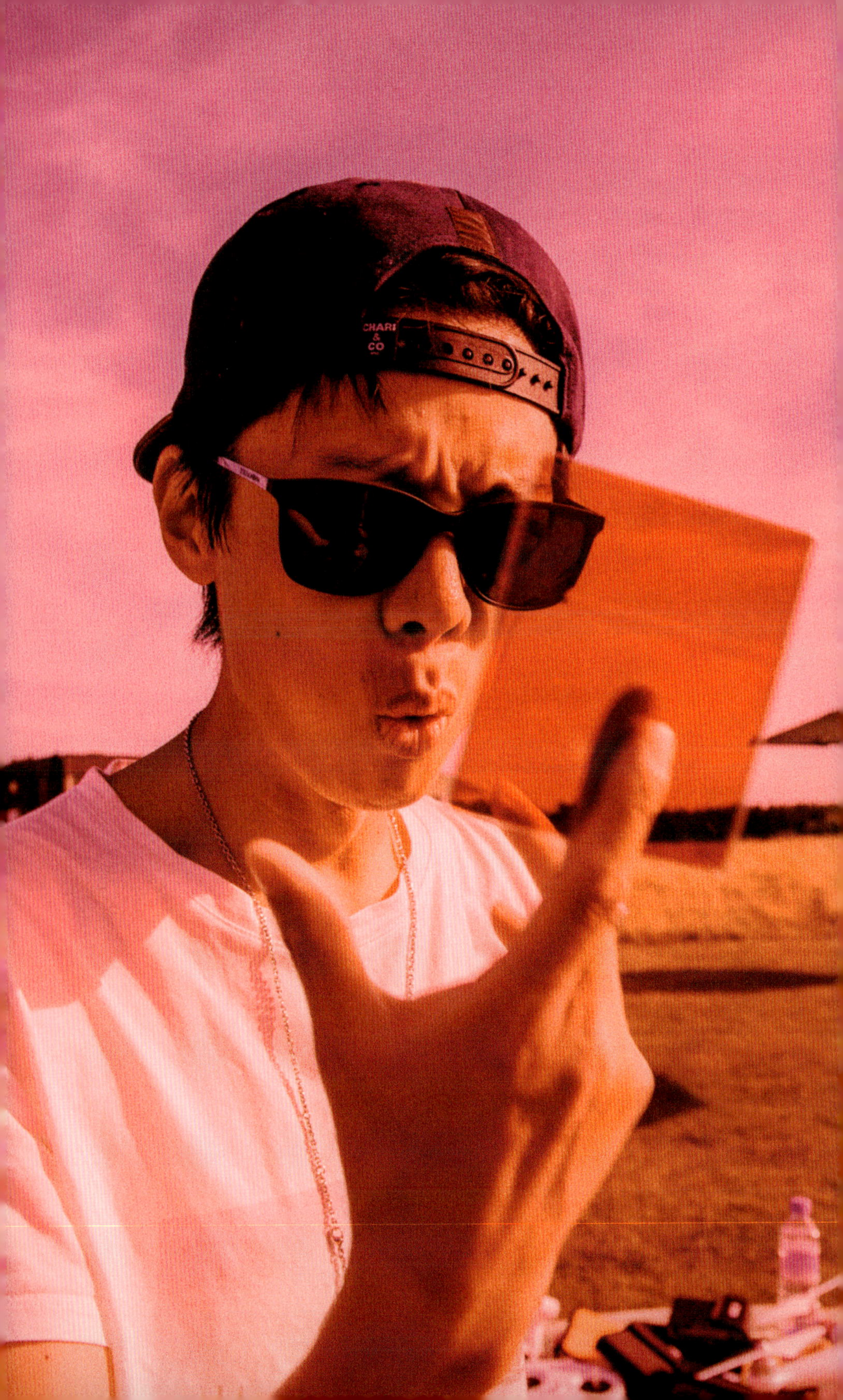
CHARI
&
CO

#34 FILTERS YOU NEED

With filters, less really is more. Start off with the basics; work on improving your photos and then consider adding more later on.

Here are my picks of the best and worst filters you can get:

The Essentials

Neutral Density Filters

They reduce the amount of light coming through your lens, which is useful for getting slower shutter speeds—to blur the motion of clouds or water—or using large aperture settings for shallow depth of field in the daylight. ND filters are available in different strengths, reducing the light by varying levels of stops of exposure.

Graduated Neutral Density Filters

Graduated ND filters are much darker on one half of the filter, with the other half being completely transparent. The purpose of this is to balance the exposure of a scene—the dark part is mainly used for reducing the exposure of the sky to bring it closer to the exposure level of the land, which tends to be darker than the sky. Without the filter, if you expose correctly for the sky, the land will end up too dark. Correctly exposing for the land will result in skies that are too bright, and some of the details will be lost as a result. With a graduated ND, you should be able to get a balanced exposure for the whole scene, keeping the details in the sky and land.

Colour Filters for Black-and-White

A yellow filter is a must-have filter for black-and-white photography, working to make the clouds more prominent by making the blue of the sky a darker shade; skin tones will look great, too. An orange filter will do all of this, but take the intensity up a notch. A red filter will go even further, giving a dramatic look, making the sky look deep, dark, and moody.

Worth Having

Circular Polariser

Polarisers are often used to make colours pop more by cutting out reflections, but you can't just slap this on the front of your lens and expect to magically get a beautiful, deep blue sky and punchy colours even on a cloudy day—you will need some sun to make your images shine with a polariser. Circular polarisers can be rotated to give different amounts of a polarising effect, but if you want to get the best results from a circular polariser, you should shoot when the sun is at its highest point in the sky.

Warm-Up Filters

If you're photographing on a cloudy, overcast day, the light might make your image look a bit cool and blue. A warming filter will add a bit of, well, warmth to your image. Obviously. Take a look at 81A, 81B, and 81C filters. They represent the different levels of warmth: A being weaker, C being stronger. Eighty-five filters will give a more orange colour, for more intense warming up, but I think you'll get more use out of the 81 filters.

Blue Filters

80A, 80B, or 80C work in the opposite way of the warm-up filters by making the light look cooler. Useful for reducing the orange cast from tungsten lighting.

Waste of Money

UV Filters

Although they are supposed to reduce haze caused by UV light, most people tend to use them to add a protective element to the front of their lens in case they accidentally drop it. Don't bother with a UV filter, and be careful not to drop your lens.

Tobacco Filters

Sounds like something you'd get inside a cigarette—they'll make your sky look kind of nicotine-stained, too.

Star Filters

Add some cheesy retro vibes to your photos with this filter, which has the effect of little points of light looking like stars.

Soft Focus

For a double helping of cheese, stack this filter on top of a star filter.

Diffractor Universe and Diffractor Galaxy

If filters were haircuts, these would be a pair of mullets.

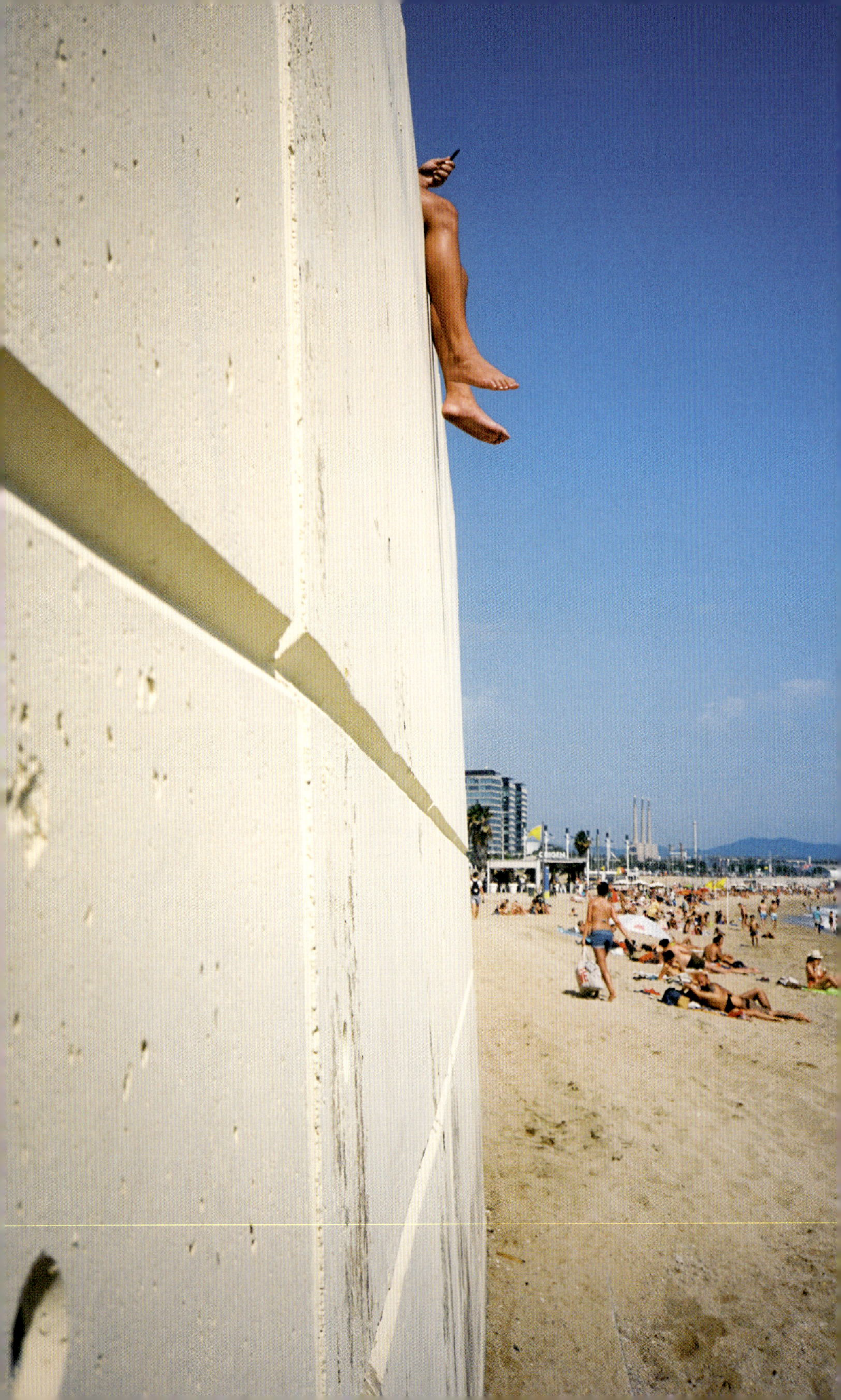

#35
THREE LEGS ARE BETTER THAN TWO

I've flattened enough tripods to be able to safely say that when you're looking for a tripod, you should just go all out and invest in the best one you can possibly afford.

A tripod will give your camera the stability you need when your limbs fail to do so. If you're looking to take photos with slower shutter speeds, or keep your camera in one position for a long time, then a three-legged thing is the perfect tool for propping up your camera.

Weight

Tripods are usually made out of aluminium, carbon fibre, or wood. There are plastic ones, too, but you don't need me to tell you why putting an expensive camera on top of three plastic legs is a bad idea. I wouldn't recommend wooden tripods unless you want to feel like you're taking a piece of furniture out with you. Aluminium is the most common material used due to its reasonable cost and light-ish weight. Carbon fibre tends to be seen on the more expensive tripods—the carbon fibre production process is more complicated, which contributes to the higher price—and is used because it makes them incredibly light, yet strong.

You'll probably spend more time carrying a tripod than actually using it, so make sure it's a weight that you're happy to carry, because it can feel like a long, hard slog when you're lugging some heavy sticks around with you.

Height

Different tripods extend to different heights. Some people prefer a tripod that reaches up to your eye level, just so you don't have to stoop down every time you look through the viewfinder; but it's not an absolute must-have unless you've got a bad back.

If anything, I think it's more important if a tripod can flatten its legs so that you can get it down for some low-angle shooting. Look for tripods with multi-angle leg locks that allow your tripod to do the splits.

Leg Locks

The legs need to be extended and retracted, and to keep them in position they have a locking mechanism, which comes in the form of either a twist or flip lock. Although the flip method feels a little faster to release and tighten, it's a bit more prone to knocks and damages when compared to the twist lock, which also tends to benefit from better weather sealing.

Centre Column

The column in the middle of the tripod can go up and down, but some of them can also be removed completely and inverted so you can mount your camera even lower to the ground. Look for a hook on the butt end of centre columns—these come in handy when you want to hang your bag somewhere, and that will also add stability to your tripod with extra downforce.

Use Your Head

The most common choices will be: three-way/pan-tilt head or ball head. The three-way is a classic setup, allowing you to unlock each axis separately and make little precise adjustments easily. The ball head doesn't allow the same ability to make super-accurate adjustments to just one axis as the three-way does, but it makes up for it by being far more compact.

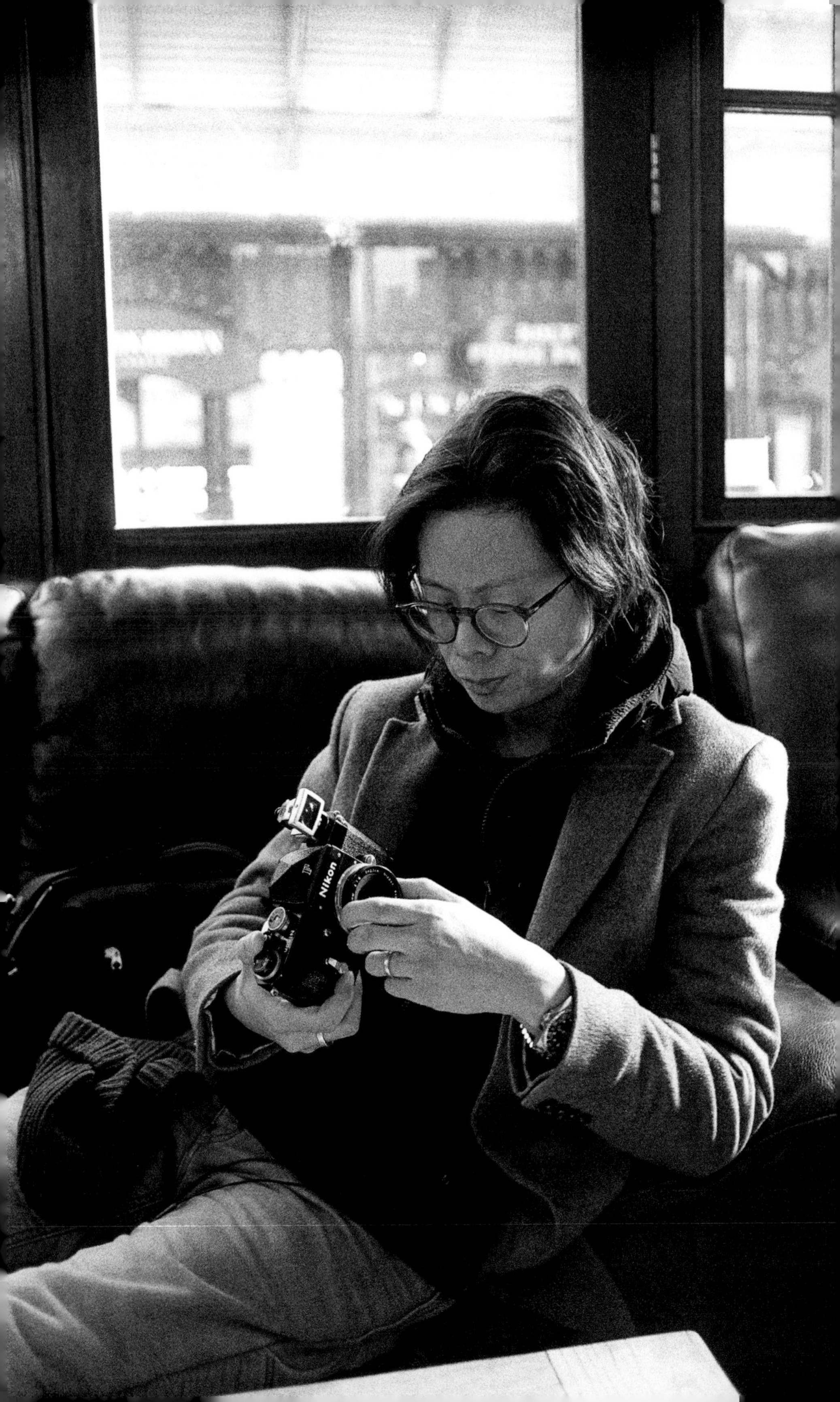
Nikon

#36
WHAT'S IN MY BAG? THE ESSENTIALS

Nobody likes a nosy parker, but if there's any place where you're welcome to stick your schnoz in, it's the inside of one's camera bag. Taking a cheeky sneak peak at what another photographer is packing is one of those little guilty pleasures that surely every camera-loving photography enthusiast has indulged in at some point.

The joy isn't just in the coveting, though—checking out what someone else is carrying in their camera bag can be a great source of inspiration, to give you an idea of what you should you chuck in your own satchel.

Hitherto, there's been a lot of gear talk, but as we transition into the not-so-gear-centric tips, I want to give you a glimpse of what I actually put in my camera bag, and why:

Billingham Hadley Pro

Billingham bags are just so British. They look like they should be teamed with an ensemble of tweed trousers, wax jacket, and flat cap, but they look good with anything. It's not just the sweet styling; the quality is sublime. They're made in England, using leather and canvas, or a fancy fabric called FibreNyte—and they're just very thoughtfully made bags.

Whereas other over-the-shoulder bags might use cheaper Velcro fastenings to keep flaps closed, Billinghams use metal stud or button fastenings that make hardly any noise. The last thing you need when you're photographing a subject is an almighty krrrrrrrrccccchhhhhhhhhhhhaaaaaaa Velcro sound, alerting everyone around that you are about to take a photo (you might as well just sound off a Klaxon every time you take a photo).

Also, the padding insert is a splendid British racing green, not just for the sake of making it look so quintessentially British, but also to make it a little easier to find your black-coloured gear and accessories inside a dark camera bag.

My Main Camera

One doesn't need to carry more than three lenses or, in my case, I don't need to take more than three camera bodies. Why take more than one cam? Well, if you've put one type of film in your camera, you're stuck with that ISO and also can't switch from colour to black-and-white until you've finished the roll. With two cameras, you have two types of film to use for two different styles or scenes.

Still, my main camera is what I expect to use for most, if not all, of my shots, so it has to be the best camera. And that doesn't mean best in specs—the Leica M5 is a rangefinder camera that doesn't do much other than focus, meter, and look good. I don't need anything more than a camera that quietly takes photos, does it reliably, and feels good in the hands.

Alternatively, if I still want that minimalist, all-manual control feel in an SLR, I'd go for the Nikon F. Otherwise, the Canon EOS 1V HS is a great camera to use because it's such a solid, reliable tool that autofocuses quickly and accurately. Unfortunately, it shreds up those batteries like there's no climate change—it takes eight AA batteries and guzzles through all that battery juice like a thirsty, electronic beast.

Fast (Enough) Fifty

I like to keep a lens mounted on my main camera so I'm ready for some snap-snap action at any time. A 50 mm lens is what I'd have mounted on the camera from the get-go because it is my most-used focal length.

I've tried super-fast 50 mm lenses—Leica Noctilux f/1.0, Canon 50mm f/1.2L—but tend not to use them because they're heavy, chunky things that require a bit more care with focusing; and f/1.4 or f/1.8 lenses are fast enough while still producing sufficiently shallow depth of field.

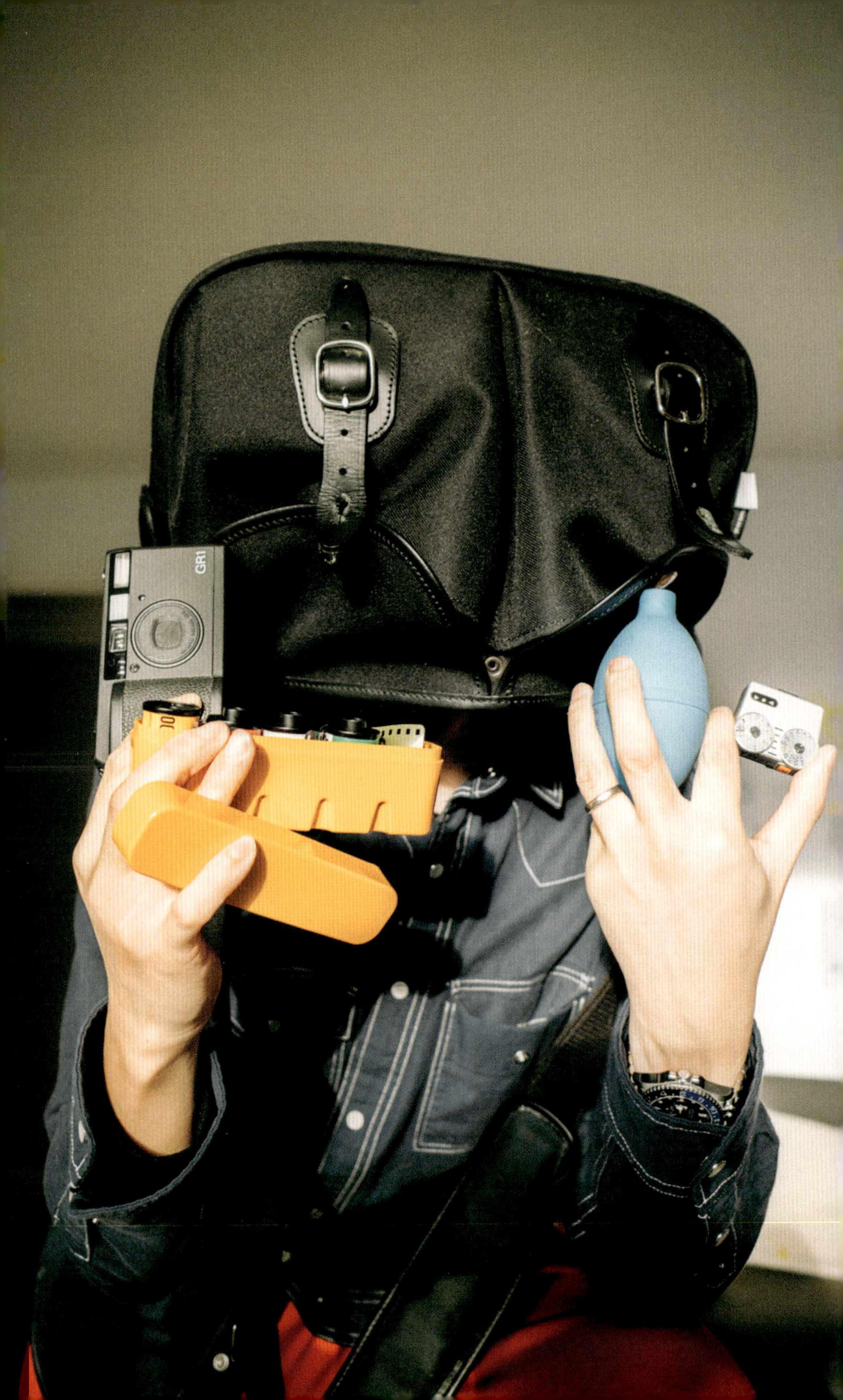
GR1

#37

WHAT'S IN MY BAG? THE BEST OF THE REST

Second Camera

The second camera I pack in my sack is a Ricoh GR1. Its size, shape, and weight gives me a stealthy option for quick and easy snapshots with minimal fuss, while providing maximum amounts of fun. The 28 mm focal length is a wider focal length than the 50 mm, which makes it great for shooting in tight spaces.

Wide-Angle Lens

Honestly speaking, I hardly ever use it, so mostly it's there to make my bag look more full. But it is one of those in-case-of-emergency lenses: a lens that you might regret not carrying when an opportunity arises where you absolutely need that ridiculously wide field of view in a tight space, or for creating an exaggerated look.

Wides with larger maximum apertures are savagely sized. I'd rather lose out on the speed and have a more compact bit of glass, and the Voigtlander 15mm f/4.5 fits the bill, being a tiny little thing with hugely impressive image quality. I've also got a Nikon 20 mm, which isn't quite so sharp, but it looks so very cool.

Voigtlander VC II

There are other options for light meters—iPhone accessories, other hot-shoe-mounted meters—but this little Voigtlander is probably the classiest-looking on-camera meter I've seen.

Artisan and Artist Straps

You could use the standard strap that came with the camera, but if it's as old as the camera, it's likely soaked up with decades of salty secretions of owners past.

Artisan and artist straps are made in Japan, are elegantly proportioned, and look great attached to the lugs of classic film cameras. The leather strap feels like it will last for many years of use, on top of the ten years I've already got out of it. But if animal skin is not your thing, they also make silk cord and cloth straps.

Japan Camera Hunter Film Case

As fun as it is to open up those little boxes and pop open those plastic containers containing the film, doing it on the go will make you look a right clumsy oaf. These JCH cases are the coolest way to carry your film, while still giving you the pleasure of popping open a plastic container to access your films.

Filters

If I'm out taking street photos, I'll leave my filters at home. The only time I'll pack filters is if I'm out shooting landscapes. For me, it'll only be the neutral density—a graduated ND filter for bringing the brightness of the sky closer to the land, and a regular ND filter to bring down the exposure of the whole scene—if I want to get a slower shutter speed to blur the movement of the clouds or water.

Notebook

Digital photos have EXIF data, which has all the data (and more) that you will need to refer to after you've taken a shot. All you get with film is the name of the film and the ISO along the film strip; use a notebook to jot down your exposure settings, so you can gain a better understanding of exposure and figure out if you could've used better settings to get a better result.

Cable Release

It takes up hardly any space in my bag, so it's something to keep in there even if I probably won't get any use of it that day.

Blower

It blows ... dust.

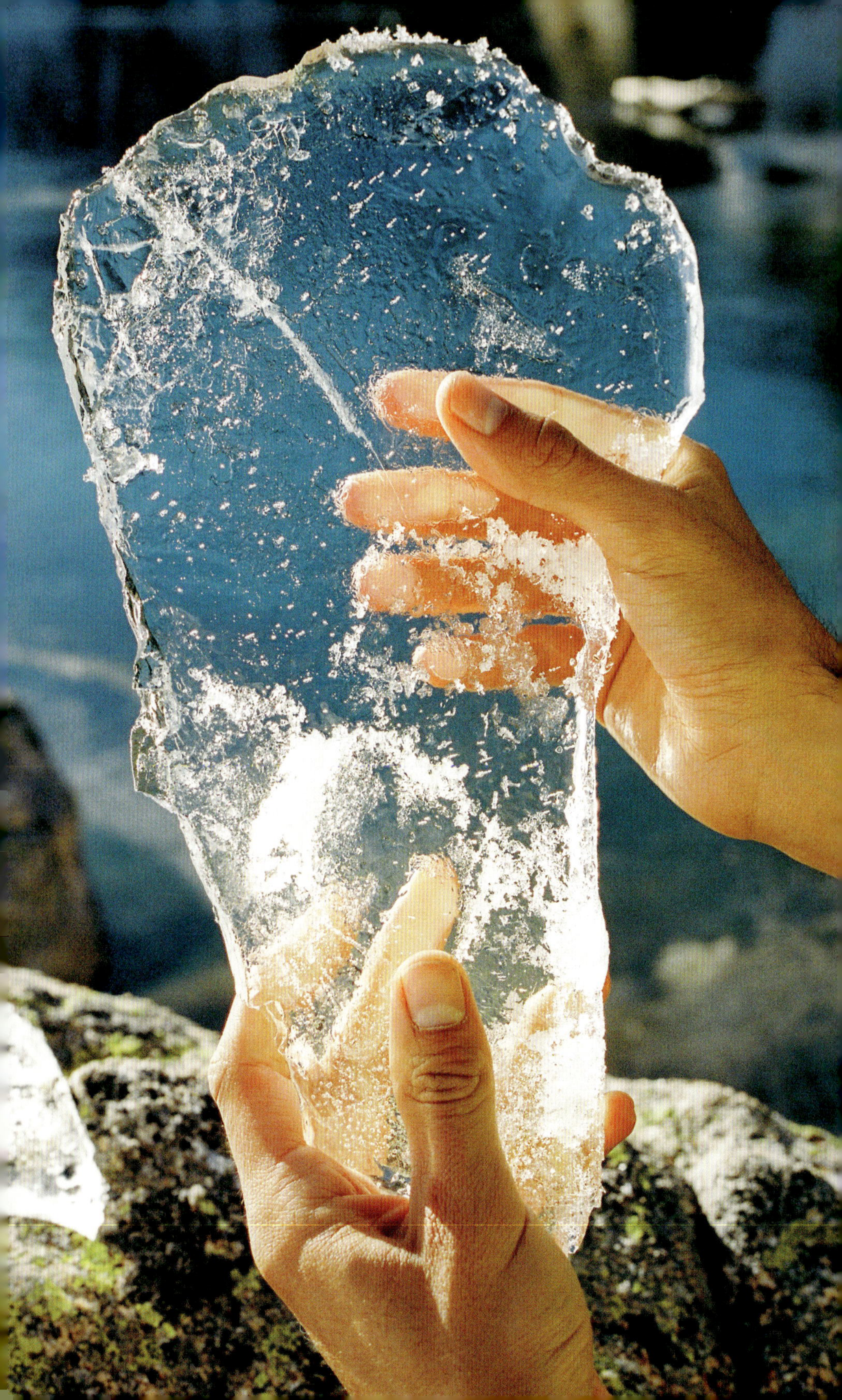

#38 AVAILABLE LIGHT: WHAT YOU SEE IS WHAT YOU GET

The best way to start taking photos is with available light. There's plenty of it, as you're dealing with whatever light you see in front of you, and what you see is what you'll get; but that also means that you have no direct control of it. As long as you weigh up the scene and pay attention to the light, you should be able to nail that shot easily.

Light Temperature

Throughout the day, you'll notice that the light has different colours and levels of harshness. Midday sun is the harshest, most squint-inducing light, with the bright sunlight coming directly from above, casting some not-too-complimentary shadows on the subject's face.

The light at sunrise or sunset is the lushest of them all, softly illuminating your subjects with a warm, flattering light that will make anyone look good.

Having said that, you can still take flattering photos of people in bright daylight; you just need to place them under open shade—somewhere where they are just about shaded from the sun, but looking out towards the light—which will provide for some soft, even lighting.

Perfect Weather Is Not Always Perfect

A perfect, sunny day isn't always ideal for photography—featureless blue skies can look rather plain and parts of the scene may be cast into a deep, dark shadow; on an overcast day, you'll get softer shadows, and you'll see more details in the shadows. The clouds act as a diffuser for the sunlight, creating an even, soft light, which will look great if you're shooting on black-and-white film. However, sometimes the stark contrast on a bright, sunny day can inject a bit of drama into your image.

Window Light Is Your Best Friend (if You Don't Have Friends)

Available light doesn't need to be limited to photography done outdoors—light still comes in through your windows. If you want to take studio-like portraits without resorting to costly, studio lighting, open those curtains and flood your room with light.

As long as the sunshine isn't beaming straight through the window and onto your subject's face, the light coming through will be nice and diffused. If you are getting harsh, direct light, you can try using net curtains or tracing paper to cover the windows and take the edge off that light.

Try placing your human subject angled partially toward the window instead of having the subject looking straight at the window. The partial side lighting will add a bit of depth by casting some shadows on the subject's face, whereas full-frontal lighting will make the face look a bit flat.

Invest in a reflector—or a big bit of card wrapped in foil if you're feeling thrifty—to place on the darker side of the subject. This will bounce any light coming in back onto your subject to act as a fill light, and lighten some of the shadows cast from the light shining through the window.

Use Your Hand

With Google Maps and basic knowledge of which direction the sun rises from and sets in, you can get a good idea of where the light is coming from, in any location, at any point in the day.

Sometimes, though, it's easier to just hold your hand out in front of you, and see how that catches the light. Where is the light coming from? Is it back-lit? Are the shadows harsh? You might get some odd looks, but it works without having to unlock your phone and open up an app.

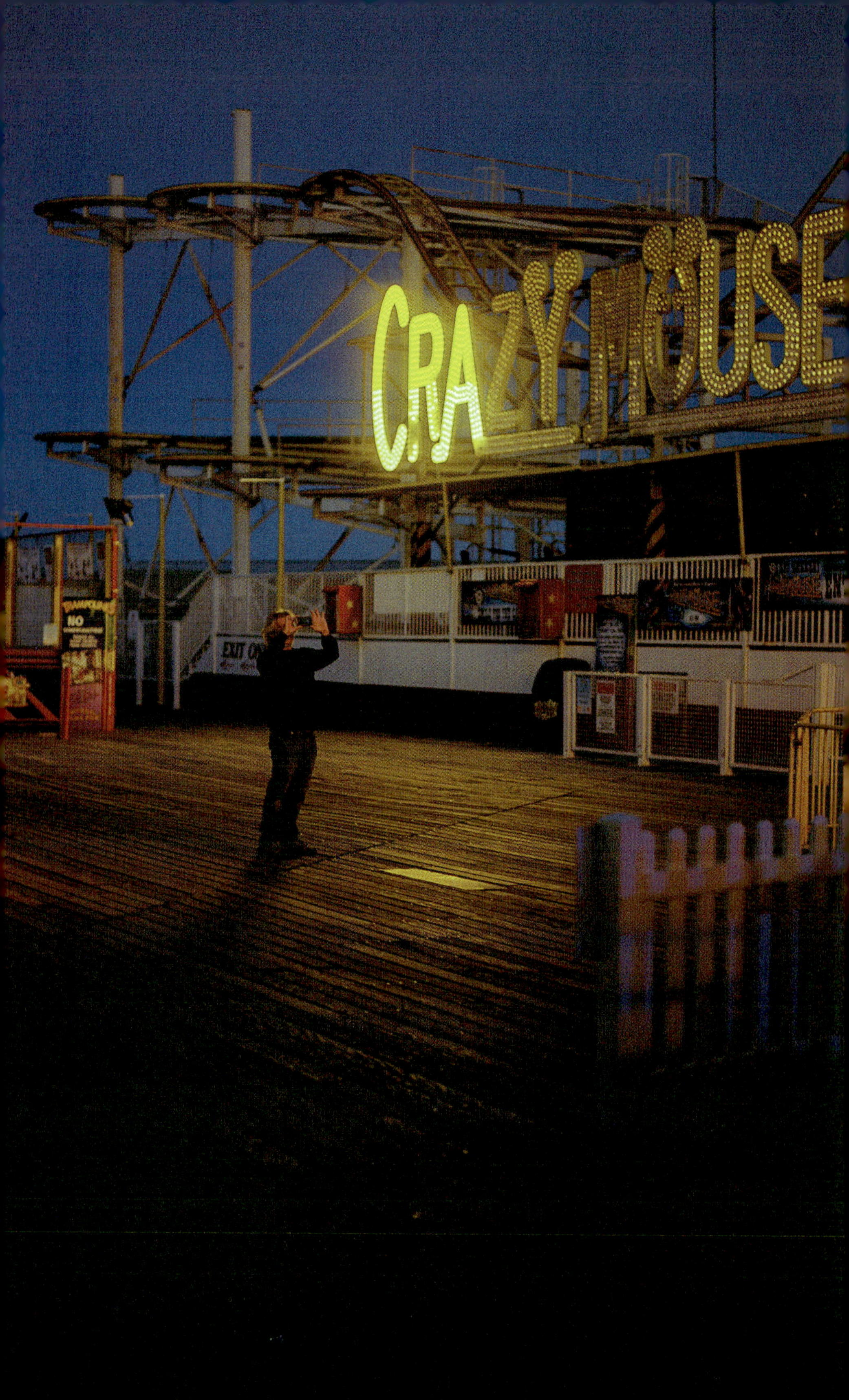
CRAZY MOUSE
NO

#39
MAKING THE BEST OF BAD LIGHT

At night, light is a valuable commodity, and it doesn't matter if you're shooting indoors or out, you're going to struggle to get enough of it to make a decent exposure. As it's not really a reasonable request to ask the local council to turn up the street lights just so you can take better photos, your best bet is to make the most of what light you have.

ISO: Go High or Go Home

Before you start taking low-light photos, make sure you've loaded some high-sensitivity film in your camera. ISO 400 film would be stretching it, as you'll be struggling with getting fast-enough shutter speeds, but some black-and-white ISO 400 films, like Kodak Tri-X, work well with push processing (explained in #48), which allows you to expose it as if it's a higher-speed film.

If you want higher ISO black and white, you have the ISO 3200 films from Kodak and Ilford—T-Max and Delta, respectively—and if you're sticking with colour, the choice is pretty much limited to Kodak Portra 800, Fujifilm Superia Venus 800, and CineStill 800T. Fujifilm Natura 1600 was a pretty fab high-ISO colour film, but it is sadly now discontinued (only available for extortionate prices on eBay).

Be in Control of Shutter Speed

With light in such short supply, and film ISO only going so high, the challenge is getting fast-enough shutter speeds to take steady, shake-free shots.

Ideally, you don't want to stick your camera in auto, P mode, or even aperture priority because your camera will just choose the shutter speed required to get a balanced exposure, not one that it thinks you'll be able to get stable, handheld results with. Use manual mode or shutter priority, so you know what the shutter speed is and that it's one you're comfortable using.

If you don't need to be handholding your camera, and your subjects don't move around, then it's not as important to use such a high-ISO film, or worry about having a fast-enough shutter speed, because you can just mount the camera on a tripod and fire off the shutter with a cable release.

Manual Focus

Autofocusing systems on old film cameras aren't always reliable in the best of light. In the worst of light, you might completely end up missing the shot altogether. This is one of the times when it's better having complete control of the focusing, because your eyes are much better designed for dealing with low light than early-days autofocusing tech.

Kai's Tips

- Try placing your subjects closer to a source of light to make sure there's a greater intensity of light illuminating them.
- Use your phone. Whack the brightness up on your phone screen and use that to light up your subject.
- Try light painting. Use a longer shutter speed and a flashlight to paint part of the scene with light. Imagine the point of light is paint and cover all the parts that you want painted with light.

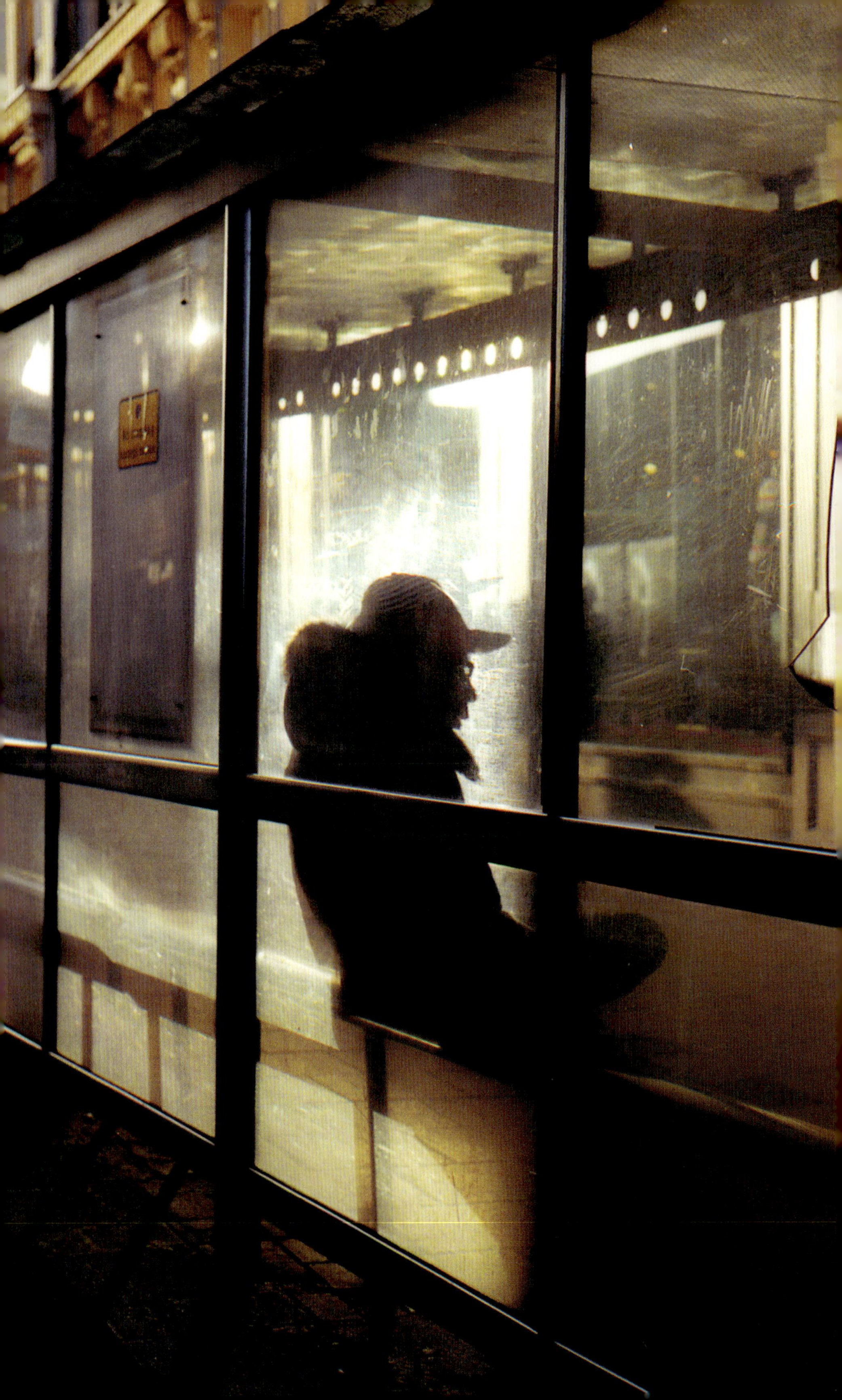

#40 USE FAST GLASS IN LOW LIGHT

Investing in fast glass is the first thing a low-light shooter should do—those gorgeous, large-aperture lenses will suck up what little light there is. It's not going to come cheap, but look at it this way: every time you bump up the maximum aperture by one stop, you're doubling the amount of light that is coming through the lens.

Low-Light Lenses for Leica M

The Noctilux 50 mm f/1.0 is one of the large-aperture legends. Introduced in 1966, the first version was an f/1.2 aspherical lens, which has now become a bit of a collector's item. Revisions came in 1976, taking away the aspherical elements but bumping up the maximum aperture to f/1.0. This is the one to get if you want a lens that you'll actually use, not put in a display cabinet.

In 2008, Leica announced that they were stopping production and released a limited last run that came in a glossy humidor; the Leica world weeped for the loss of a legend. Then, even before the last tear was shed, Leica introduced an even faster 50 mm f/0.95 aspherical. Although technically a superior lens, it lacks some of the soul of the f/1.0, so save a (little) bit of money and go for the classic.

For even less money, one of the finest lenses you could ever use is the 50 mm Summilux f/1.4 ASPH—it's sharp, fast, and produces gorgeous bokeh. If 50 mm isn't your thing, pretty much any other Leica lens with Summilux in the name will guarantee some sweet, low-light goodness.

Also in M-mount, the Konica M-Hexanon 50 mm f/1.2 is sharp and fast (but with not-so-hot bokeh); however, the price isn't much lower than the Leica Noctilux, making it harder to justify getting the Hexanon when you can have a Noctilux. Voigtlander's Noktons are cracking low-light monsters for minuscule prices, and are worth a look if you don't mind harsh bokeh.

Nikon's Finest Fast Lenses

If you end up buying a Nikon S rangefinder, which you probably won't, because hardly anyone does, then the fast fifty that you don't need is the super-rare 50 mm f/1.1. It's magnificent, it's rare, it's gorgeous, and it'll cost the same as a used car; but you can't take photos with a car, so the 50 mm f/1.1 makes a heck of a lot more sense.

For Nikon F SLRs, there are a number of fast-lens options for the thrifty: the 50 mm f/1.4 AI or AI-S are great manual-focus choices, the 50 mm f/1.4D for autofocus, and all can be had for not much money at all. If you're willing to push the boat out a bit more, the 35 mm f/1.4 AI-S and 85 mm f/1.4 AI-S are excellent fast lenses; and if you're feeling properly lavish, the 58 mm f/1.2 Noct-Nikkor is pretty sexual.

Canon's Wide-Open Wonders

The Canon 7 rangefinder is not as cool as the Nikon S, but perhaps a more popular and affordable choice. The fastest glass for the 7 is a rather audacious 50 mm f/0.95, and it's neither easy to find nor affordable. Wide-open performance is pretty mediocre, producing images that are a bit mushy. They were once called the poor man's Noctilux but have since increased in value thanks to large-aperture-obsessing collectors; it would now seem more appropriate to call them the middle-class man's Noctilux.

For SLRs, Canon made some finest fast lenses ever: 50 mm f/1.2L (equally magnificent in FD-mount and EOS-mount); 85 mm f/1.2L; 35 mm f/1.4L ... basically you can't go wrong with anything with a "f/1.4" and "L" tagged on the end.

Others

I love the eight-element Pentax Takumar 50mm f/1.4 and Olympus 50mm f/1.2, but even if you end up with another brand of camera—or you don't want to go for some of the lenses mentioned above—if you want to shoot low light, you can pick any reasonably priced 50 mm f/1.4 and get decent results from most of them.

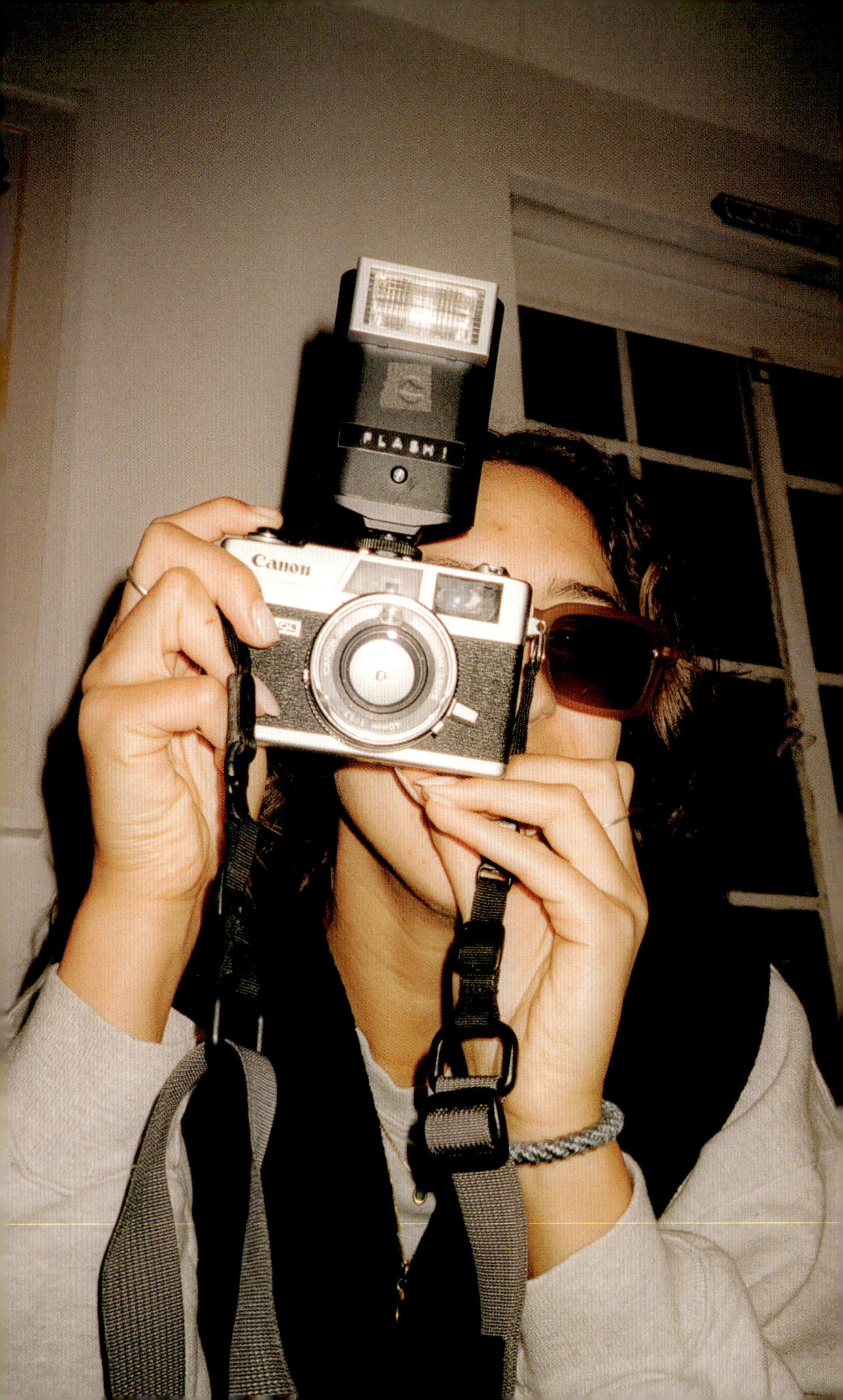
FLASH!
Canon

#41
FLASHING PEOPLE

Photographing in available light isn't limited to light from the big, bright round thing in the sky. Any form of man-made lights not under your direct manipulation can be considered available or ambient lighting—think street lamps and shop signs—but the great thing with lights that you do have control of is the ability to light a subject more precisely.

Continuous lighting will still give you the same what-you-see-is-what-you-get perks of available lighting because the lights are always on, which makes metering straightforward and lighting your subject decently an easy task.

Some Like It Hot

The problem with some continuous lighting setups (tungsten/quartz) is that they can run hot—known as hot lights, unsurprisingly—which is never fun when you're photographing for a prolonged period of time and everyone is melting their faces off. LED or fluorescent lighting won't run as hot, but the thing with any continuous lighting setup is that you're pretty limited with what you can shoot—they need a continuous source of power and tend to be not so portable—and that's why you might want to use flash/strobe lighting.

Key/Fill/Rim

The most obvious use for a flash is as your key light—the main source of lighting for your subject—by ensuring it is the most dominant light source. It can also be used for a bit of fill light, to fill up the shadows that come from the primary source of light. A fill should be weaker and softer than the key light.

You could also try placing the flash pointed toward the back of your subject, making sure the flash itself isn't visible, to create a rim light. The purpose of this is to add a highlighting light around the edge of your subject that will separate them from the background.

Start with One

There's no need to buy a load of flash units in one go; start off with one, keep things simple, and learn how to get the most out of a modest, one-flash setup before you make things more complicated. Mix it up with available light sources and try using the flash for the key, fill, or rim light.

Off Camera

If you're going for the snapshot or paparazzi kind of vibe, it's fine to keep the flash mounted on the camera (or to use the built-in flash). For flash lighting that will flatter, keep it off camera, whether it be mounted on a light stand or held by your non-camera-holding hand. Try placing the flash 45 degrees horizontally from your subject, and 45 degrees vertically, so that your flash is slightly to the side and above, pointed down at your subject. It's nice, flattering light for faces.

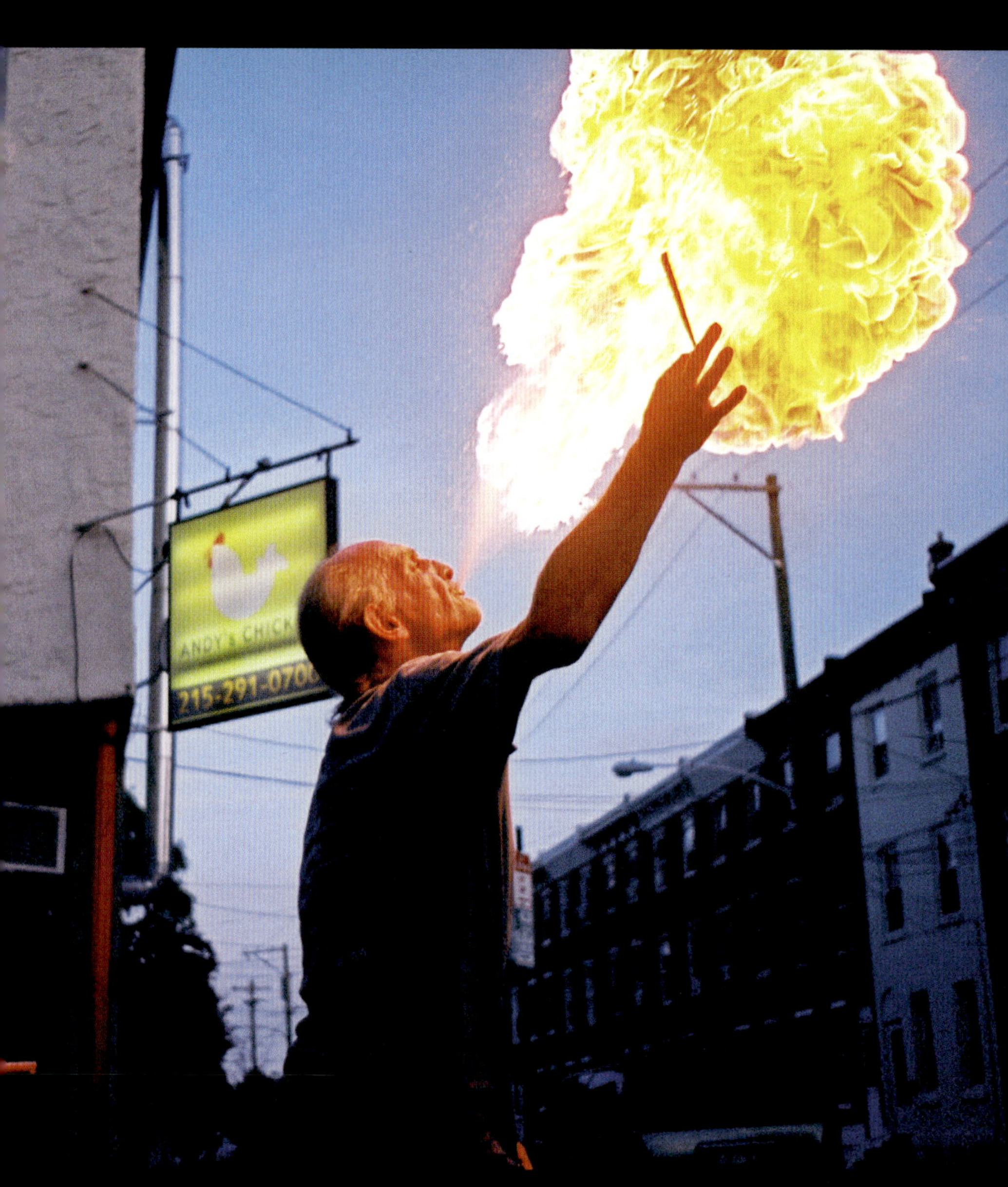
ANDY'S CHICK
215-291-070

#42

COLOUR TEMP: FEELING HOT AND COLD

Most film is daylight balanced—they will give the most accurate colours when shot on a nice sunny day; but use that same film to take photos indoors in a room lit by artificial lighting, and you might end up thinking that the colours look a bit squiffy-iffy.

Daylight has a colour temperature of 5500 K, which looks a neutral white; lower-colour temperatures take on a warmer, yellowy-orange hue, whereas higher-colour temps will look a cooler shade of blue.

Tungsten has a colour temperature of 3200 K—it's meant to look warmer, and that is exactly what you're going to get on daylight film. By the bucket load. And that's gonna look a bit off because, whereas your eyes and brain can adapt to different lighting and perceive different colours—you'll still see white as white in daylight or under tungsten lighting—film is not quite so flexible. White will look yellowy-orange, and that doesn't feel right because we know that's not what we would see.

With film, you've got three options to make your tungsten-lit photos look right:

Filter

As mentioned previously (#34), you can use a blue filter to balance out the warm look of tungsten lighting. The problem with that, though, is the filter will reduce the amount of light coming through your lens, which is never a good thing when you're already shooting in a dimly lit room and you need all the light you can get. Consequently, if you're using an SLR, you'll have to put up with peering through a gloomier-looking viewfinder thanks to that blue-tinted bit of glass on the front of your lens.

On a positive note, though, you can take off the filter whenever you like, so if you're going to take photos throughout the day—in daylight and artificial lighting—all on the same roll of film, then correcting the different colour temperatures is as easy as slapping a filter on or taking it off.

Film

Tungsten film is a bit of a niche product—this is not the kind of film you're going to find stocked in supermarkets, and you're really not going to be spoilt for choice. CineStill 800T is really your only option for 35 mm, actually.

CineStill 800T is essentially Kodak's VISION3 500T 5219 with the Remjet layer removed. WTF is a Remjet layer? It's a black protective layer on the film that is anti-halation and anti-static. Its removal means that your images might suffer from a rather distinctive glow in the highlights, but the good thing is that it means most good labs should be able to develop this without an issue using the C41 process. Although, having said that, a lab I used to process a roll of 800T somehow managed to mess it up.

In the daylight, tungsten film will produce a cool, blue look, which you can correct with an 85 filter, or leave it as is if you fancy that blue vibe. The loss of light from using a filter won't seem as problematic in the daytime, because you're shooting with fast ISO 800 film in the daylight, and could probably do with less light.

Photoshop

If you're making prints, it makes a lot of sense to get the right look straight out of camera. But chances are: the photos will end up being scanned and then uploaded, so the easiest way is to use Photoshop to correct the colour. Not only does it have the option of applying different colour filters, it's also very easy to tweak the colours, meaning you don't need to spend money on bits of coloured glass; don't need to worry about whether you're getting enough light; and don't need to go to the hassle of sourcing rather expensive tungsten film that some lab might mess up anyway.

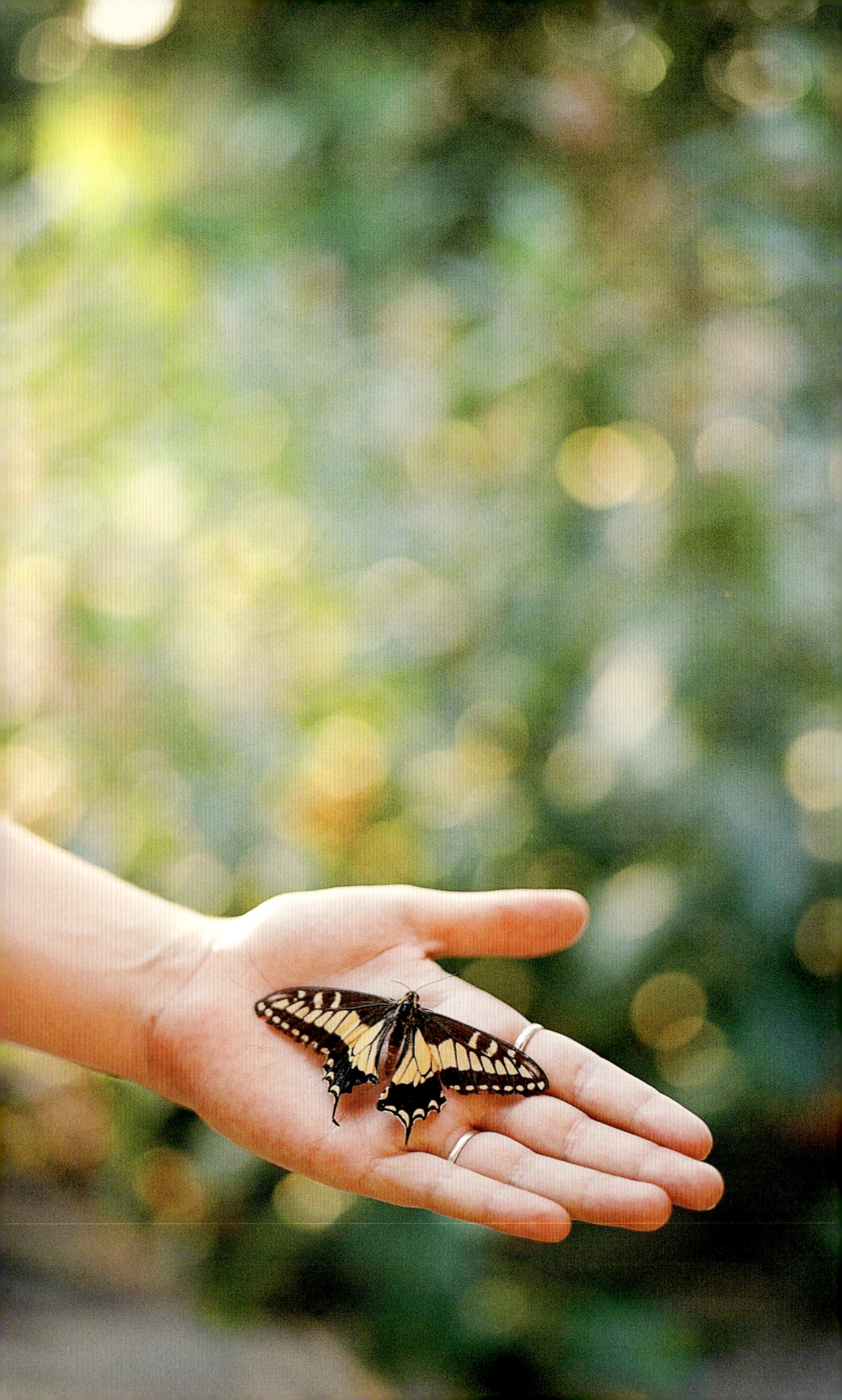

#43
BONKERS ABOUT BOKEH

Bokeh: you're not going to find this one in the Oxford English Dictionary, but that's because it's an anglicisation of a Japanese word 暈け that means blur or haze. It's also a word that can be used to call someone stupid or an idiot, but for photography it relates to the quality of the out-of-focus elements in a photo (unless you want to call a photographer an idiot).

It sounds like such a bonkers thing to obsess about—the quality of the blurry bits—but it's such an important aesthetic element of the image that can really make or break a photo.

As mentioned in the first half of the book, a small f number (a large aperture) will give you shallow depth of field—making the subject really pop by putting them on a thin plane of focus, throwing anything centimetres in front and behind completely out of focus. These blurry bits can look really smooth and creamy, melting away like gooey, hot, melted mozzarella—that's good bokeh. It can also look like a load of fairy lights after you've had one too many shandies—bad bokeh.

Having good bokeh is every bit as important as having sharp, in-focus bits, perhaps even more so. Bad bokeh can look harsh, with hard outer edges that are incredibly distracting. You don't want people to end up looking at those crazy little rings of light; you want them to look at the subject. Superb bokeh is there, but it isn't; they're properly blurry, which makes your eyes naturally look toward the in-focus bits.

Bokeh is not used to talk about the amount or intensity of the blur—that's depth of field—so buying a lens with a larger aperture doesn't mean you're getting more bokeh, and it doesn't necessarily mean you're getting good bokeh either.

Buy a lens with your eyes. Well, and your credit card, too. But definitely google for bokeh sample shots from a lens before you commit to the purchase. There are very obvious examples of good bokeh and bad bokeh. Then it gets to a point where blurry bits just look like blurry bits, and it gets all subjective about whether the bokeh is good or not.

Know how to tell the difference between obviously good and bad bokeh, and buy a lens that keeps those blurry bits blurry. When you start trying to differentiate between decent bokeh and excellent bokeh, you're mainly buying for yourself and the approval of your peers.

Kai's Top Five Bokeh-licious Lenses

1. Leica 50mm Noctilux f/1.0: The dreamiest bokeh balls of all.
2. Canon 85mm f/1.2L : A beast of a lens with beastly bokeh.
3. Nikon 85mm f/1.4 AI-S: Good bokeh needn't cost all that much.
4. Nikon 105mm DC: Defocus control lets you tweak your bokeh ball softness.
5. Leica 50mm Summilux ASPH: Not as mental as the Nocti, but super bokeh nonetheless.

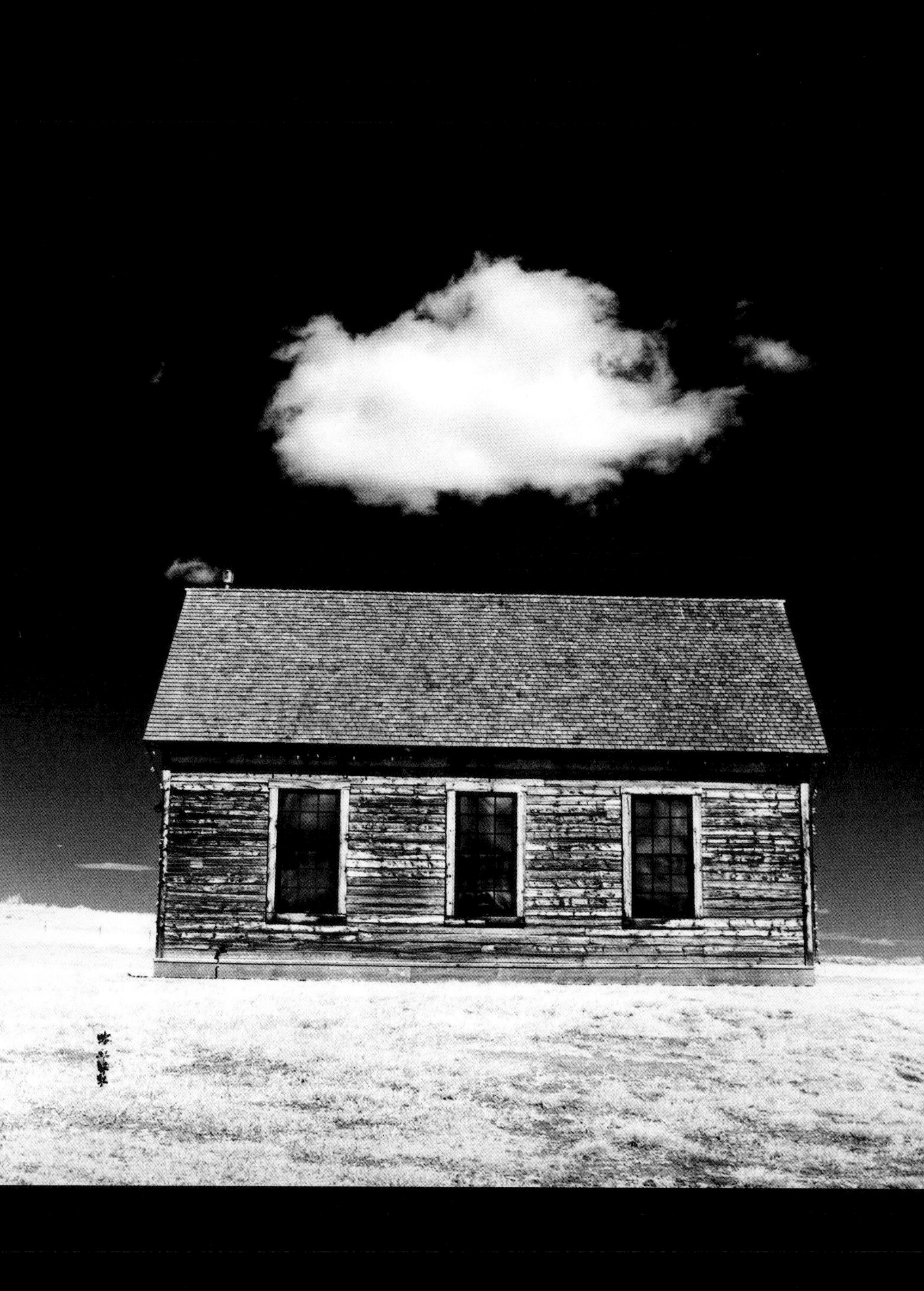

#44

INFRARED FILM: INDULGE IN THE ETHEREAL

Infrared photos are some of the most stunningly surreal, out-of-this-world images you will ever see. But, oh boy, can it be a bit of a botty-bothering process to deal with.

For a start, infrared photography involves capturing something you can't actually see—the human eye can't see infrared light. And it's not just you; light meters can't pick up IR light either, so you can't use it to check exposure.

Then there's the finicky way of storing and loading them. The film is so sensitive to light that it needs to be kept in the light-tight canister until you load it into your camera; and even then, it still needs to be put into your camera in a completely dark room.

On top of that, you'll need an all-manual camera that doesn't read the DX coding on film cases and doesn't automatically wind your film, because the LED lights could fog up your film.

Infrared Film

Infrared film can be seen as a colour or black-and-white image: Colour infrared film will make familiar places look like alien lands; trees will look like troll hair. Black-and-white gives a great balance, with a look that is not too wild, while injecting a magical look to the image that you simply won't get with boring, regular light. Foliage reflects a lot of IR light, which will make trees and grass appear as almost bright white; and the sky, which doesn't reflect IR light, will show up as near black—creating an aesthetic that is gorgeously ethereal.

Unfortunately, colour infrared film has been discontinued, so no troll-hair action for you, but thankfully black-and-white IR film is still available. Check out Ilford SFX or Rollei Infrared to get started with shooting infrared photos.

Filters to Make IR Photos Pop

You've got your film, and now you need a filter; to get the right one, you need to know your nanometers. In infrared photography, the film is sensitive to wavelengths in the near-infrared spectrum (700–900 nm), and it picks up visible light as well (400–700 nm). You could start off with a 550 nm filter that would allow some visible light through, giving a mild IR effect. A 720 nm filter is the one I'd recommend, as it gives a healthy dose of bright foliage and moody skies. A 850 nm filter takes the effect up a notch further, but I wouldn't start off with this for your first crack at infrared photography.

It would be wise to frame your shot before slapping on the filter, because you won't see much with the filter on. Make sure you're manual focusing, as infrared light is a bit weird—it focuses slightly in front of regular, visible light. Some old lenses have a little red dot on the focusing scale to give a little indicator of that shift.

For best results, shoot on a sunny day, because that's when you'll get loads of IR light, and it will make figuring out exposure settings much easier—you just use the Sunny 16 Rule (see, it is handy to know). Bear in mind that you've got a filter on the front and you're probably looking at f/8 instead of f/16 on a sunny day, but it would be advisable to bracket your exposures (try a few different settings) just to make sure you get a keeper.

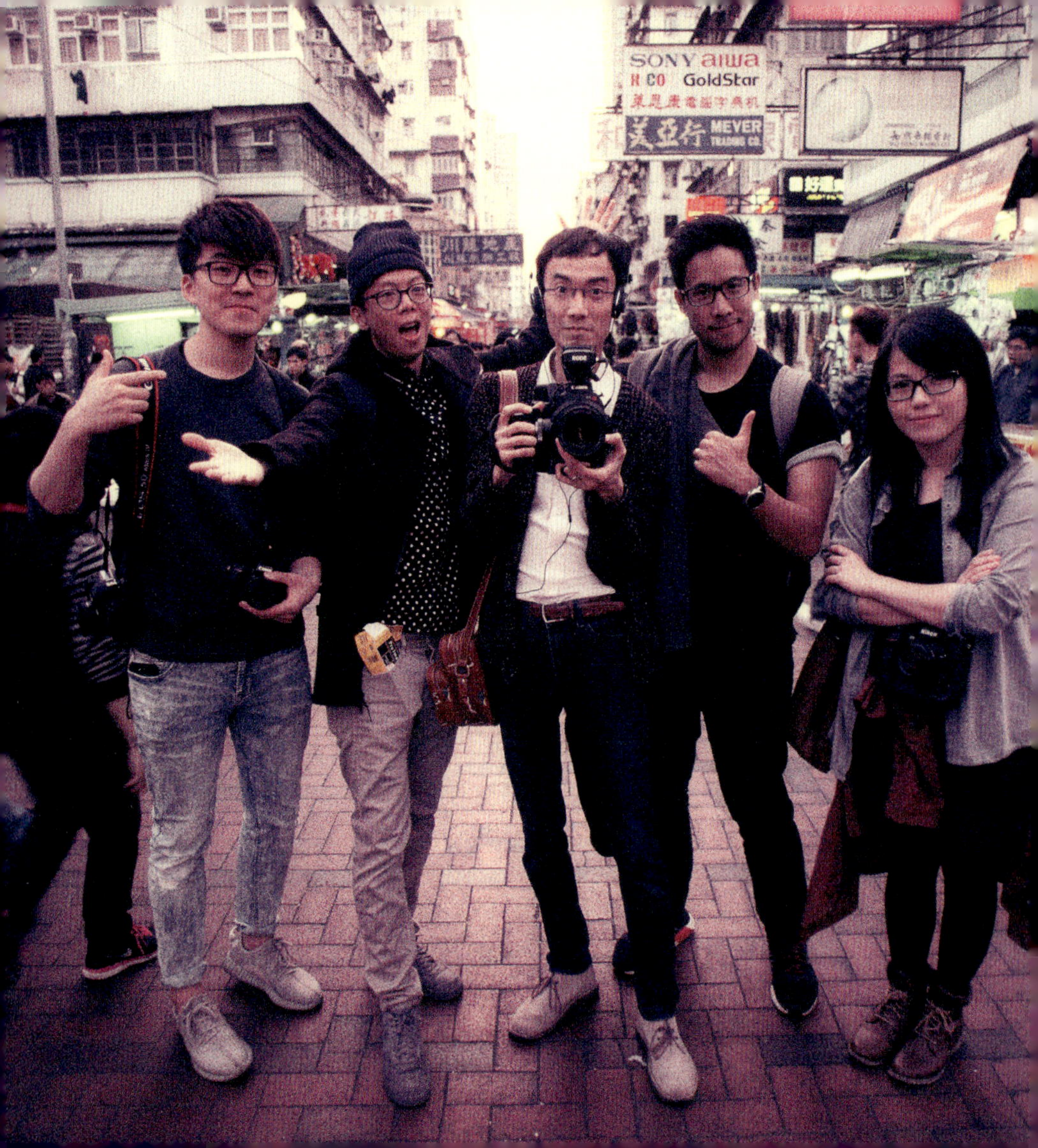
SONY aiwa
GoldStar
美亞行 MEYER TRADING CO.

#45

USE EXPIRED FILM FOR A FRESH, NEW LOOK

Think of film as an egg—not in the sense that it came out of a chicken's arse and tastes great poached with some hollandaise sauce—in the sense that you can store them in room temperature without too many ill effects. But if you want them to last longer, without spoiling, you should keep them in the fridge until you need to use them.

Film has a best-before date, so you might want to use them before then—I say might because some people like the unpredictable look—because once it does expire, it starts to deviate from its intended, original aesthetic.

Silver halide crystals are the key, image-forming bits of the film—when they're exposed to light, chemicals react, some magic happens, and the image gets recorded on film. The longer the film is left past its expiration date, unexposed, the less sensitive those crystals become. In other words, the film speed is no longer accurate to what is specified on the film packaging, so you might need to overexpose your shot to ensure you're getting enough light—and the key word is might.

Recommendations vary, from overexposing by one half stop to one stop for every decade after its expiration date. There is no saying for sure how much more light you need, simply because there's no way of knowing how much the film is going to degrade—it's made of organic substances that react to environmental factors. If it has been kept in a fridge for the ten years after its expiration, it could still function almost in the same way as a fresh roll of film, whereas poorly stored film could start turning to crap even before its expiration date. The problem with buying expired film is that you don't know if it has been stored properly or not.

Expired film will become less sensitive to light, show signs of fogging, and exhibit more noise. And if it's colour film, there's more: Black-and-white film only has one layer of silver halide crystals, but colour film has at least three of those layers, along with dyes. So not only may the effects of expired film be more pronounced with colour but you'll also start to see colour shifts; and it might look less saturated. It might.

Honestly, I don't think expired film is something that you should try out for your first few rolls of film. If you're trying your best to learn how to get your exposures right with film, it would be counterproductive to try doing that with film that is not guaranteed to expose in the way it was intended to. Also, if you're going to take photos that you intend to look absolutely gorgeous, or it's an image that you're going to cherish, don't use expired film yet.

Still, shooting with expired film is something that is worth trying because there is a wabi-sabi (that's not the stuff you put on your sushi) appeal to it. The key to taking good photos with expired film is to not care too much, and just accept what you might get as the end result. Might.

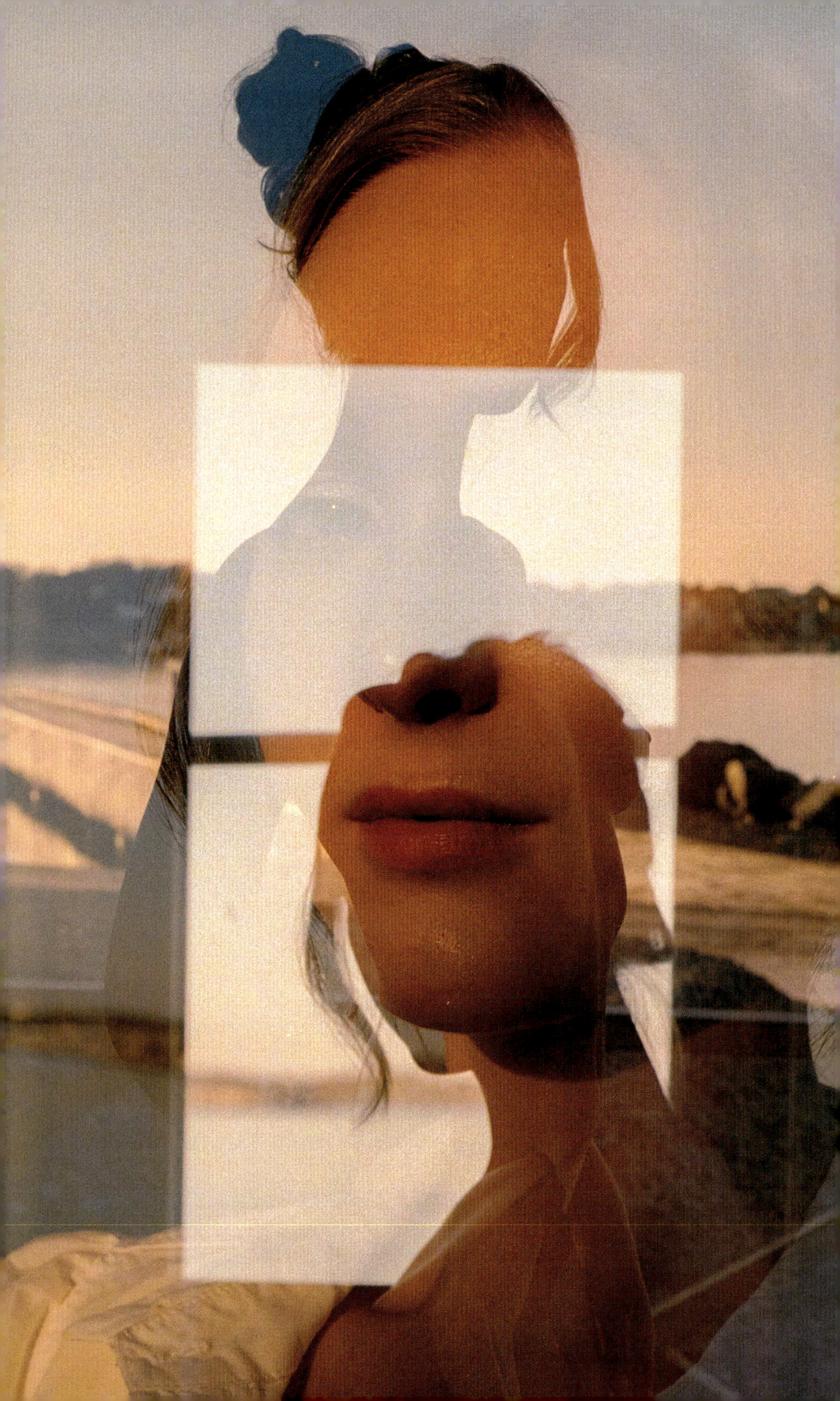

#46 DOUBLE EXPOSURES FOR TWICE THE FUN

Slapping one image on top of another in a single frame of film sounds like a surefire way of ruining two images, and that is essentially what you're doing with double exposures—ruining two shots to create one.

Double exposures can feel like a refreshing approach to making an image because, even though there is a chance that the resulting image will look crap, when it does work out well, it feels awesome. Doubly awesome.

Not all cameras will have a double-exposure function—most toy cameras will just let you keep exposing on the same frame. Some cameras will have a little lever or button to flick/push to allow you to double expose—but you can trick those cameras by pressing the rewind button on the base of the camera and winding the film advance lever once. The film will stay in place, and the shutter will be re-cocked and ready.

Luck does play its part in the making of a magnificent double exposure, but that doesn't mean it has to be a haphazard mishmash of two half-arsed photos. It does take a bit of good technique and creative vision to make something interesting.

Shoot in Pairs

One way of taking double exposures is to finish a roll of film, rewind it back to the start, and then take another load of photos until you finish the roll a second time. That's fine if you don't mind risking a whole roll of film.

The more rewarding way is to pair off each double exposure, taking the second of the exposures not too long after the first—you'll have a fresh memory of what the first shot looked like—so if the final result is good, it'll feel like it was all your doing.

Perfection Not Needed

If you've taken a superb shot—a magically lit, perfectly composed, unrepeatable moment—I'd recommend that you wind on without making it a double exposure. You have a lot more to lose than you could gain.

Each exposure doesn't have to be amazing to begin with, but you should consider how they will fit together and complement each other.

Underexpose Twice to Make It Nice

As you have two times the exposures on one frame, you will need each exposure to have half the amount of light. Underexposing by one stop will half the amount of light—e.g., stopping down from f/2.8 to f/4 or increasing the shutter speed from 1/50s to 1/100s—and that will make sure your final image doesn't look too bright.

All About the Shadows

The details of the second exposure will show up more clearly on the shadows of the first exposure. So if you're photographing, for example, someone with a bright sky in the background, and then you take a photo of some flowers for your second exposure, those little floral details will show up more clearly on the darker parts of your subject than the bright sky in the background.

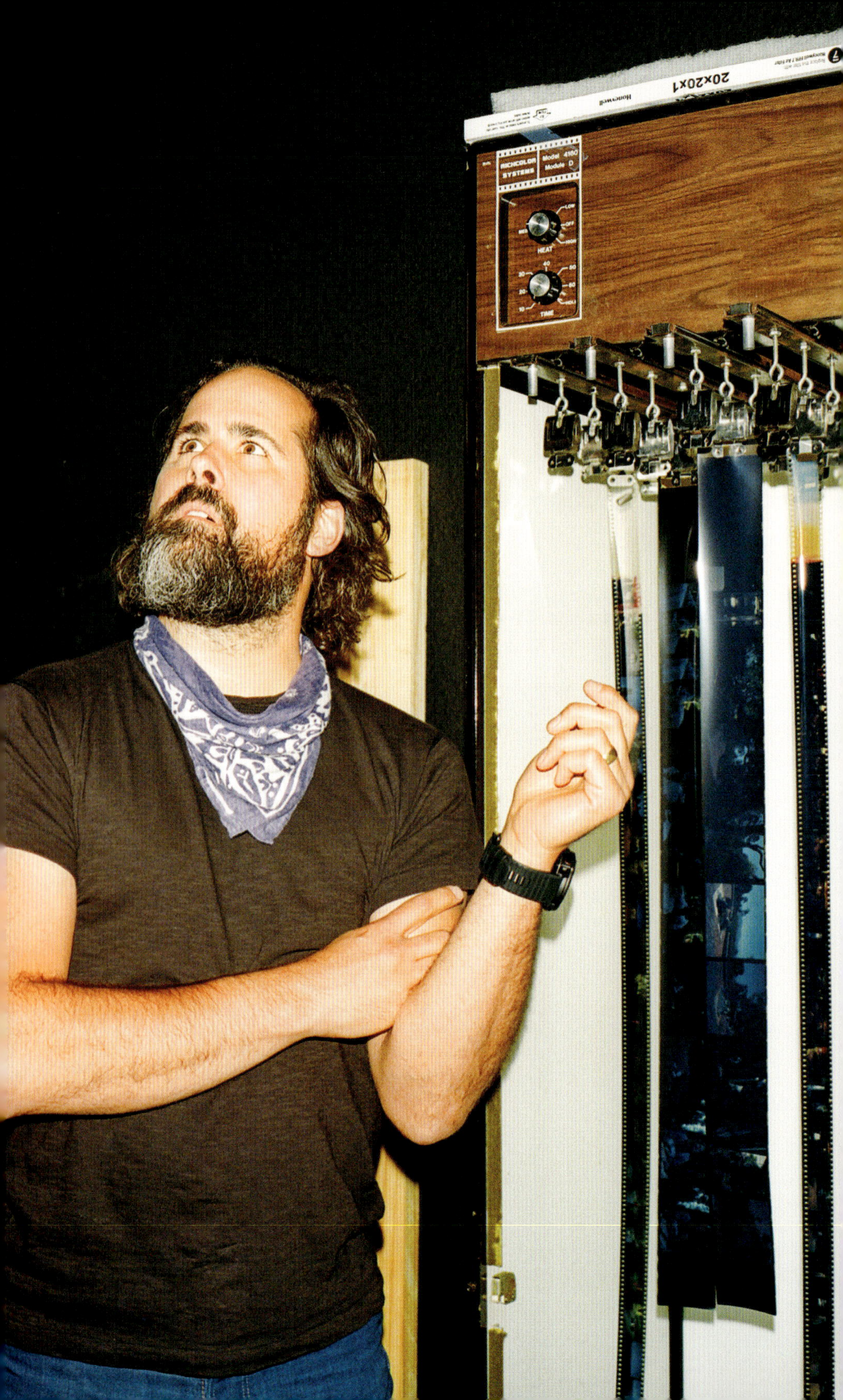
RICHCOLOR SYSTEMS
Model 4160
Module D
LOW
OFF
HIGH
HEAT
TIME

#47
DEVELOPING FILM: THE BEST WAY IS YOUR WAY

Once your film is fully exposed, it'll need to be developed or processed (they mean the same thing) before you can see the final images on film. This can be done by the happy chappy at your favourite photo lab, or by yourself. But just so you know: If you're planning on having a crack at it, processing colour film is a monumental pain in the orifice. In comparison, black-and-white film developing is an absolute doddle.

Some film photography enthusiasts wish to perpetuate the idea that a good film photographer should develop their own film. Knowing how to process your own doesn't make you a good photographer; taking good photos does. As long as the final result looks good, no one other than yourself is going to give a crap if you developed it or not.

Colour-negative film is relatively cheap to process, and it shouldn't be a problem finding a lab that will develop it with a quick turnaround time. Given the option of developing colour negatives myself, or dropping it off at a random chemist for a one-hour process, I'd choose the latter. Given the option of developing it at a chemist and getting the developed film back within an hour, or using a film-processing lab and waiting a week to get it back, I'd go for the latter.

Don't just settle for the first lab that you can find, and don't pick one just because it's cheap, or assume that it's good because it's expensive. There's a bit of trial and error involved, which is a bummer given that the cost of developing film is not cheap; but once you've found a place that provides a good service and produces great-looking results, stick with them. If it means sending your film to a lab that you can trust, do that, rather than making do with the mediocre.

Some labs will keep you in the loop with the progress, letting you know if there are any issues, and will refund you for the cost of scanning if it turns out the film was improperly exposed. And if you're happy with the way your film turned out, you should keep using them.

For scanning, I'd just pay a little extra to have the lab scan the film after they've processed it. Buying your own scanner is not a problem—spending the time to scan through a whole roll of film is the soul-sapping task. Scan them as TIFF files to have top-quality scans with maximum tweakability in editing, and then you can save them as JPEGs once you've finished editing the scanned images.

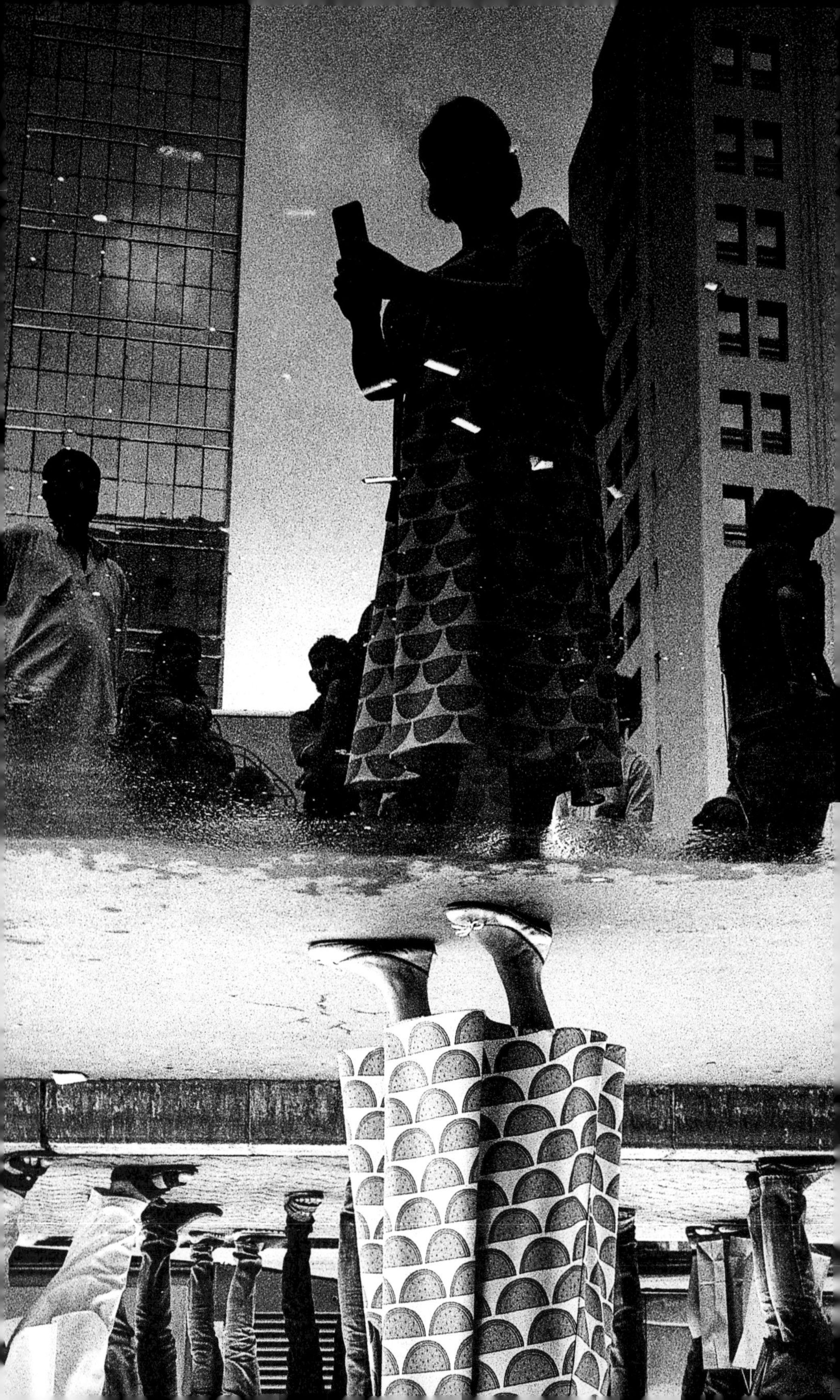

#48
PUSH AND PULL: THE GOOD, THE BAD, AND SOMETIMES UGLY

Push and pull processing are always mentioned together in the same sentence because they both involve film developing, are used to correct exposures, and will also change the look of the image; it's just that they go in completely opposite directions (hence the names).

When film is processed, they take the film and put it in a developer (FYI: it's a liquid, not a person) for the recommended amount of time. If you're push processing, you're overdeveloping the film by leaving it in the developer for a longer time; pull processing means underdeveloping the film by leaving it in the developer for less time.

Now, if all of your film is properly exposed, you don't need to go for push or pull processing. Even if you think only half your film is properly exposed, you should just develop it as normal. The only times you should push or pull process is if you took light-meter readings based on the wrong ISO for the whole roll of film, or you purposely underexposed or overexposed your film—but why exactly would you want to do that?

When Two Wrongs Do Make a Right

Wrong #1: Underexposing

If you've got an ISO 400 film in your camera but tricked your light meter into thinking it's an ISO 800 film (you can set this on the ISO dial), the film will be underexposed by one stop. The light meter will think it doesn't need as much light with a film that is one stop higher in sensitivity, and you will end up using a faster shutter speed or a smaller aperture.

Wrong #2: Overdeveloping

To compensate for the one-stop underexposure, you can push process the film by one stop.

The Right

This allows you to shoot in lower light, despite only having an ISO 400 film in your camera, with fast-enough shutter speeds to allow you to handhold them without getting shaky shots. Alternatively, it could be useful for allowing you get deeper depth of field.

Pull processing allows you to overexpose the film and then pull process to bring back the exposure. This will allow you to use a larger aperture for shallow depth of field or a slower shutter speed.

Useful. But push or pull processing are mostly used for the effects that come as a result of putting the film in the developer for a shorter or longer time.

The Effects of Push/Pull Processing

Pushing the film will not only lighten the image but it will also bump up the contrast and increase the graininess, creating a striking, in-your-face look. Pulling the film decreases the contrast, making everything look a bit wishy-washy. Pull processing is definitely not as popular as push processing, but then that's understandable, as I can't imagine many people want the dirty-dishwater look in their images.

The more stops you push or pull the film, the more pronounced those effects will be. Having said that, for best results I wouldn't recommend pushing or pulling any more than two stops because the effect will become too overbearing.

Push/pull processing works best with black-and-white film, less so with E6 colour slide film, and even less so with C41 colour negatives. The problem with colour film is that it will start to take on some unpredictable colour shifts when you push or pull process them. By all means experiment with push or pull processing colour film; just don't keep your hopes up about the final results.

#49

CROSS PROCESSING: THE FLAVOUR ENHANCER

If wild and wacky colours are what you're after, then cross processing is guaranteed to provide some batshit-bonkers colour palettes.

Cross processing (or X-pro) is a technique of running the film through the wrong chemicals—putting E6 film in C41 chemicals, or developing C41 film as if it were E6 film. Different film stock reacts differently to cross processing, so the best way is to experiment to figure out which one produces a look that you like.

Subjectively speaking, C41 to E6 gives results that can end up looking more awful than arty. That's probably why cross processing tends to be done with images exposed on E6 film and developed in C41 chemicals—the look is lower in contrast, with more pastel colours. If you want to give it a go, try out different films, keep your expectations low, and overexpose by at least a couple of stops.

E6 to C41 X-pro will result in super contrasted images with some odd but likeable colour casts; and although it's not always easy to predict the final results, when it works out well you'll get some super-saturated, vibrant-looking images. When shooting with E6 slide film, expose the film correctly.

X-pro is like a flavour enhancer—the monosodium glutamate of film—it may not be natural, too much of it is never a good thing, and it won't be everyone's idea of good taste, but there are certainly times when it can give instant, kick-up-the-bum appeal to an image. Some photographers might turn their noses up at the thought of cross processing their film, perhaps due to its association with Lomographers and lo-fi photography. But as long as you're enjoying it, and you don't use cross processing to mask the mediocre with over-the-top colours, then who cares what others think?

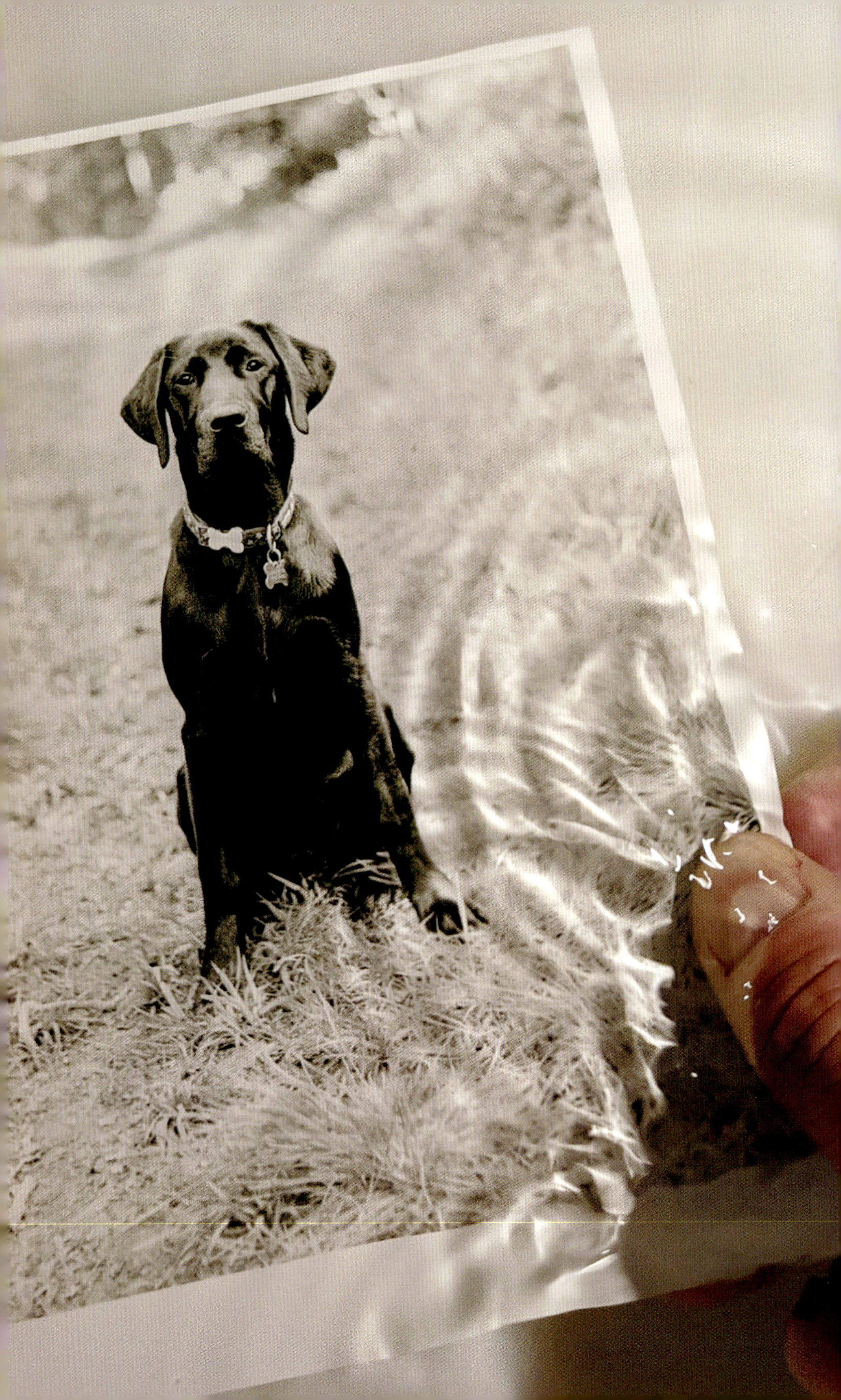

#50 WHY YOU NEED TO PRINT YOUR FILM PHOTOS

As with processing, I'm not going to go into detail about how you should get started printing from home. As fun as it is to print your own photos, not everyone wants the hassle of doing your own. But whether you decide to do it yourself the old-school way, get the lab to do it, or simply use your printer to print from the film scans, it is something that I recommend you do.

Pride of Work

Part of being a good photographer is a healthy dose of hubris. Photography is not about hiding your work—so print your photos and proudly place them on the most prominent walls in your house. Be proud of your work and you'll inevitably take great pride in the way you make those photos.

Motivation

Perhaps not everyone else in your house will be so pleased to let you take on the non-democratically elected role of chief wall decorator, but even if it means putting them up in the garage, the thought of filling a number of walls with your favourite photos will give you the motivation to produce some fine-looking pics.

Always Better in Physical Form

It's easier to appreciate photos in physical form versus seeing them on the screen. It's easier to flick through the archives and refer back to some old photos you've taken, instead of switching on a computer and looking through your external hard drives.

When you've got the prints there in front of you, it feels easier to evaluate and consider how you could improve that shot (if needed).

Perfect for Sharing

Sharing a photo now has less to do with slide film and more to do with sliding into someone's DMs, but if you want to give the gift of a photo, the best way is to give an actual print. The success of instant film is proof of its appeal, and the recipient is more likely to cherish a print than a photo down in the depths of their downloads folder.

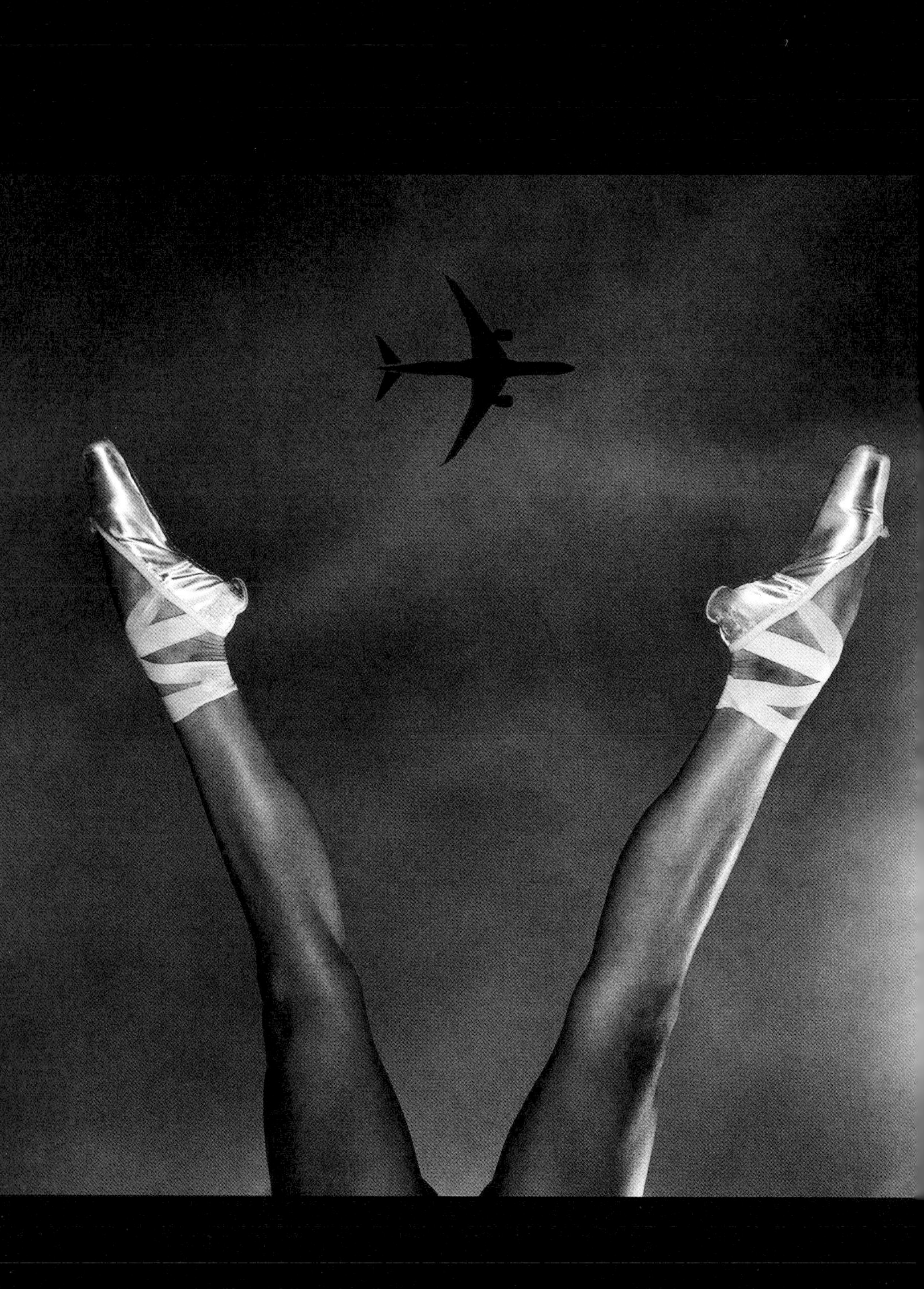

#51 LEARN THE RULES; THEN FORGET THEM

My photography teacher at uni was a bit of a rule breaker. I mean, the dude never turned up to his own bloody lessons, so I guess you could say he wasn't one for walking the line.

I haven't got a clue why he didn't teach any lessons (there was a pub conveniently located next to the university building, though). But to be honest, I'm glad that I didn't have to sit in a classroom to learn about photography, and it's not just because it gave me Thursday mornings off. I spent that time plodding through muddy fields, looking for the perfect place to capture first light. That, in my mind, is the best way to learn about how to take better photos—by going out to take photos—not listening to how the frickin' exposure triangle works.

The technical aspects, the gear, the f-stops, the triangles, all that tear-jerkingly dry stuff—that can all be learnt on the go, fit in around the photo-taking, at your own pace.

Comprehension of all the techie stuff is going to come eventually, and it'll come quicker when you're putting what you're learning into practice at the same time. Do it at your own pace, and dive only as deep as necessary.

The creative part of photography is something that is already there in your head; it just needs to be developed through taking photos, being inspired by things you see—photos, culture, places—and making yourself aware of the guidelines for composition. It's good to understand the conventions—some might call them rules—for making well-composed shots, but to be truly creative with your photography it is better if you challenge those conventions.

The only rule in photography you need to know is that there are no rules—that's what my photography teacher taught me anyway.

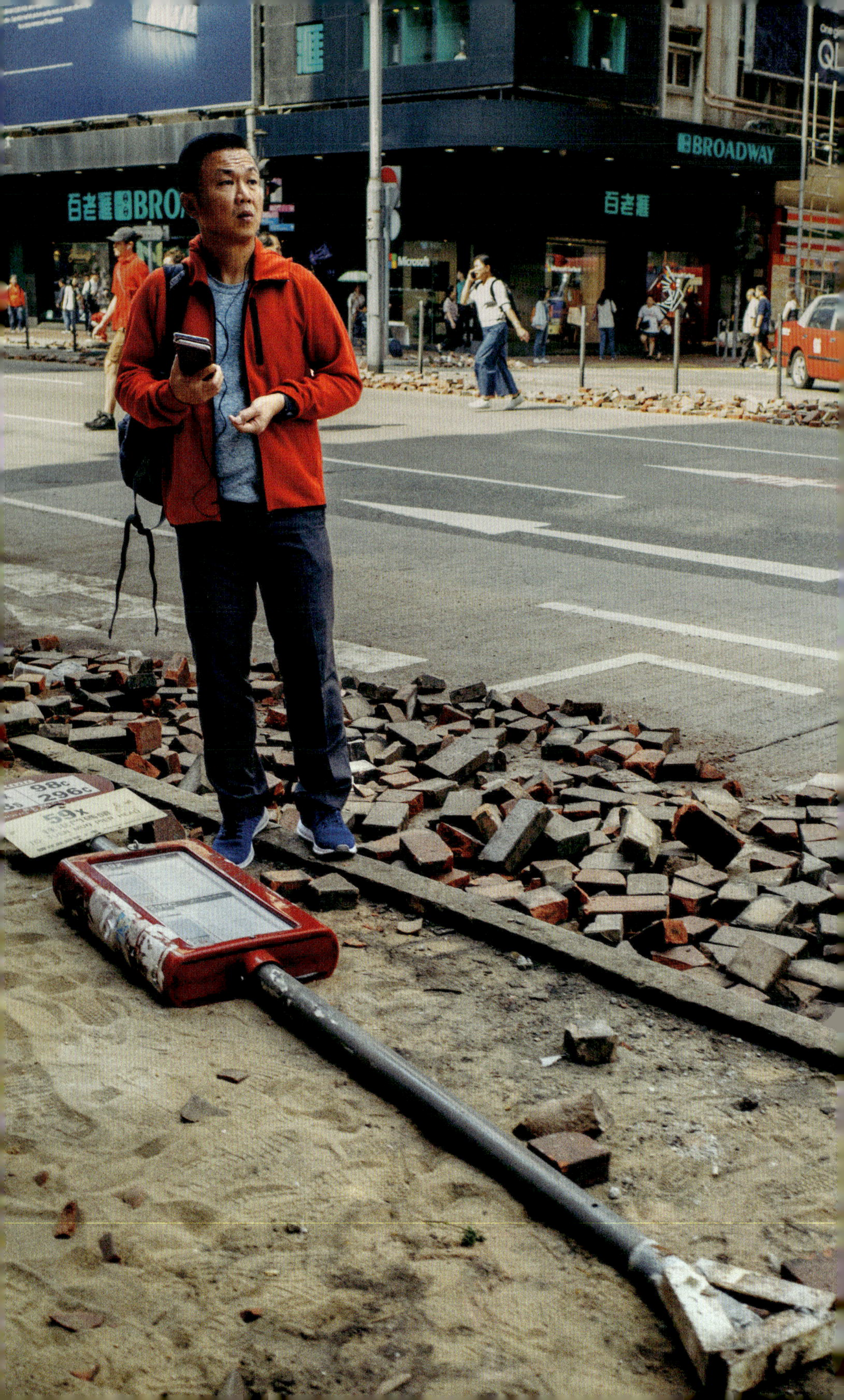

百老滙BROADWAY
百老滙
59x

#52 BENDING THE RULE OF THIRDS

You will see this compositional rule recycled and regurgitated in numerous books, magazines, blogs, and vlogs, all explaining the same thing—with a few tweaks courtesy of a thesaurus—accompanied by some carefully selected photos with a rule of thirds grid slapped on top.

The premise of the rule of thirds is that you divide your frame with two equally spaced horizontal lines, and two equally spaced vertical lines—to form nine squares of equal proportions over your frame. Then what you're supposed to do is to place the most interesting visual elements on those intersecting points for a simple and effective way of creating a strong composition.

Composition must be one of our constant preoccupations, but at the moment of shooting it can stem only from our intuition, for we are out to capture the fugitive moment, and all the interrelationships involved are on the move. In applying the Golden Rule, the only pair of compasses at the photographer's disposal is his own pair of eyes.

—Henri Cartier-Bresson

The beef I have with all of this is not the rule itself but the way the rule is presented as the best way to make perfect compositions, when it simply doesn't work in all situations. Haphazardly slapping the rule of thirds onto anything could easily make the image look wildly unbalanced, leaving masses of awkward dead space by putting a subject off-centre.

It does work really well for some things—with landscapes, the idea is that you place the horizon along one of the two horizontal lines on the grid; place it along the top line to emphasise the land, or on the lower line to highlight the sky. This is a great way of showing someone new to photography how careful placement of horizon can work wonders for the look of a photo. But everything doesn't have to be that precise; treat the grid as guidance and play around with what feels correct to your eye and not correct to the grid.

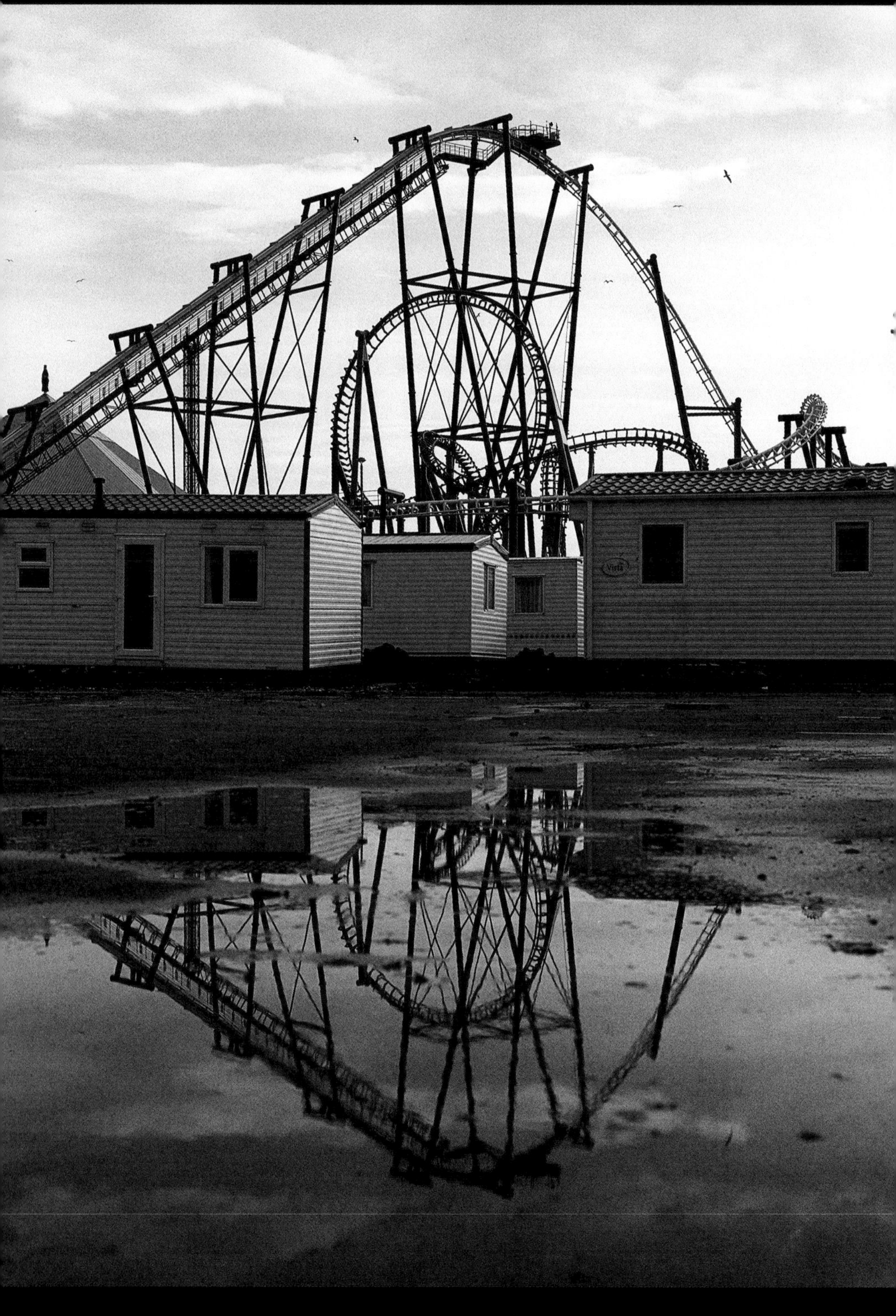

#53
STRIKING A BALANCE

To start slayin' it with your compositions, sling the rule of thirds aside for a moment and concentrate on one very important thing that makes a truly kick-ass compo: balance.

Formal Balance/Symmetrical Balance

Otherwise known as symmetrical balance. Some trolls might write off this everything-dead-centre composition, but it works a treat for things that have perfect symmetry—e.g., faces, architecture, eggs—and some other things with near perfect symmetry—e.g., landscapes reflected in the water. The perfectly centred framing accentuates the shape, giving your image a harmonious balance.

Informal Balance/Asymmetrical Balance

This is a more complex way of composing a shot that involves placing subjects or elements off-centre or asymmetrically.

This means you might end up with a load of awkward, boring dead space in the other part of the frame. Sound familiar? Yes; that's because the rule of thirds is asymmetrical balance.

The quick fix for that is to place something else in the frame to provide the balance. For example, if you're taking a photo of a mountain, placed in the background, it could be balanced by putting something less visually overwhelming, like a small tree, some flowers, or a gate, in the foreground. Images with asymmetric balance work best when there are two elements of visual interest, one of greater importance than the other.

There are other ways to create an asymmetrical balance:

Tonal Balance

This one works best with black-and-white film because the simple stark contrast between the dark and light tones create a nice and simple balance. It really can be as easy as using a darker foreground balanced out with a light sky.

Colour Balance

Not too dissimilar to tonal balance, it involves placing something colourful amongst more muted colours to create a contrast—a balance that helps the brightness of the subject pop more.

Conceptual Balance

A conceptual balance is when you place two subjects in the frame, with separate meanings that can relate to each other: e.g., an old car next to a new car, a flower next to a gun, rough textures next to soft.

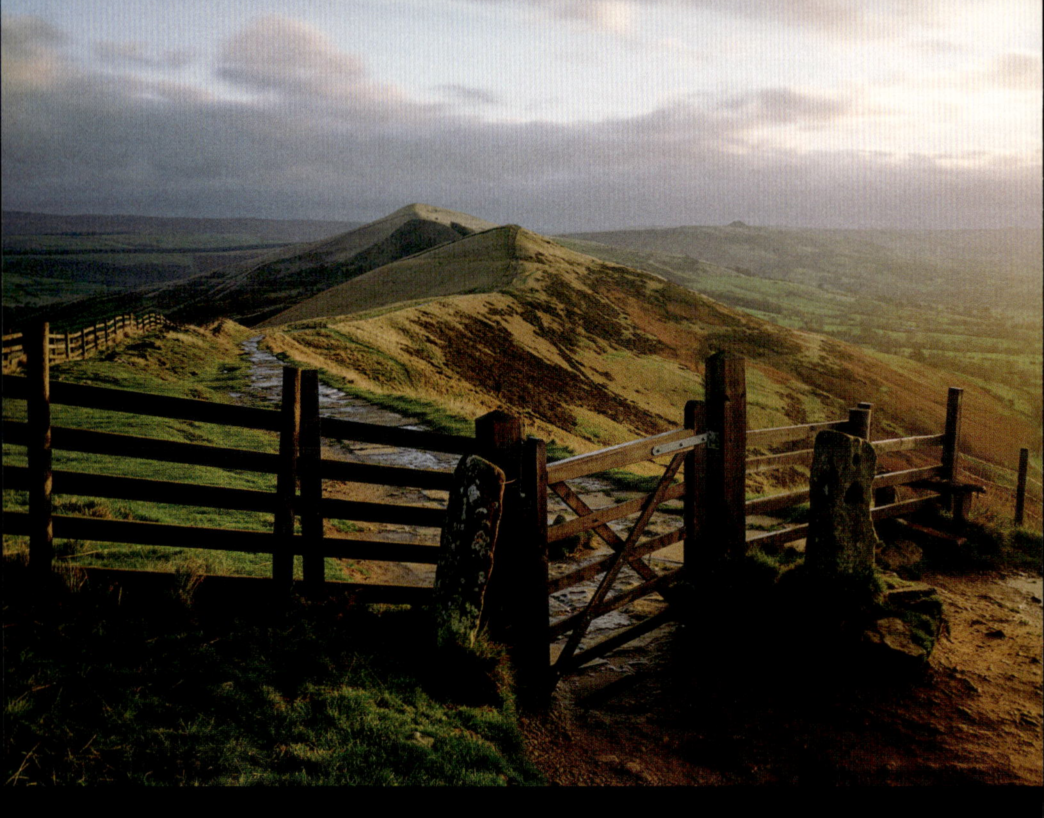

#54
LINE THEM UP

Everyone's a sucker for a leading line—it draws you in and directs your eyeballs on a one-way route toward a focal point. For a photographer, it's one of those simple and effective visual tricks that can make a decent photo great. It's super easy to get started with using leading lines in a composition; just consider the following points first:

Something to Lead To

Just in case it wasn't clear enough, you need to have an actual focal point, a subject, something of visual interest at the end of those leading lines, otherwise they're just lines. It doesn't even have to be an amazing subject; at least having something there in the line of sight is still going to look more interesting than having your eye directed down a long, straight road, only to see more long, straight road.

Get Down Low

A great way to connect the viewer from the foreground to as far as the lens can see is to position the camera down low, which will really give the feeling of those lines bursting out from the bottom of the frame.

Not Always Down the Middle

The most obvious way to start is with a leading line that starts from the middle, especially great for photos with symmetry, and they just work so well. But there will be times when it will work out better to have the leading lines on one side (sometimes you won't have a choice but to have the leading lines on the side). Experiment with placement of the leading lines from the side, but I prefer having them start from one of the corners of the frame.

Not Always Visible

Some leading lines are not quite as blatantly obvious as a railway track or a road; it might be a log or a row of pillars. They will still serve the same purpose as a straight line that has been painted on a road. Look at the natural contours on the ground or very subtle markings, too, that will work well as a leading line.

Lines Don't Have to Be Straight

Don't just go hunting for those impossibly long, straight lines. Those wobbly lines will serve not only the same purpose as your linear ones but perhaps also inject a little more drama to your image. With landscapes, there are lots of naturally curvy leading lines—rivers, natural contours, or coastlines—that will work fantastically, too. Just remember to have a focal point at the end of it!

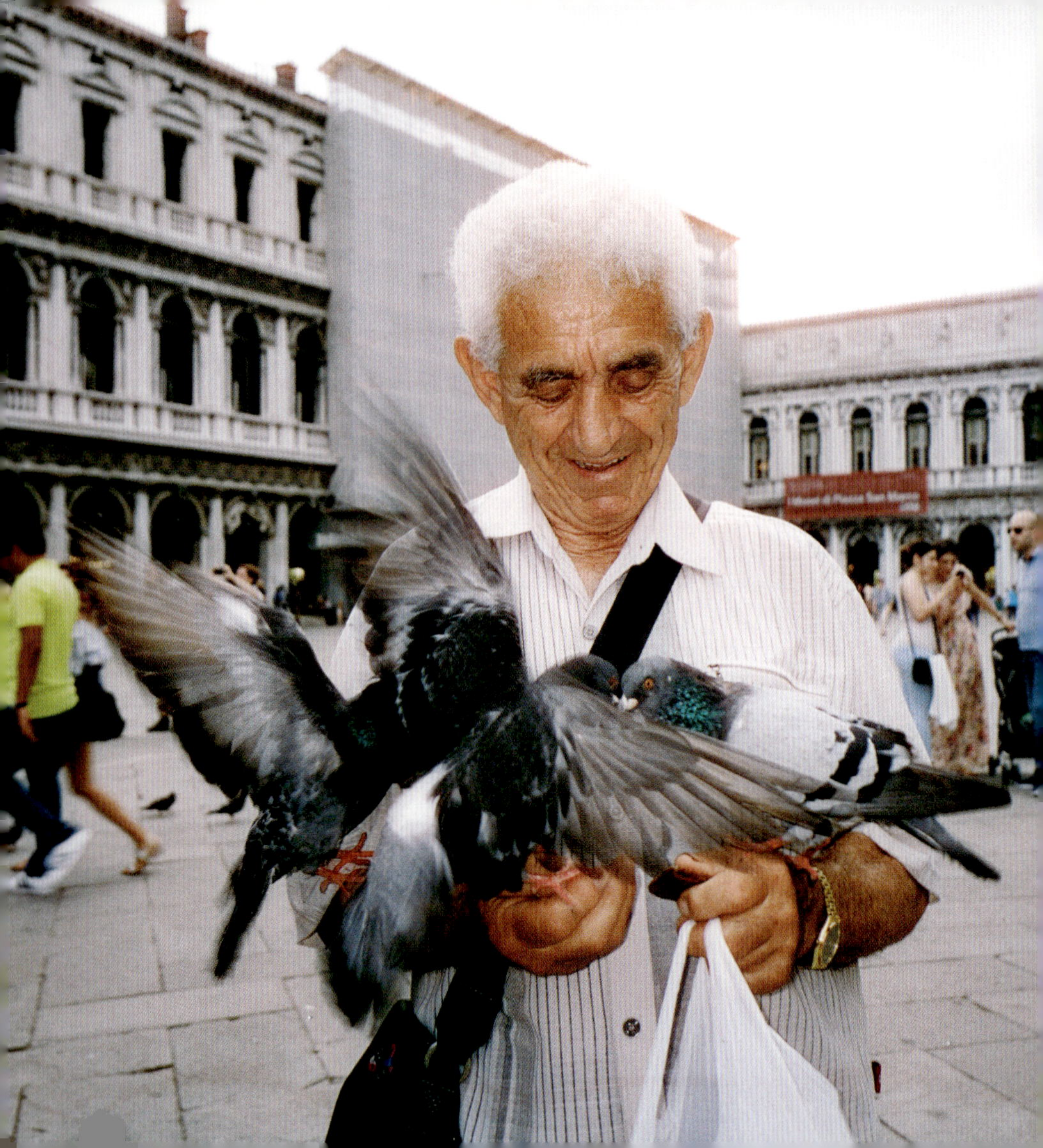

#55
GET UP CLOSE

If your picture isn't good enough, you're not close enough.

—Robert Capa

Famous wise words from the legendary war photographer. Sadly, for Capa, he ended up getting a little too close and stepped on a landmine (RIP).

Imagining the courage needed to take photos in the midst of a war zone makes this most quoted of maxims even more inspiring. If Capa can do it in such a hostile environment, then it should be easy for us to get close to our subjects in more peaceful settings.

Taking a couple of steps closer toward your subject can work wonders for your photography. It's the perfect remedy for loose framing—compositions with too much unnecessary dead space around the subject—which can make it difficult to determine the focal point of the image. For people photos, the closeness works for both the photographer and viewer, helping to understand the subject more, to feel like you're part of the scene.

When I first started taking street photos, I stood too far away from the subject—it's a common mistake for those new to street photography. It happens because it's not a normal thing, to walk up to a stranger and shove a camera in their face, so you stand back. You're keeping a distance to be less intrusive, to look less aggressive. But by not being part of the scene, not wanting to get closer to the subject, the image ends up looking cold, clinical, and distant.

Getting close is important for any street photographer wanting to take interesting photos, but you need to overcome that awkwardness. The key to being confident enough to get closer to a human subject to take their photo is quite simple: have empathy. You already understand that they might feel uneasy, so it's not too difficult to try to understand what would make someone more comfortable with having their photo taken by a complete stranger. It could be as easy as acting more friendly, or simply talking to them to explain what it is you're doing.

Capa's words are often interpreted to mean that you should literally, physically, move closer to your subject. It's not like you need to take a couple of steps forward just to improve your photo—some photographers need to take steps back, if anything. But any photographer wanting to take better photos could do with getting closer in the sense of investing yourself more, emotionally, to the subject and the scene—to want to know more about what it is you're seeing and feel connected to it.

Closeness, whether it be physical or not, is certainly something that can help us all to take better photos.

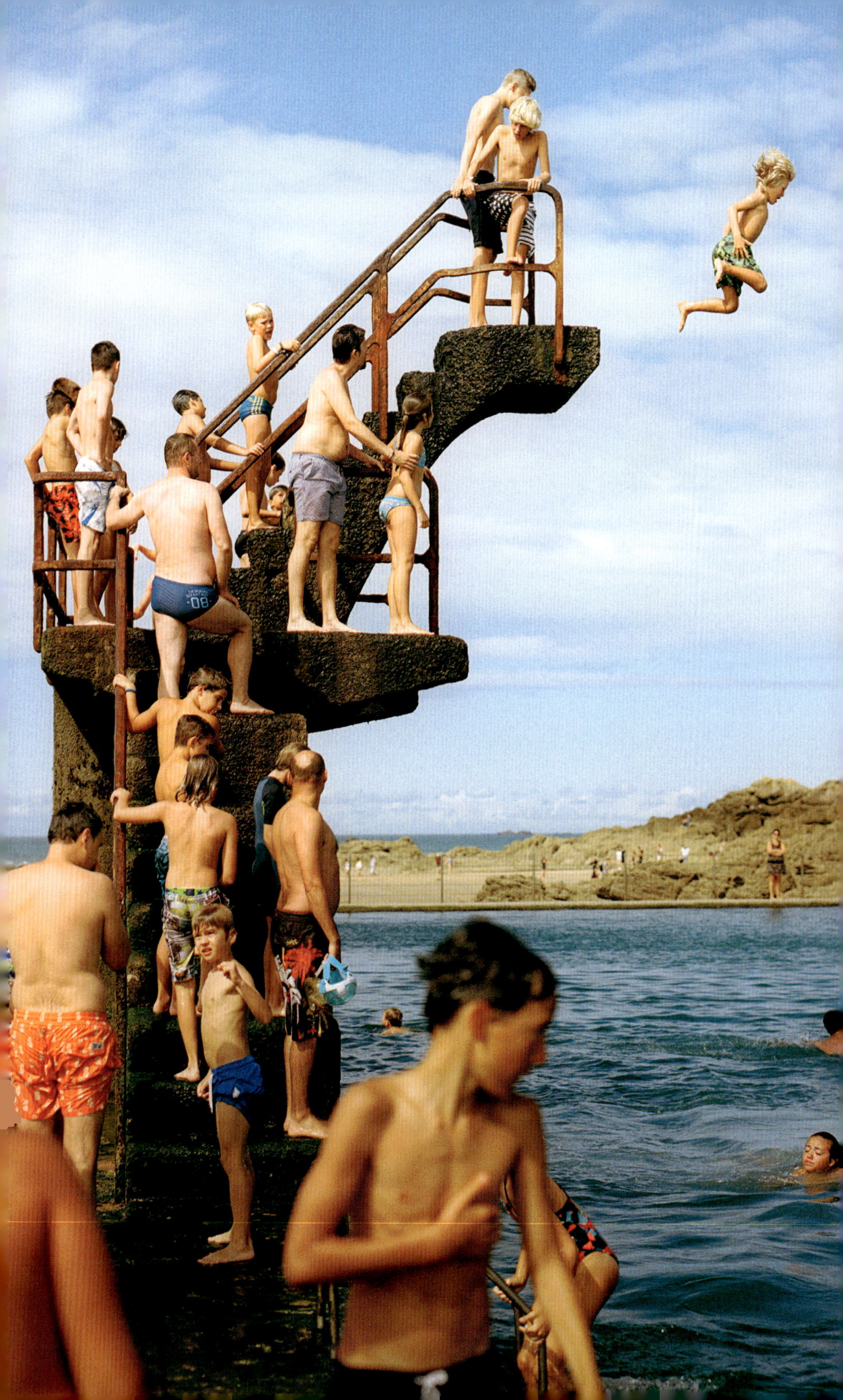

#56
FILL THOSE FOREGROUNDS

The foreground is like the front garden to your photo—a seemingly useless bit of space but, executed well, it can make for a pretty inviting path that leads to the big, obvious thing. It will not only give your image balance but also serves as a nice visual lead-up to the middle ground and beyond.

Use Wide Angles for Maximum Foreground Action

A great way to make that little bit of foreground pop is to use a wide-angle lens. As they have a wickedly wide angle of view, they will suck in foreground details from more extreme angles, like a crazy optical vacuum, and will stretch and skew those shapes and lines, elongating, widening, and making them look more dramatic overall.

Get Down Low

The wide-angle lens will draw in more of the foreground, but with a bit of careful camera positioning you can bring even more in and put more emphasis on it. Instead of having the front of the lens completely parallel to the subject, point it down a little bit. Angling the wide-angle down slightly will show a bit more of the foreground, while not taking the attention away from the subject. Positioning the camera closer to the ground will make the foreground more prominent, making it more connected to the bottom of the frame. Still, it's best not to go over the top and make it all about the foreground—it's there to complement your main focal point, not to steal the show.

Use a Smaller Aperture

The foreground is right by your feet; the subject is much farther away. To get that all in focus, stop down and use a smaller aperture to get a deeper depth of field. An aperture of f/11 or f/13 should give you enough depth of field to keep most of the foreground and background in focus. Then use the double-distance method—find out the distance between the camera and the closest part of the foreground in your frame, and double that distance. That's where you should be concentrating on to make sure everything is in focus.

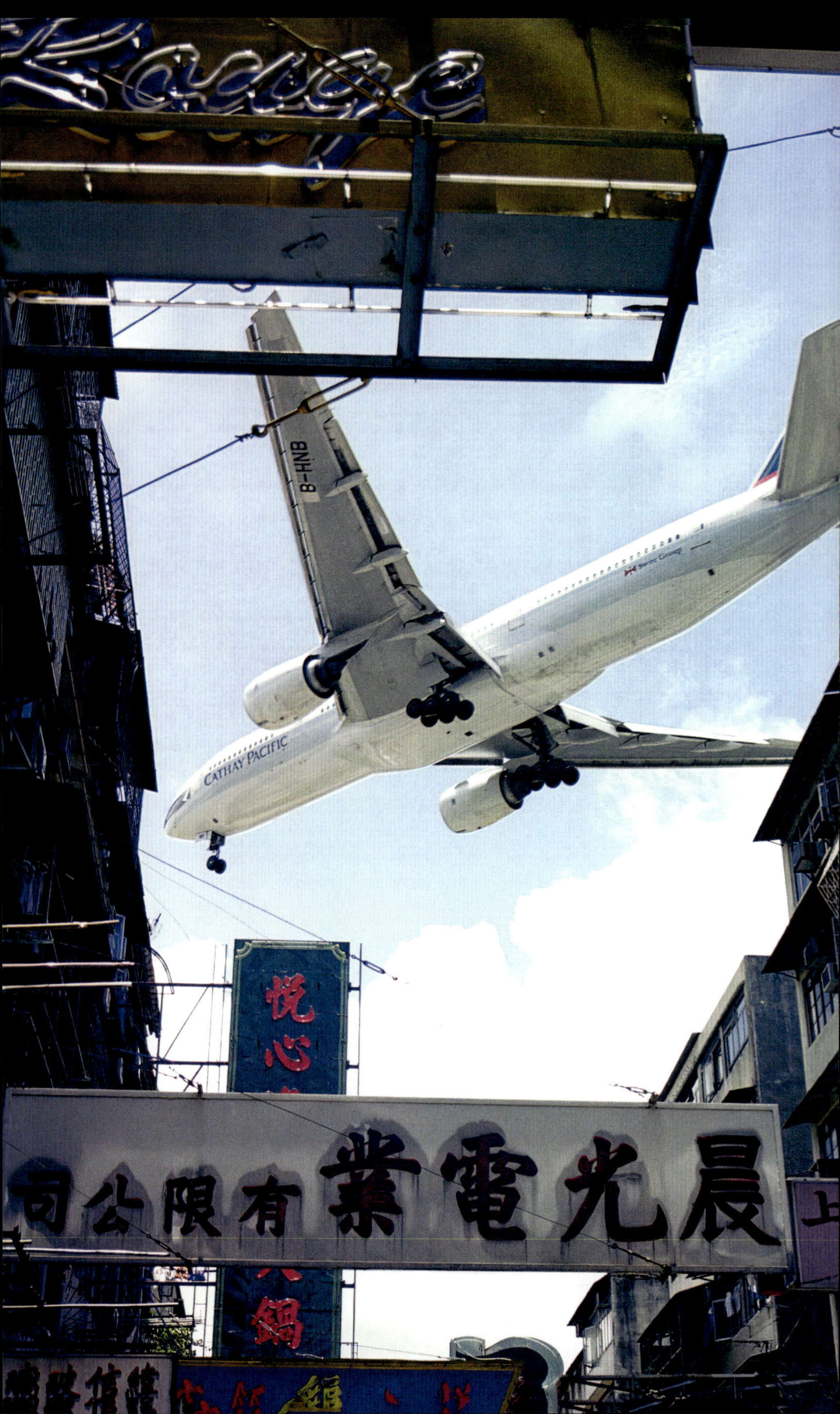
B-HNB
CATHAY PACIFIC
悅心
晨光電業有限公司
鍋

#57 FRAMING WITH THE FRAME WITHIN THE FRAME

Warning: the word frame is going to be used a hell of a lot in this chapter.

Composing a photo involves putting visual elements within a four-sided frame. Sometimes you might chance upon a visual element within your frame that looks a bit frame-like, which can be used as a frame within a frame. Using that frame inside the frame is, like leading lines, a visual effect that is guaranteed to grab your viewer by the (eye)balls and force them to look at what's within that frame within a frame.

As that secondary frame is smaller than the main frame, it can help to highlight the focal point of the image. Adding that frame within a frame is also a neat way of adding extra depth to an image, which is especially handy when the focal point looks too flat and boring without that frame inside of the frame.

Being able to add a frame within a frame is all dependent on what frame-like things can be found at the location, though. I suppose you could use your index fingers and thumbs to form a frame, but that would be downright cheesy. The most commonly used frames are man-made structures, such as window frames, doorways, arches, and bridges. There's plenty of them around, and they look great as a frame because they are so perfectly formed. Frames don't have be completely enclosed, though.

You can find naturally formed frames, such as caves or trees, that also do the trick even if they aren't as in-your-face obvious as a window frame. The frame can be really subtle, like just a few branches and leaves positioned at the top of the frame, which also work great to cover up and cordon off the sky—great on overcast days or when there are no clouds in the sky—averting eyes away from the boring bits and toward the cool stuff.

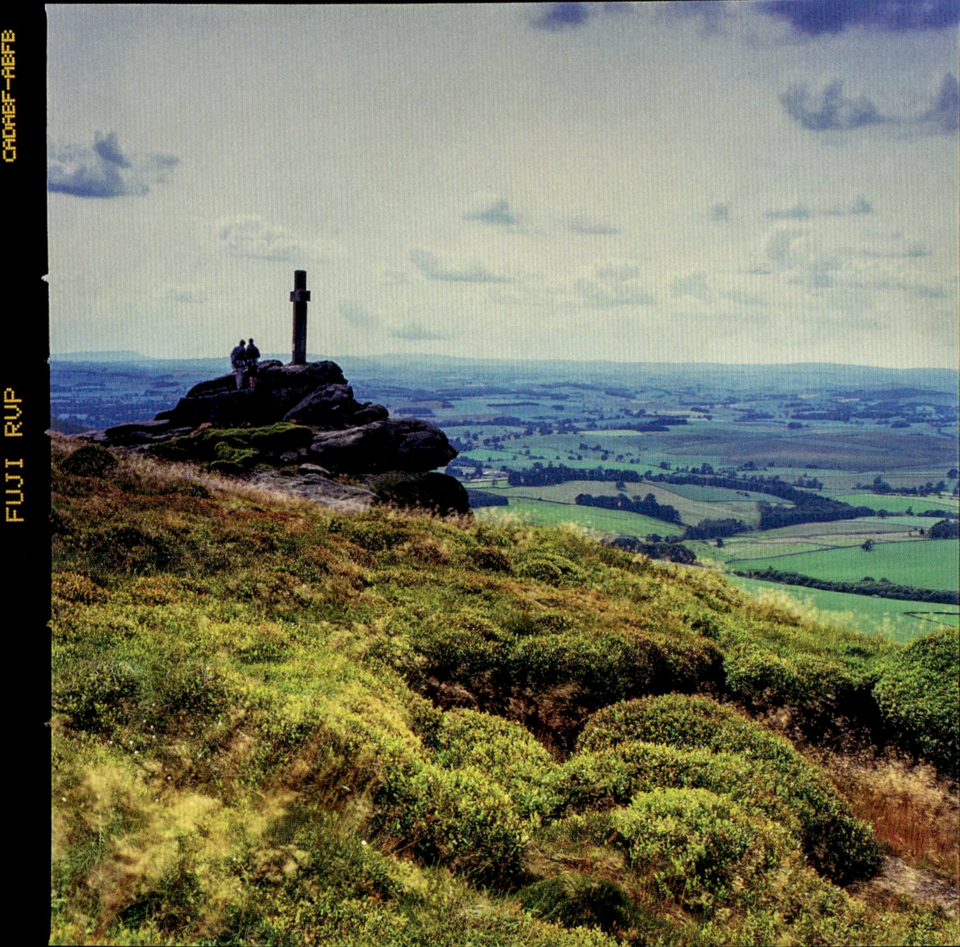

#58
THE POSITIVES OF NEGATIVE SPACE

Although dead space, or negative space as it is also known, is often seen as undesirable, at times the use of negative space can be a positive thing. (Just to be clear, though, negative space is not positive space.) Positive space is a part of the photo that is packed with detail, something for your eyes to feast on; negative space is devoid of detail. The subject, or anything that visually stands out, is positive space, and any bland or blank areas are negative space.

It's more obvious what you should do with positive space because it is something that adds immediate value to your image; whereas negative space seems to be a waste of precious frame space, which could've been filled up with something more interesting. If there's a little bit of negative space in a frame packed with lots of detail, it's going to look odd to have just a teeny-tiny bit of negative space in there.

Filling the frame with all positive space makes sense—packing the picture with visual interest—as you want people to look, but using negative space in a photo can have a huge impact on a photo, too. If you're going to use negative space, make sure there's plenty of it in your frame. The best use of negative space is to create a sense of scale— making the main subject a tiny part of the frame in the middle of a vast expanse of negative space. For example, a human subject in front of a big blue sky, or swimming in the sea, gives you a sense of scale, emphasising the difference in size.

The use of negative space can also convey a sense of loneliness, with a human subject surrounded by nothing but cold, blank space. But negative space doesn't always have negative connotations; it can be incredibly soothing, refreshing even, to see a photo with lots of negative space. It feels like such a contrast to the images that we often see that are packed with elements of visual interest splashed all over the frame. The subject is still the subject—it's still a focal point—but with all that negative space, the scene and subject become of equal importance, which can make for a tranquil, minimalist composition.

Kai's Tips

- We're so used to filling frames with positive space—it's not going to be simple to make a photo with lots of negative space work well at first. Spend some time to experiment.
- The negative space draws you in to the subject, but don't overlook the importance of choosing aesthetically pleasing negative space.
- Don't forget to think about composition. It should be easier to figure out where to place your subject, but you have to be very careful with how much negative space you show. The smaller the subject gets, the less it becomes about that subject.

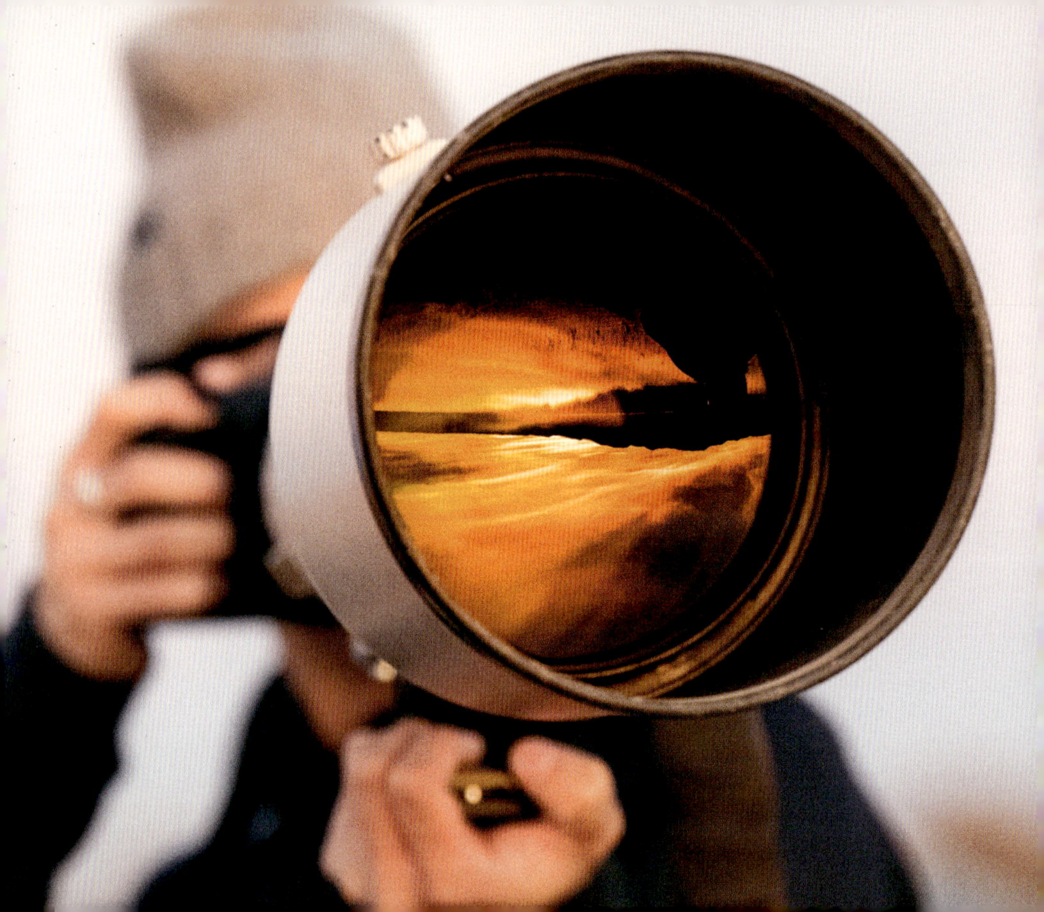

#59
STRIKE GOLD IN GOLDEN HOUR

Taking photos during golden hour can be dangerously addictive. Once you get used to taking photos with everything bathed in a gorgeous, golden light, there's every possibility that you won't want to shoot during any other time of the day.

Four Things You Need to Know about Golden Hour

1. Golden hour happens right before sunrise and just after the sun sets.
2. It doesn't necessarily last for one hour. It all depends on where in the world you are and what season it is.
3. Sunlight is made up of different colours, each with different wavelengths. At midday, the light has less atmosphere to travel through. During golden hour, the sun is coming at a lower angle, so it has to travel through more atmosphere. The blue light, which has a shorter wavelength, gets scattered, and it's mainly the longer wavelength colours, red and yellow, that reach us.
4. Having to travel through more atmosphere means the light is more diffused, making it a nice, soft, even light that doesn't cast any harsh shadows.

Slide Film vs. Negatives

As mentioned in a previous chapter, slide film will render everything in a beautiful palette of rich colours, but if overexposed, it will lose the details easier than negative film. Negative film retains the details in the bright parts better, but the colours aren't as lush as slide film.

Velvia is a fantastic slide film for a super-saturated look that will bring out the best of the glory of golden hour.

But if you want to get the part of the sky with the gorgeous colours, you want to be looking in the direction that the sun is setting. This can be problematic if you want to have a subject in the foreground because the subject will be backlit, and will be much darker than the sky. Then you have the choice of either having the subject properly exposed and the sky overblown, with some of the details lost because it's slide film, or you can properly expose the sky, keeping the beautiful colours but making your subject dark. You could use a saturated colour negative film, like Kodak Ektar 100, but you definitely should use some graduated ND filters if you want to balance the exposure for the sky and land.

Kai's Tips

- Plan ahead. Check what time the sun rises or sets, so you can turn up to the location in advance (don't rock up to the scene ten minutes before it happens), set up your camera, and get your composition ready before the golden goodness happens. The light changes very quickly, and it will be over before you know it, especially when you're faffing about with a camera.
- If you're photographing people, the golden light looks splendid shone directly on them, or when put behind them. That will make them almost silhouetted, albeit with a nice, golden-highlight glow running through their hair.
- For people shots, it'll look more flattering to use a film that produces more subdued tones, like Kodak Portra, rather than Velvia, unless you want to make your subjects look jaundiced.

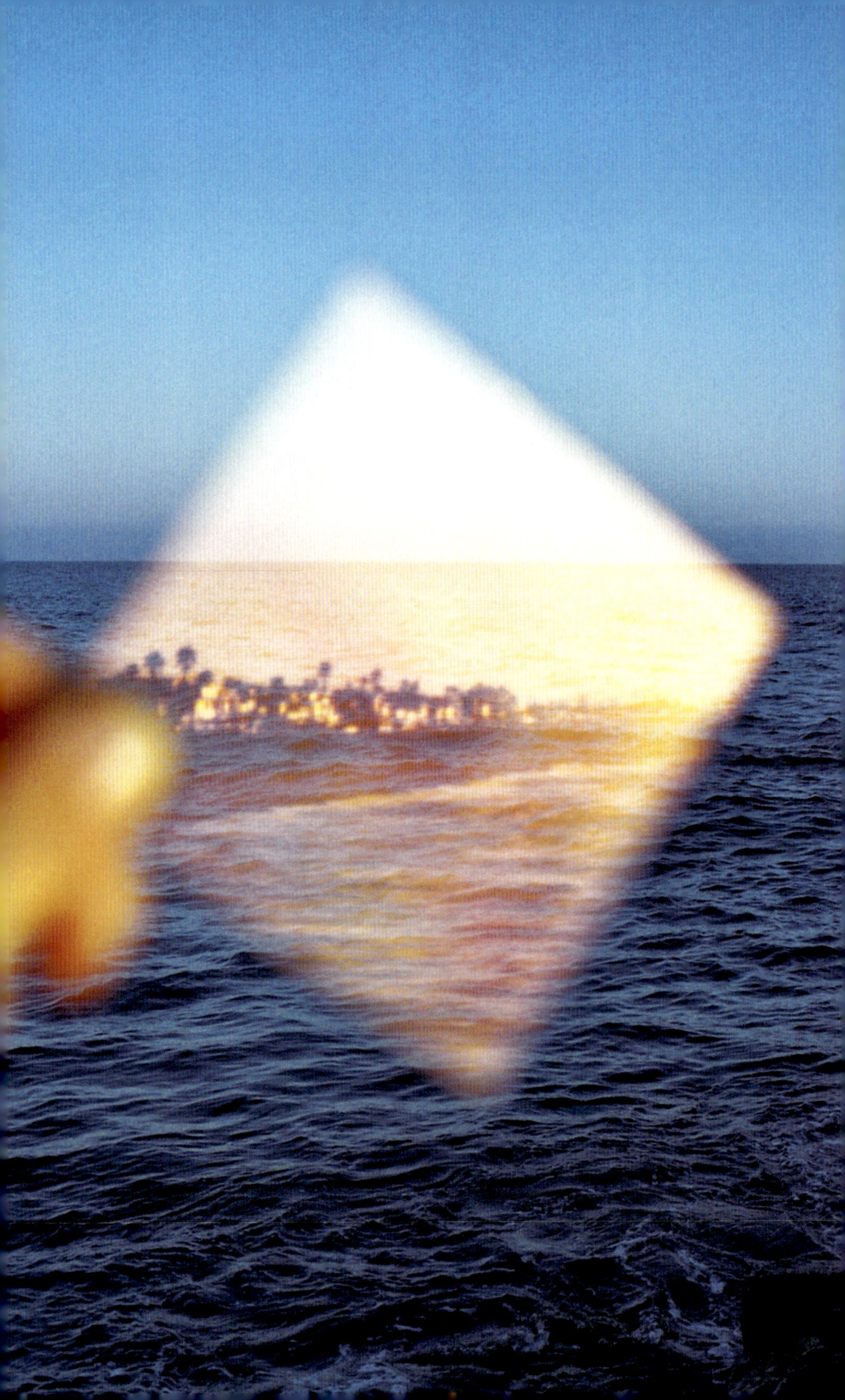

#60

PHOTOGRAPHY IS NOT A SCIENCE

Sharpness is a bourgeois concept.

—Henri Cartier-Bresson

People can become too obsessed with the wrong kind of things in photography, like the technical elements—how to balance the aperture and shutter-speed settings to make the perfect exposure; how to get tack sharp focus—and then there will be those that spend too much time worrying about whether their camera performs well enough. They'll want faster focus, smarter features, and a lens that will producer sharper images. On the grand scale of things, none of that really matters.

Owning what might be thought of as better gear doesn't do anything for developing your photography, and knowing the technical side of things just means you know how to use a camera.

Sure, there are types of photography, like landscapes, that require a bit of technical excellence to produce an attractive image. But the appreciation of a good landscape photo is not just about how sharp and well-exposed it is; it's primarily about the photographer's artistic vision.

A photo taken by someone who has mastered their camera but doesn't have an idea what they want to shoot will never be as interesting as a photo taken by someone who is using their camera in full auto mode but has a great eye for a fantastic photo.

If there is one thing you should become obsessed with, it's understanding how to see what would make a good photo.

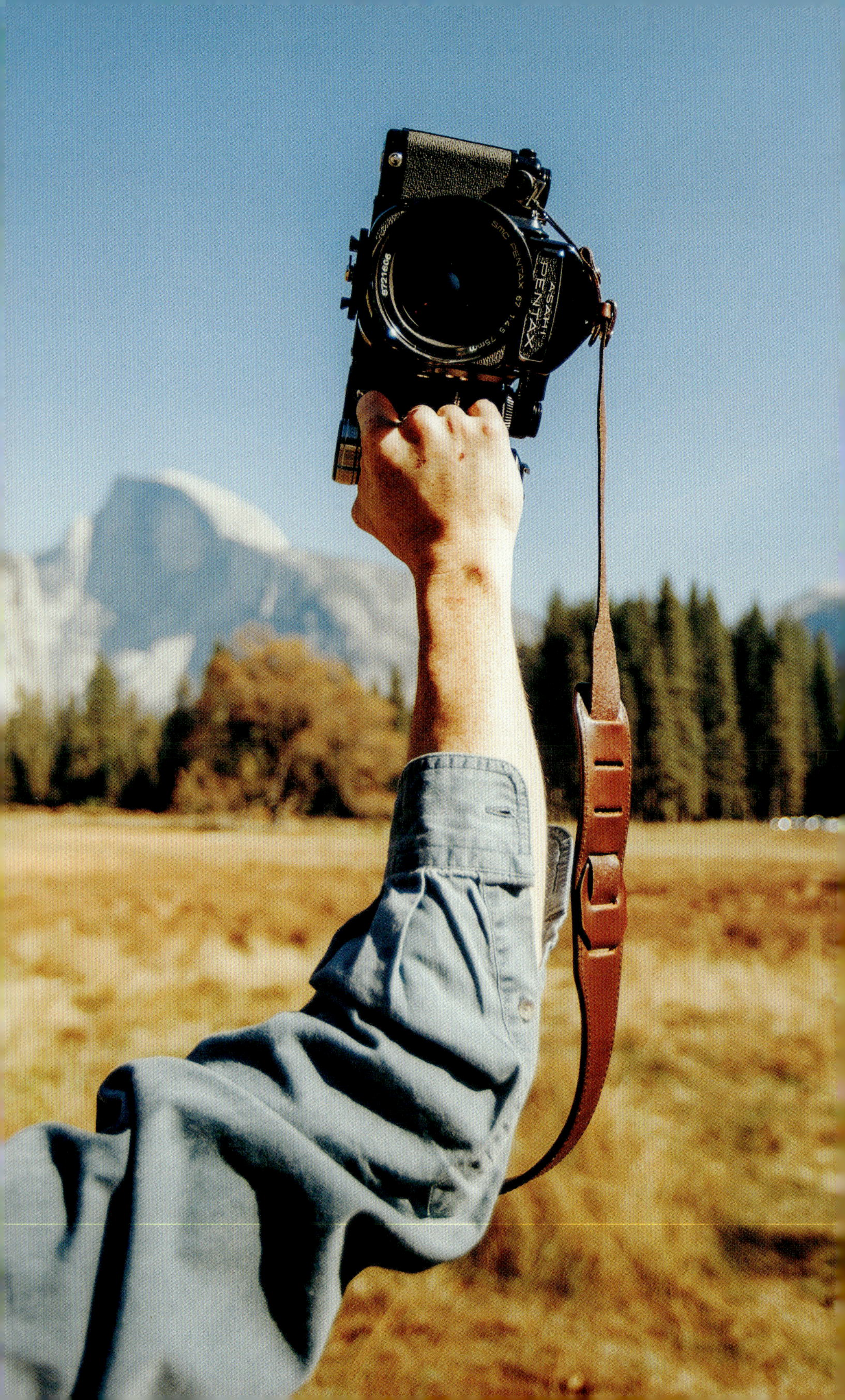
ASAHI PENTAX

#61 THE MOST IMPORTANT COMPONENT OF A CAMERA

The single most important component of a camera is the twelve inches behind it.

—Ansel Adams

I don't want to be the pedant that points out that humans aren't technically a component of a camera, especially given that ol' A.A. is a bit of legend. Plus, he makes a damn good point: nothing on any camera is as important as the flesh-and-bones thing controlling it.

A Camera Is a Tool

When it comes to gear, I'm as guilty as the next geek for acquiring new cameras, so it would be uber hypocritical of me to tell you not to obsess about cameras. Still, even though I have this dirty habit of buying cameras, I understand that they are just tools for taking photos. Some cameras might be better suited for some types of photography, but it's still the person using it that makes that shot happen. A basic camera in good hands can make a better shot than a high-end camera in the hands of someone who doesn't care all that much about photography.

Upgrading Your Camera Doesn't Upgrade Your Photos

Buying a new camera is not a major issue, just as long as you know that upgrading your gear does't upgrade your photos. An expensive 35 mm film camera takes exactly the same film as a cheap 35 mm film camera, so don't expect to see a huge impact on your photography. Good photos come from good ideas, not from what some might call a good camera.

Obsess over Settings First

When I was a photo noob back in uni, I used to read photo magazines (yes, people actually bought magazines back then), admire other people's photos, and obsess about the little captions that would detail what aperture, shutter speed, film, focal length, and filters the photographer used. I wanted to know how they made those clouds look creamy smooth, why the sky looked so evenly exposed with the land, and why those colours looked so great. The camera obsession came much later, and I can tell you this now—the obsession with settings has been way more useful (and better for the bank balance) for my photography than obsessing about cameras.

Stick to One Camera at First

My first camera was a gift from my sister—it was a Pentax MZ-M SLR—and I used that, along with the standard-kit zoom lens, for many years as my main camera; I still have it. It was an all-manual camera with no frills or fancy features, which worked out great for learning how to focus manually and to figure out all that exposure-triangle shiz. I can understand the temptation to upgrade cameras when you feel like your camera is too basic, but you should upgrade your skills first before upgrading your gear.

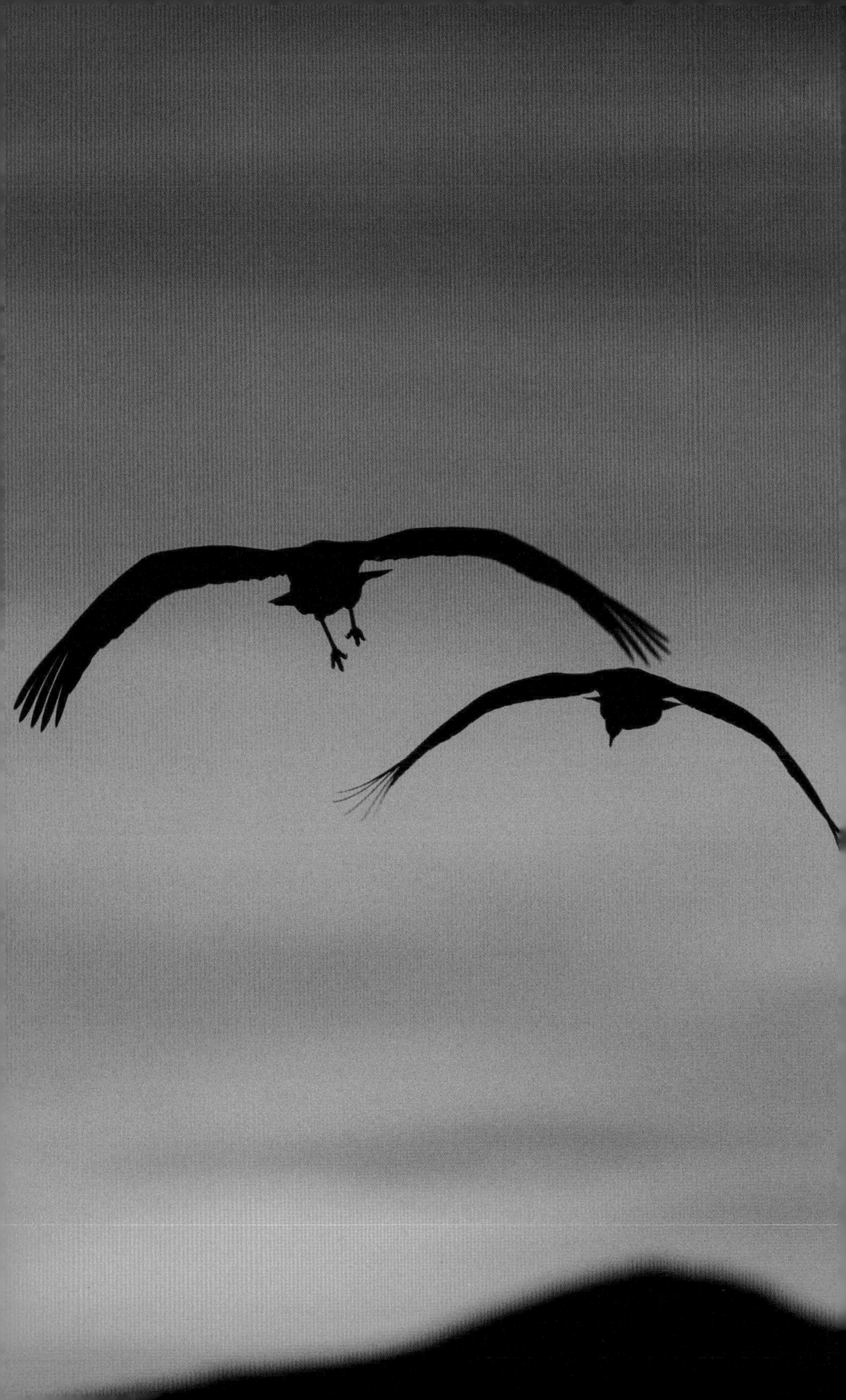

#62
REPLICATE BEFORE YOU INNOVATE

Figuring how to create your own style is difficult. For me, figuring out what to wear is a daily struggle—is it a hoodie kind of day or is a suit best suited? Or maybe I should wear a hoodie under the suit? Actually, it doesn't really matter what one chooses to wear—unless it's a birthday suit—because style is all about self-expression (even if I do end up looking like a hobo going to a business meeting).

Photography is no different—the most important thing is that the style is true to you. But as a beginner, it can be difficult to define your own style because you're starting from scratch, while concentrating on mastering the gear and learning about the different kinds of composition.

One thing I did when I got into shooting landscapes was to try to replicate shots that I'd seen in magazines, by finding out the locations they were shot and visiting those places to try to nail the shot myself. By doing so it gave me a clear visual goal, and made it easier to comprehend how to compose and apply the settings to get the desired result. It's a great way to get you up and running, to give you enough confidence to build your own style by developing three aspects of your photography:

Subject Specifics

Within each genre of photography, there are very broad terms for subjects, such as people or landscapes; but to find your own style, you need to start focusing on the specifics. For the landscape project I did at university, I photographed the hills and mountains in the Yorkshire Dales, and had a soft spot for using man-made objects as a focal point, to contrast with the natural landscapes. It's all about obsessing over the little details.

Composition

Photography books can teach you about composition, but they can't show you how to compose your shots. Following someone else's compositions gives you a foundation to build upon; but when you start taking your own photos, you need to react to what you see, and move your camera to fit those visual elements in the frame so that they look pleasing to your eyes, and your eyes only.

Colour and Light

For that landscape project I shot only in the early morning—first light—on Fujifilm Velvia 50. In theory, there shouldn't be too much difference between the look of sunrise and sunset—the sun lies really bloody low on the horizon for both—but to me there was enough of a difference to wake up at silly o'clock in the morning, and then walk up muddy mountains in the dark just to get a sunrise shot. To me, the crisp, clear morning air makes the light look a little paler than the light at sunset, but it wasn't just about the look of the light. There would always be the possibility of seeing mist in the morning, and encounter fewer people, too.

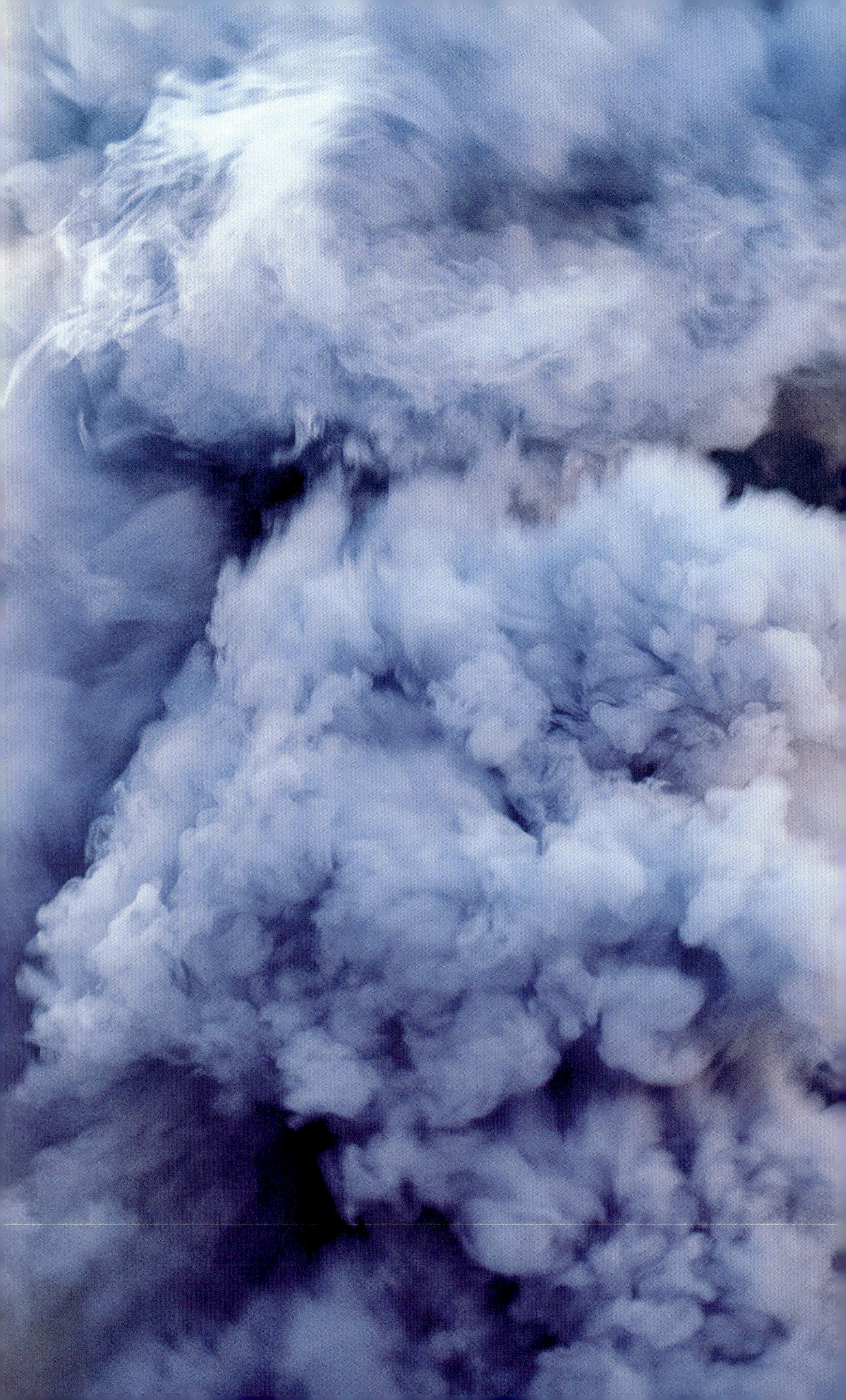

#63

CREATE YOUR OWN LUCK

Lady Luck plays a part in the process of getting those once-in-a-lifetime images, but don't expect her to turn up and make that shot happen because (apart from the fact that she's just a figure of speech) it's up to you to make the most of a good opportunity.

What, Where, When

There's nothing like a master plan! Start off strong by having a clear idea of where you want to shoot and the kind of subjects you want to shoot. Having a clear aim will mean you're not going to dillydally around, wondering whether to take the shot or not. Then think about the time of the day that will give you the best light—which direction is the light coming in, whether the light will reach the subject at that time of day, and what that light will look like. Make sure you pack the most suitable lenses and load the right film, too.

Contingency Plan

Sometimes shit happens—the weather changes; subjects don't materialise; locations end up looking lame. There is nothing worse than getting all excited about what you thought was a super-cool location, only to have your positive vibes crushed once you rock up to the location and realise the place has all the excitement of a brown, paper bag.

The place might be crap, but don't let your shoot go down the crapper—have a bail-out plan that you can easily turn to. I always have a few safety-net locations that I can rely on to get my photo fix for the day if I can't find anything better. Going home with some shots you're content with will sharpen up your photo technique and leave you with a better feeling than having gone out and not been productive at all.

Good Things Come to Those Who Wait

If the location turned out alright, but it's the weather or lacklustre subject that is pooping on the photo party, then don't feel like you need to be in a hurry to pack up and leave just yet—because sometimes, just sometimes, you might get lucky. The thick blanket of clouds might break a little to leave gorgeous rays of light beaming through, or the most amazing subject might just come along. There's no guarantee that anything will happen, but you won't know if you leave the location early.

When Things Go Wrong—Roll with It

If the plan has gone to pot, and you have some epic, torrential rain cocking things up: Instead of hastily heading for the nearest cover, you can just roll with it. Take the misery and use it to your advantage by loading up with black-and-white film to create some seriously moody vibes in your images. I think the combination of umbrellas, rain smacking against the pavement, and malevolent skies is a pretty cool look (I guess I just got used to it in London).

Don't Stop Exploring

Even if you've got everything sussed out with exactly where and what you want to take photos of, you shouldn't stop exploring the location for more interesting things to shoot. Get into the habit of looking for things of visual interest; pull the camera up to your eyeball and see what it looks like through the viewfinder. Never be content with the one really good shot you had planned; there are always many other potentially good ones nearby. Don't let Lady Luck come to you; you should actively seek her (figuratively speaking).

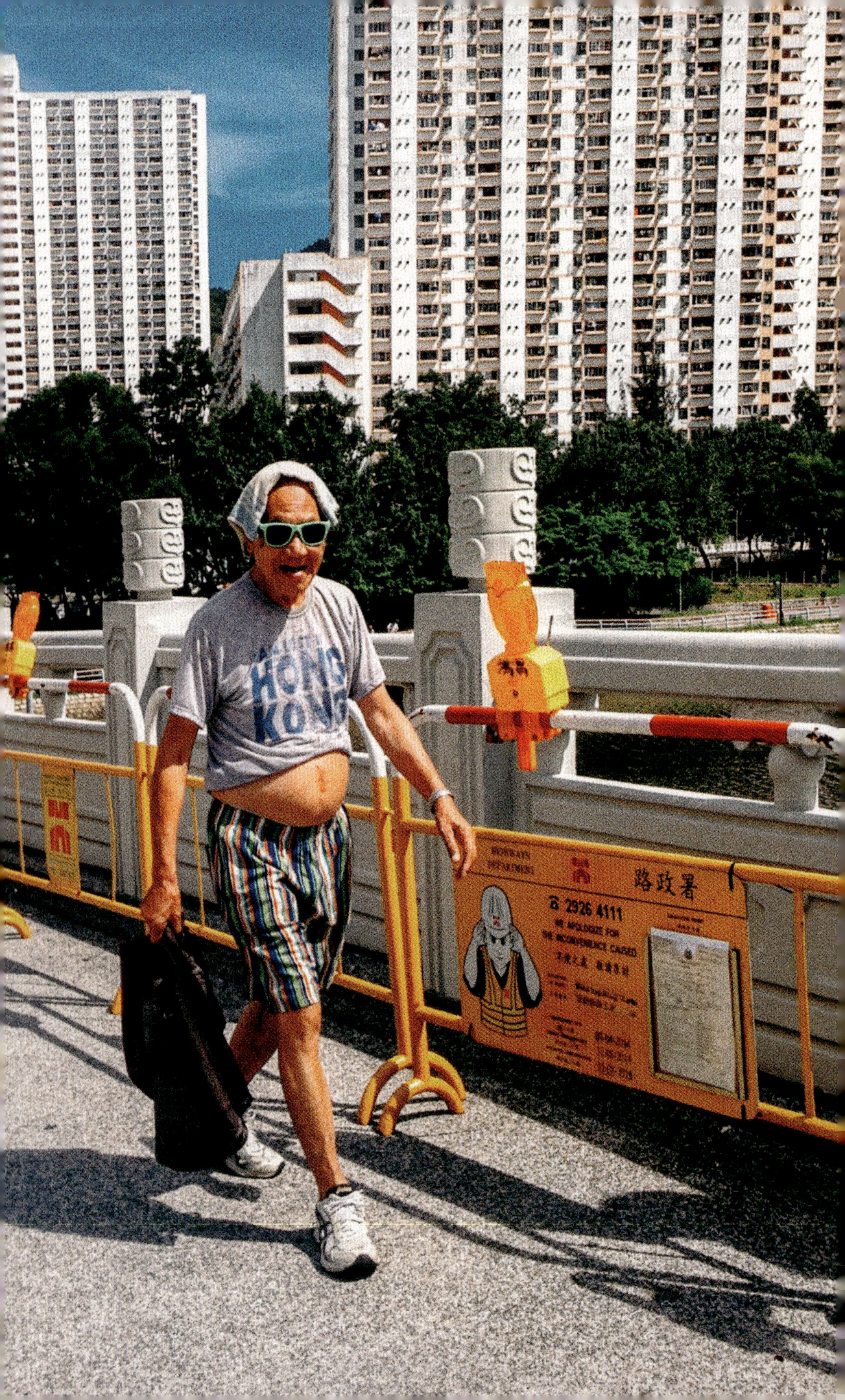
HONG KONG
路政署
2926 4111
WE APOLOGIZE FOR
THE INCONVENIENCE CAUSED

#64
EVERY PHOTO SHOULD TELL A STORY

There are always two people in every picture: the photographer and the viewer.

—Ansel Adams

As the saying goes, every picture paints a thousand words. Although photos could never replace words when it really counts—I don't think university lecturers would appreciate receiving ten pictures in lieu of a ten-thousand-word dissertation—they do have the power to tell stories. And if you want to make your photos interesting, you'll want to make sure there's more to your photos than just the surface layer.

When we're talking about telling a story, it doesn't have to be Dickens. A still image can only take you so far; it is the mind that will take it further. Without wanting to get too academic about it—because life's too short to be reading about the semantics of photography instead of actually taking photos—much-revered writer and analyser of all things with meaning, Roland Barthes, best described at great length how meaning is extracted from an image. I will summarise this in much shorter length:

Denotation

The literal meaning of the photo: a photo of an apple is exactly that.

Connotation

The implied meaning a viewer gets when looking at an image. For example, a photo of an apple might invoke feelings of freshness, healthiness, and what an apple tastes like.

Whoever is looking at your image plays a huge part in deriving meaning from the photo, but that doesn't mean you should leave it that way. Without the photographer's input, the apple photo would just be a straight-up, simple photo of an apple—it might as well be someone else's photo of an apple.

You have to use creative ideas, composition, lighting, and colour to give the photo a meaning that is all yours—to tell a story with a photo. The apple could be sprayed with little droplets of water, sliced open, lit with studio lighting, and shot with a macro lens to make the apple look crisp, juicy, and delicious—emphasising the freshness and ripeness for eating.

The story that you tell with your photo doesn't need to have a beginning, a middle, and an end; it just has to communicate a message that is clearly your own.

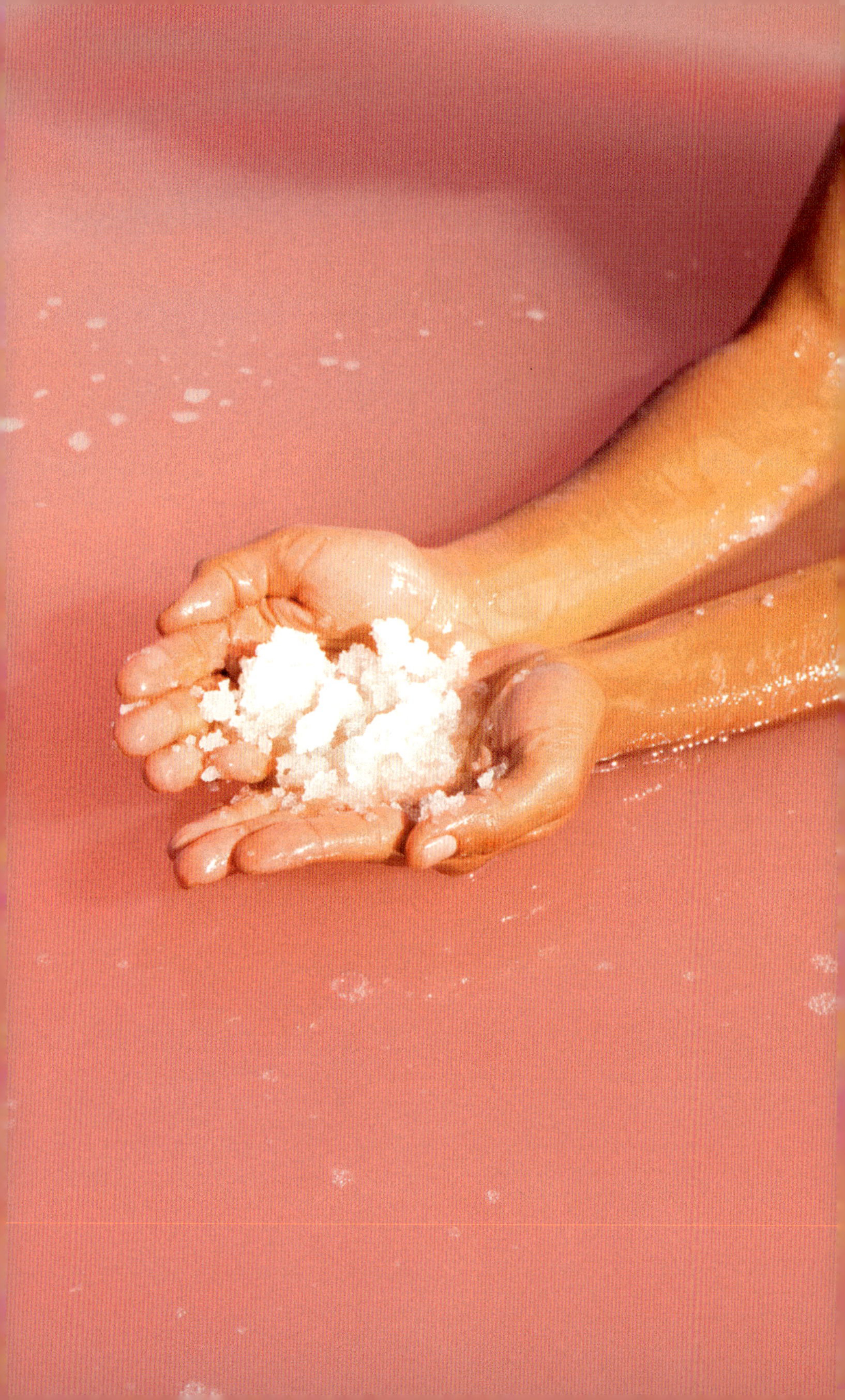

#65
FEEL WHAT YOU SEE

Seeing is not enough; you have to feel what you photograph.

—Andre Kertesz

To tell stories with your photo, you also need to be able to feel what you're photographing (not literally, of course).

When I started taking photos, I took the trigger-happy approach to shooting absolutely every bloody thing in sight. If there was any feeling in what I photographed back then, it was brief. Photography was so new and exciting that I was just happy to be taking photos of anything, because it was all about experimenting with my camera and learning how to use it, rather than having any kind of focus on what I wanted to photograph.

Thankfully, not too much film was wasted before I figured out what I really wanted to take more photos of: landscapes. For me, it wasn't just the aesthetically appealing shots of nature (and not having to deal with other people) that got me hooked. I loved the whole process of making a landscape shot happen—the planning, the journey, and the unpredictability. I was passionate to photograph landscapes and loved exploring all the different locations.

Photography for me is not looking; it's feeling. If you can't feel what you're looking at, then you're never going to get others to feel anything when they look at your pictures.

—Don McCullin

The landscape photography projects that I handed in at university got top grades; when you truly feel for what you're photographing, it will show in your images. Being passionate about your photography is what adds more depth than one that was taken purely for the sake of being technically excellent.

Hone in on a type of photography you're really passionate about, and it will give you the motivation to keep taking more photos; keep taking photos that you're passionate about, and you will improve the quality of your photos much quicker.

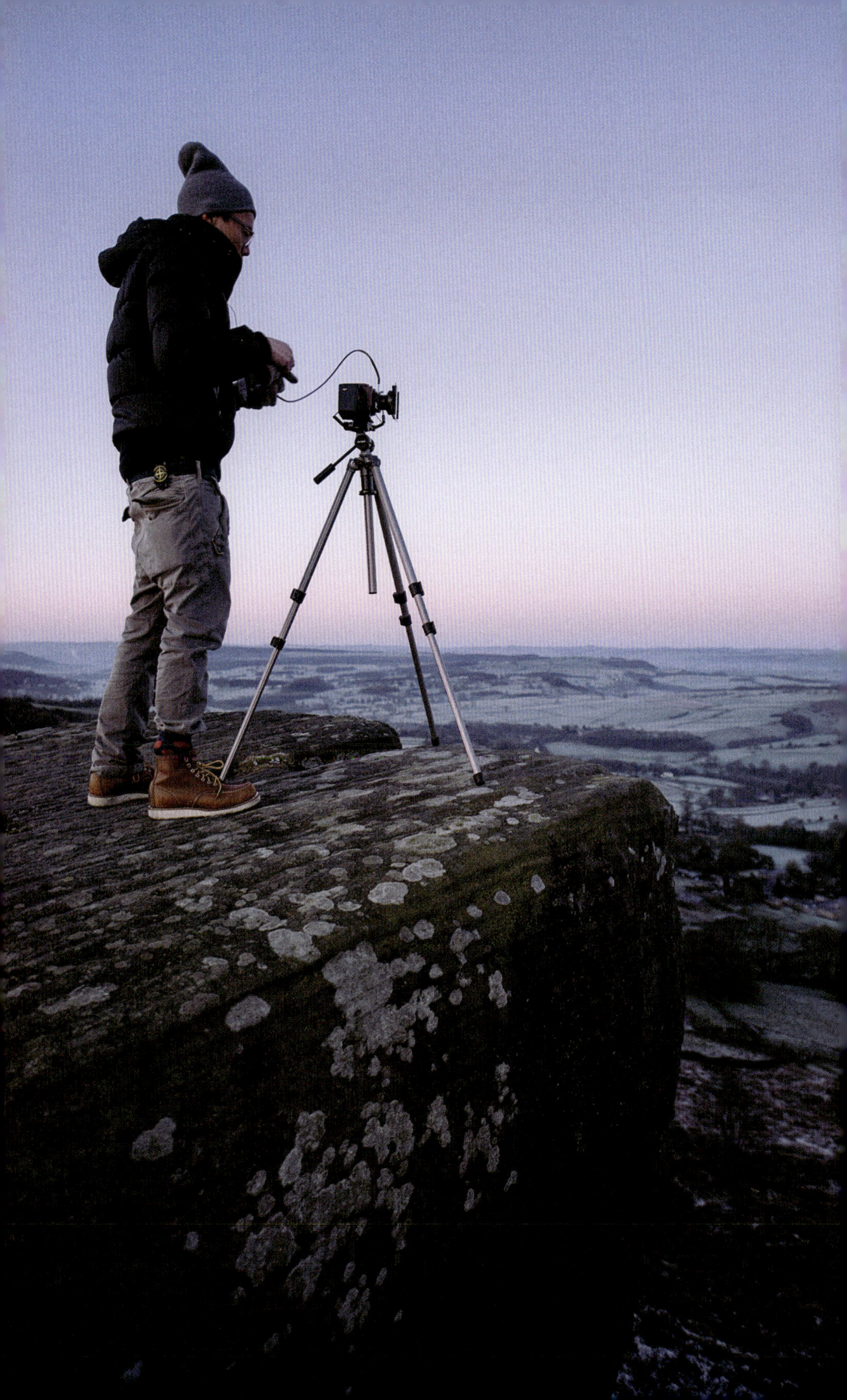

#66

9 TYPES OF PHOTOGRAPHY TO EXPLORE

Landscape

If you appreciate how those bits of earth have naturally formed to create such splendid shapes of majestic grandeur, then landscape photography might be for you. Perhaps not for those who hate the thought of an early morning shoot in a muddy field—you could always try an evening shoot in a grassy field instead.

Recommended gear: SLR with a 24–70 mm lens, plus a tripod and cable release, a warm coat, and some good walking boots (I wore one shoe and a sock in a muddy, cow-pat-filled field once).

Wildlife

It involves sitting around for long periods of time, waiting potentially hours for a few seconds of animal action. You could skip the waiting times by photographing some animals at the local zoo or pet store, but I guess it's not quite the same thing.

Recommended gear: SLR with a looooooong lens, like a 300 mm, maybe even more. Rent those really long telelenses because they're not cheap to own.

Macro

It's all about poking your lens in the private space of incredibly tiny things. Google search macro photography and you'll probably find a load of icky, close-up images of hairy spiders. Don't be put off by this; macro photography doesn't limit you to just creepy crawlies.

Recommended gear: SLR with a macro lens and a tripod.

Portraits

A great excuse to take photos of beautiful people. They can be taken indoors or outdoors, with available light or with flashes. Most people don't have the luxury of owning a studio, but outdoor locations are a great way of achieving many different looks without costing you a thing.

Recommended gear: SLR with a 50 mm or 85 mm lens.

Street Photography

Street photography is all about capturing candid moments of things that happen in real time with real people on the street. The beauty of a good street photo is the timing: getting in close and becoming part of the scene momentarily, and then taking a photo that captures the essence of the street scene.

Recommended gear: Rangefinder and a 35 mm or 50 mm lens. Nothing else needed.

Travel

The key to taking interesting travel photos is to go somewhere interesting and new; don't just go on a staycation, because that would make for boring travel photos.

Recommended gear: A compact camera would be a great, lightweight setup, or take a rangefinder with three different lenses.

Architecture

If you live in a city, you can appreciate and photograph the beauty of human-made structures. The great thing is that you can easily research the best buildings to take photos of by using Google Maps.

Recommended gear: SLR with a tilt-shift lens, plus a tripod and cable release.

Food

Food photography isn't for me—I'd eat the subject before I could take a photo of it. It's part food prep, part decoration, part photography, and being able to resist temptation.

Recommended gear: SLR with a 50 mm macro, plus a tripod and cable release.

Sports

Sports shooters probably prefer the modern-day performance of a Digital SLR (it requires fast burst rates, and that could get costly when shooting on film), but there's nothing stopping you from doing it on film. It definitely helps to be into the sport you're shooting, otherwise you might end up with a load of photos of the referee.

Recommended gear: DSLR

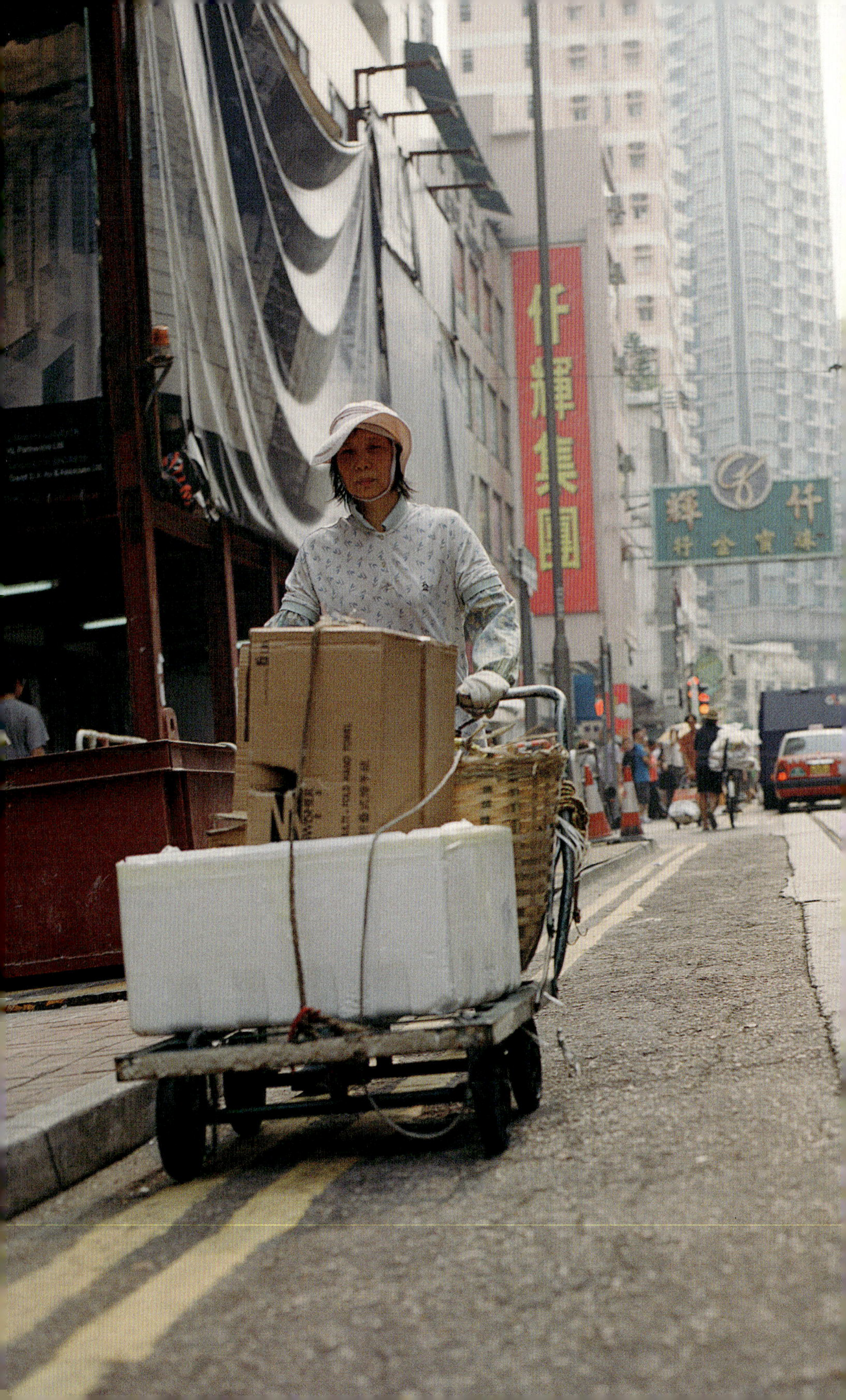
仟輝集團
仟輝
珠寶金行

#67
PHOTOGRAPH TO PLEASE YOURSELF

Film photography now is different to what film photography was like when it was simply known as photography. Enthusiasts used to print their photos and put them in photo albums, never to be seen by anyone other than uninterested relatives. Now, photos end up everywhere online, shown to anyone from all around the world.

The likes and follows from other photo enthusiasts and random, faceless people of the internet feels nice (who doesn't like a jolly-good ego stroking?), and will fill you with enough motivation to keep you coming back for more. The only problem with this is that it might be all too easy to lose track of what is actually important for your photography—are you taking photos that you love, or taking photos that will make you feel loved?

The amount of interactions can feel like an indicator of progress, a measure of success, but it's not a yardstick that you should rely on to rate the quality of your work.

There is every chance of getting an inferiority complex when you start comparing how your photos perform when compared to others. If it really is all about the likes and follows, then you should bear in mind that you will always be in the shadow of someone's oiled-up ass.

I understand the importance of a social-media presence for a photographer, but if you start shooting for likes, there's every risk that your photos will end up looking like someone else's photos. If you want consistent quality, you have to take photos that are true to yourself.

Photograph to please yourself. Even if it doesn't get as much love as some other photographer's photos, at least you can look back and really love what you shot.

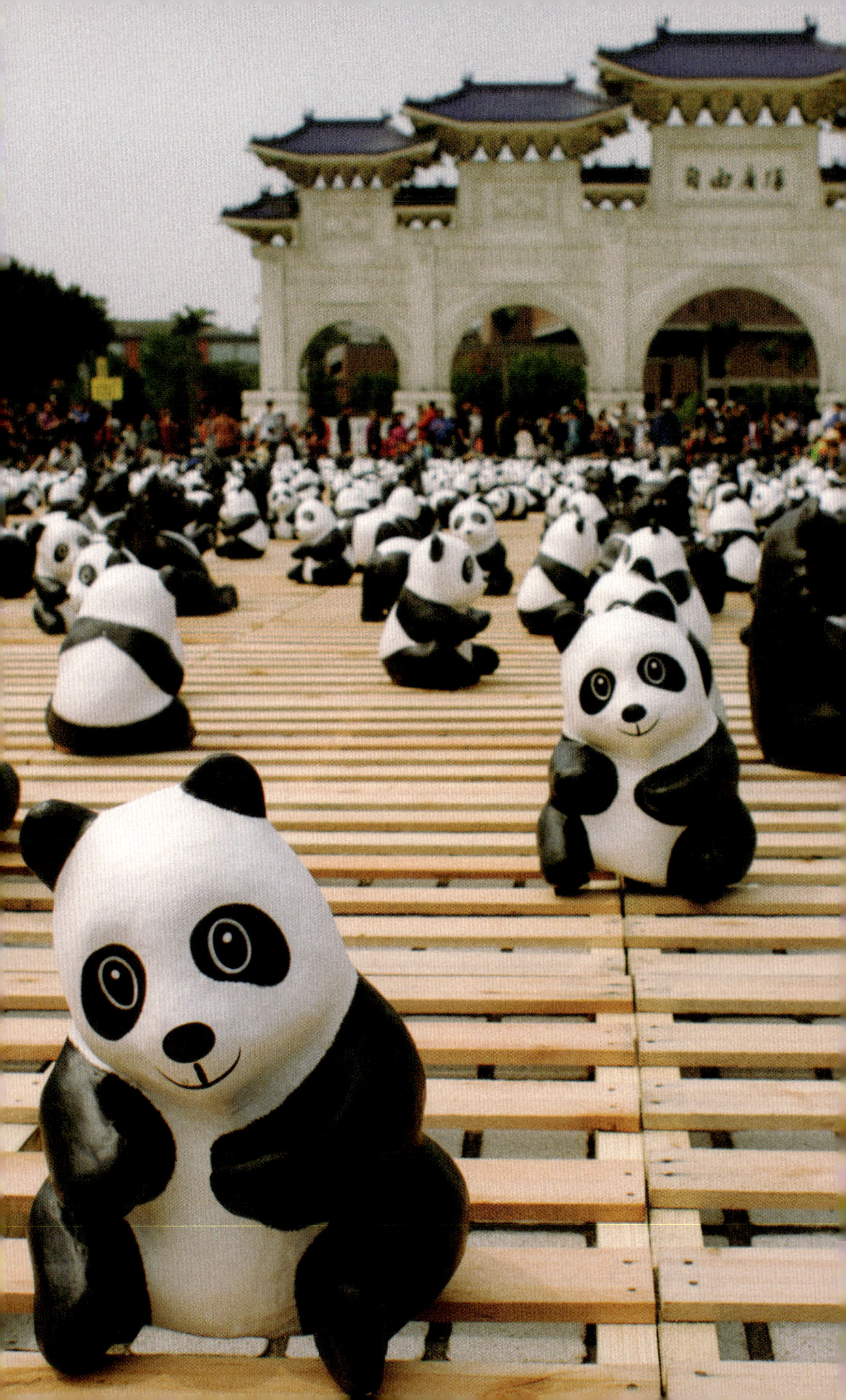

#68

EVERYONE TAKES SH*T PHOTOS (SOMETIMES)

Your first 10,000 photographs are your worst.

—Henri Cartier-Bresson

There's nothing worse than getting your freshly developed film back from the lab—the one that you were confident had some Pulitzer Prize-winning shots in there—only to find they're more shitzer than Pulitzer. I know the feeling; I've been there. It's like your whole world is about to cave in. It feels like your stomach is about to drop out of your bum. It's the kind of experience that makes you want to just jack it all in.

Before you ever think about throwing in the towel, it is important to know that everyone takes shitty photos. It doesn't matter how experienced a photographer is—whether they've actually taken a Pulitzer Prize-winning photo before or not—everyone is prone to churning out some stinkers every now and then.

If you want to learn how to take consistently better shots, you're better off taking those crap shots on film. On a digital camera or smartphone, you get to take a look at the shit shot you've just taken, and then you simply keep retaking it over and over again until you get it right, without really understanding why it was a bad shot in the first place.

With a shit shot on film, you're left with a permanent, physical reminder of how bad things can get when it goes seriously wrong. That, and the fact that you paid to develop that steaming hot pile of dung, will be enough of an incentive to make sure you get things right next time.

It's not always about learning lessons the hard way; photography is one massive, nonstop learning process. As a photographer, I don't think you'll ever be happy with just the photos you've already taken. If you're passionate about photography, you will always be on the search for the next great shot, to make an image that is better than the last. When you tread on ground that you've not explored before, there's always the possibility of failure; but you just have to keep your chin up and look in the direction you're heading, and not where you've come from.

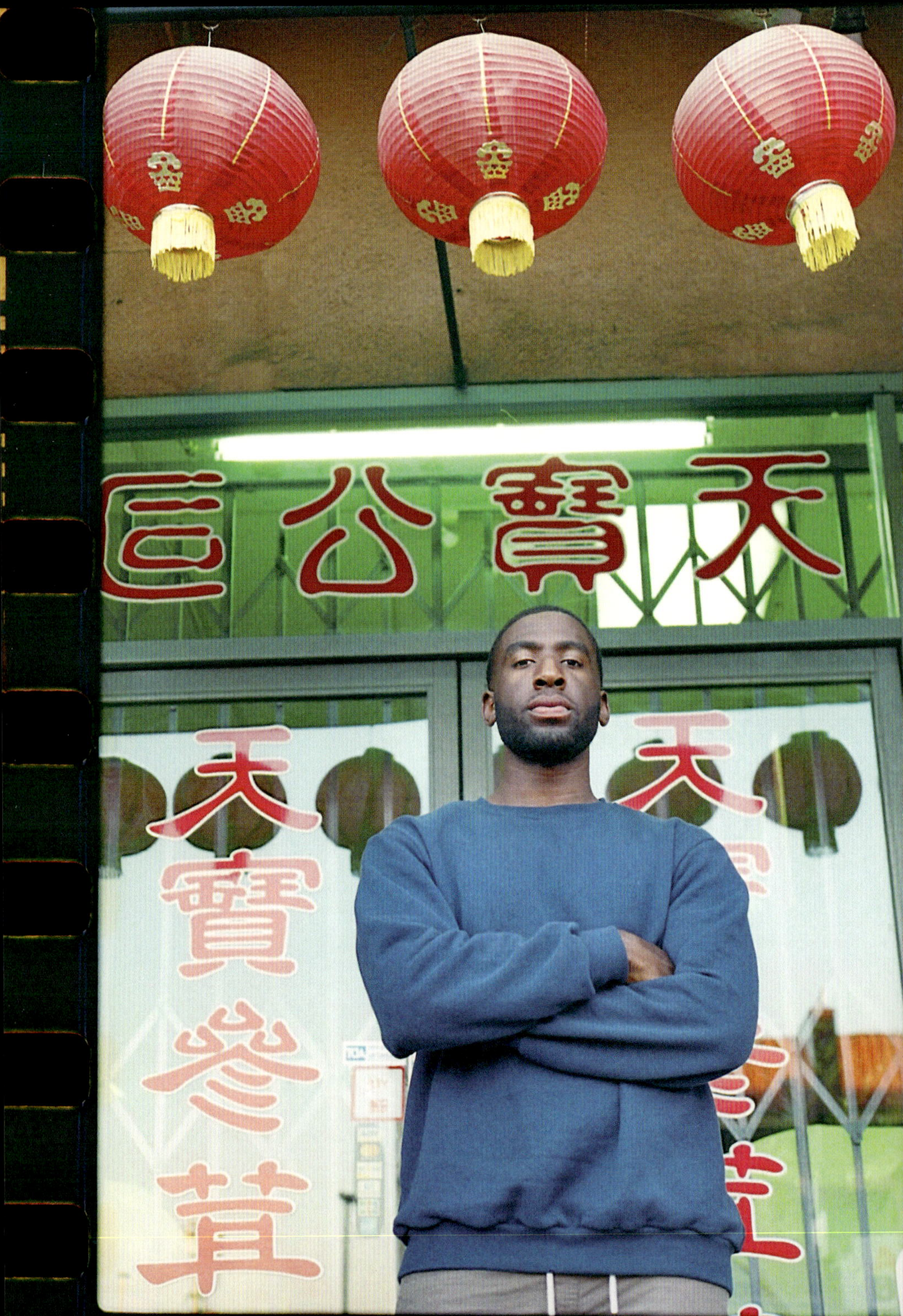

天寶公
天寶參茸

#69

THE 36:1 RATIO

A photographer once told me that he would always aim for a hit rate of 36:1—one winning frame for every roll of 35 mm film. Granted, this was his target for commercial shoots, but regardless of whether you're shooting for someone or for yourself, it's a great target to set.

It might seem like the expectations are being set way too low—to only get one good frame from thirty-six seems pretty meagre—especially given that the cost of exposing and developing one roll of film is not what you would call cheap. But if you want to take top-shelf shots, this is what you should aim for.

In the professional environment, the aim is to get one frame that would be deemed good enough for a billboard ad. For a photo enthusiast, you should use this target to aim for one amazing frame that you would happily print large and hang on your wall. On that roll of film there might be other good frames, some others that are amazing (and well done if you do), too, but you should be happy if you can take at least one top-grade shot for every roll of film you use.

Look at contact sheets of some of the most celebrated photographers of the twentieth century, and it's not uncommon to see every single frame from a roll of film used on just one subject. They would try different angles and compositions. You get a sense of how fluid the photographer was, moving closer or farther away from the subject, moving around the subject. Clearly, they have tried taking many different shots and will expect only one of those to work for them.

Photographers just need to know there is no harm in taking more photos if the subject is right, because you absolutely should try to nail that shot. Taking up to thirty-six frames on that one subject greatly increases the likelihood of getting that perfect image.

Why You Should Print Contact Sheets

Try printing off a contact sheet when you get your film developed. A contact sheet shows each frame from a roll of film, the same size as they are on film, printed out onto a sheet of paper. Get a loupe (it's a magnifier) to inspect each frame, and start scoring each frame and making notes. It's the easiest way to evaluate every frame from your film in one go. Also, I tend to find that amazing shots often look good even when not magnified. If it pops out and looks great even when seen small, it will most likely look amazing when looked at much larger.

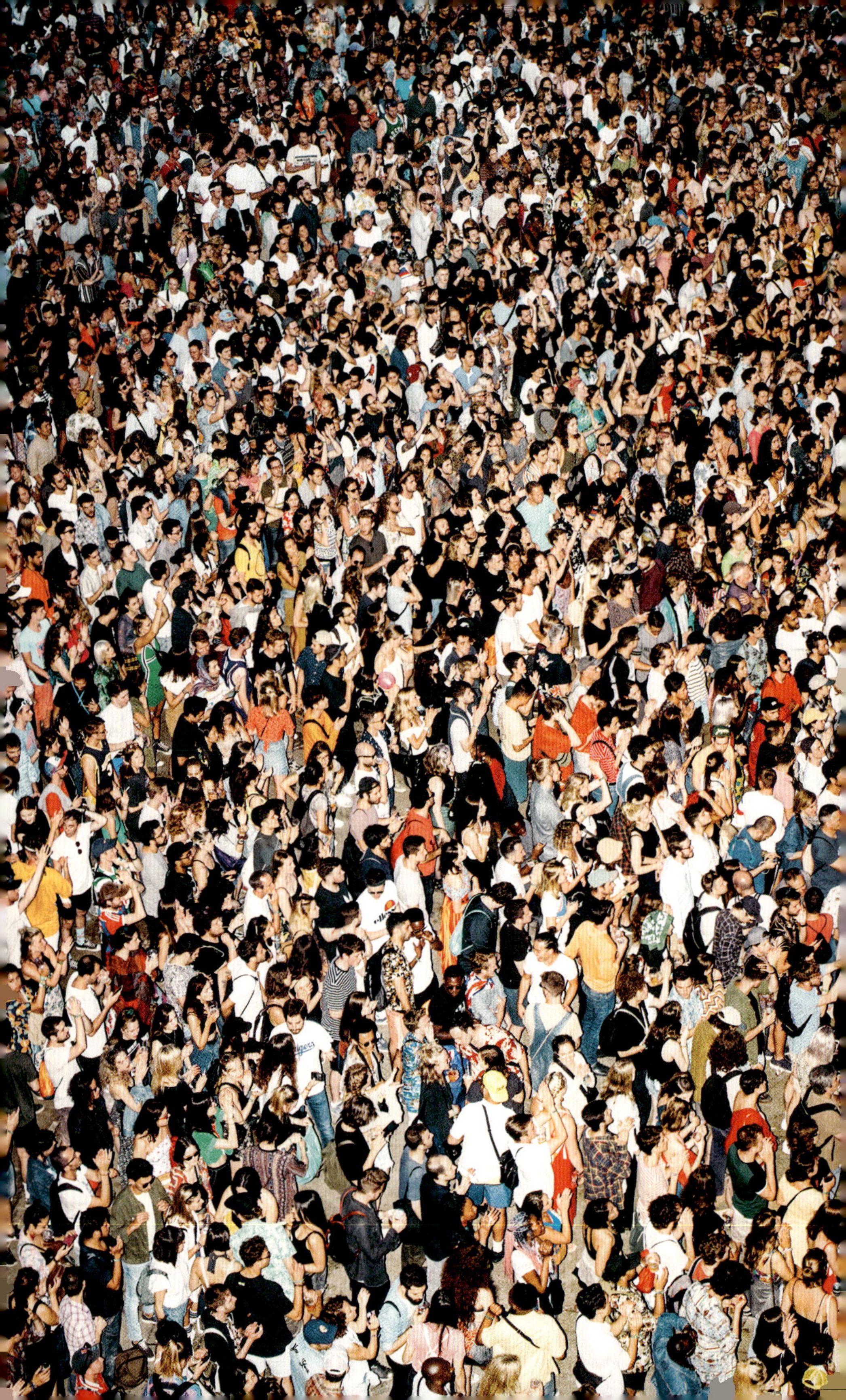

#70 SHOOT MORE OF THE SAME

Nobody wants to take photos of exactly the same thing every time—your photo collection might freak people out into thinking there's a glitch in the matrix. But as loopy as it sounds, going back to the same place again and again might just be the thing you need to up your photo game, and here's how:

- Improve on a good shot. Even if you've taken what you think is a good shot already, there's always room for improvement. If you love the location and the subject so much, then there's no harm in going back to try getting an even better shot.
- See something new. You might see something that you didn't see the first time—a better angle, interesting visual elements, or different subjects. The weather might be better, or the light might have a more interesting look, in a different season or time in the day.
- Use a new technique. You might have learnt something new in terms of technique or creativity, since you took that photo, that you think could help you take a better shot. And taking another shot will help you understand how to keep improving as well.
- To help you take a better photo the next time, you could take some of these steps:

Consider How to Improve the Shot

Look at your first photo and pick out things you would improve if you got the chance to try again. How much is based on predictable elements, and how much is based on chance? Did you use the right settings? How could you compose it better? Take note of all those questions so you can try that out if you ever get another chance.

Choose the Best Film

Now would be a good time to consider whether it was the right film choice the first time around. Does it have the right saturation? Would you have preferred a finer-grain film? Or would it work better in black and white?

Try Different Approaches

Don't just use the same composition again; try other different angles and framing. Maybe try different focal lengths, too. Don't be so fixated on shooting it from exactly the same spot as before—you might notice the next time around that it looks better from a different angle.

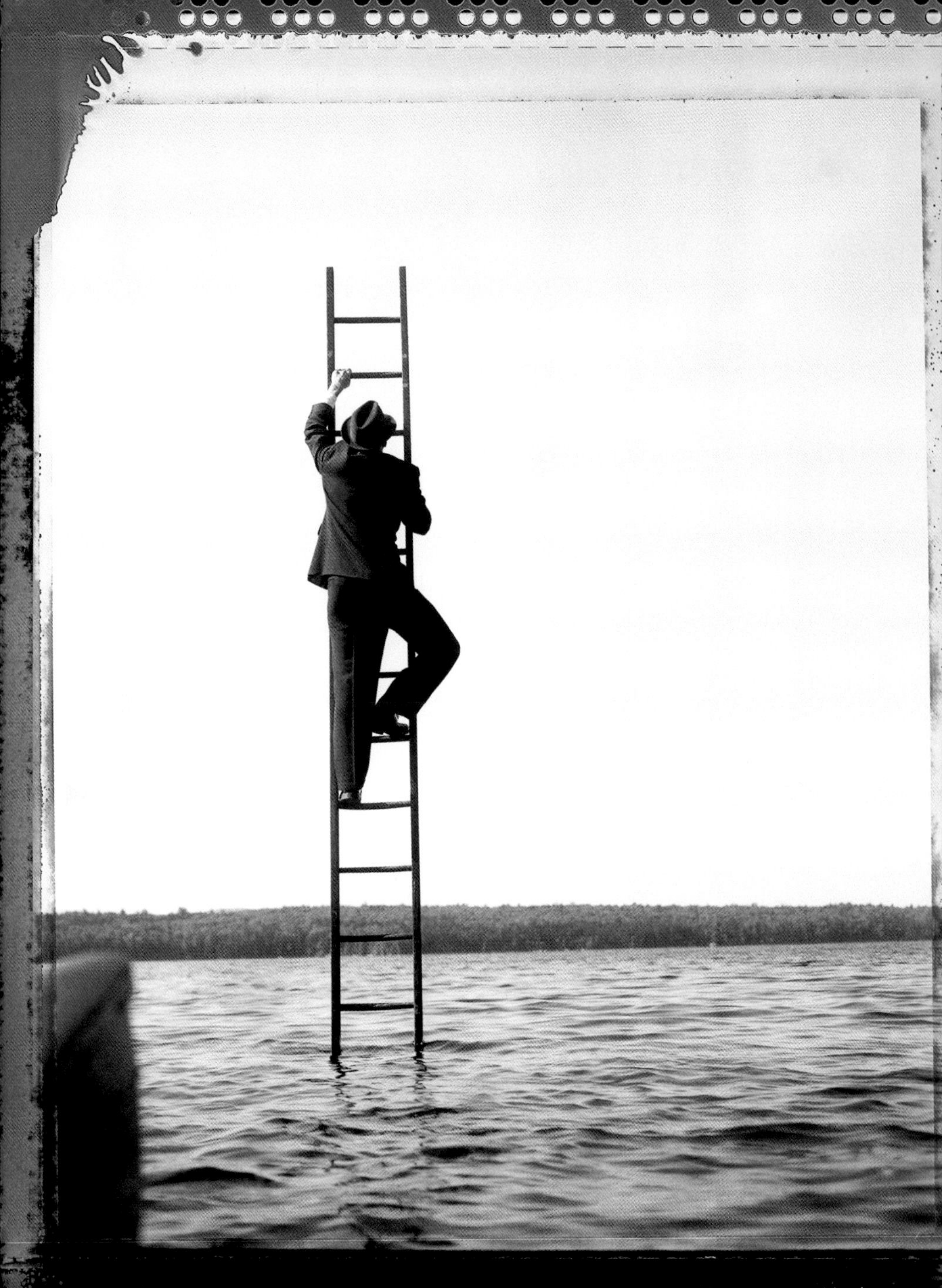

#71
KEEP INSPIRED WITH AMAZING IMAGES

The problem I had with picking up photography was that most photography-learning books of that time were heavy on the text, light on images, and seemed hell-bent on making the process of learning photography feel as enjoyable a process as having a root canal.

If you want to sink your teeth into photography, you need some visual inspiration to get you going. It's all good reading about how to take masterfully composed photos, but you won't truly appreciate a masterfully composed photo until you see one.

The quick and easy way to do that is to open up Instagram and find some photographers to follow, but it's not always easy to find some pure photography amongst all the boobs, selfies, and #ads. There are a lot of great photographers on Insta, but a smartphone screen is not the best way to truly appreciate someone's photos. In that respect, the photo book is still king.

Go to a bookstore and pick out a load of photo books; or borrow a load from the library, take them home, sit on a nice, comfy chair, with a nice cup of coffee in hand, and feast your eyes on those magnificent, printed pages. There is something about seeing a photo in physical form—having a beautiful print right in your hands—that is so magnetising. A good photo book will give you all the inspiration you need to get your creative juices flowing.

Five Photo Books That Most Inspired Me

1. Joe Cornish, *First Light*
2. Martin Parr, *The Last Resort*
3. Henri Cartier-Bresson, *The Decisive Moment*
4. Daido Moriyama, *Shinjuku*
5. Fan Ho, any of his books

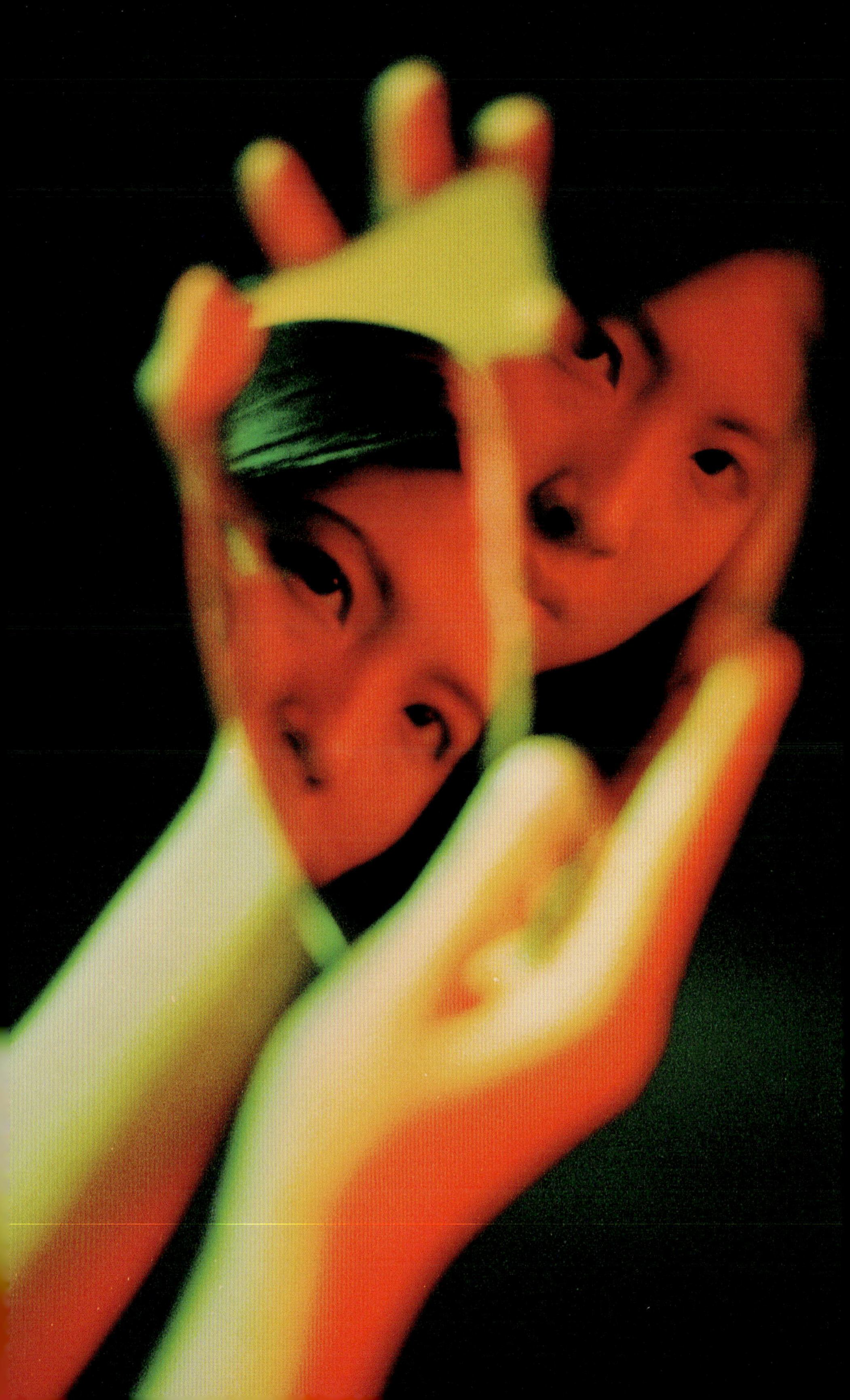

#72 BE YOUR NUMBER ONE CRITIC

There's no one more qualified for the role of criticising your own work than yourself. No one cares as much about your photos as you do. And if you care to improve the quality of your images, then you'll want to look at your own work with a critical eye.

There is a fine line between being critical about your work and just being downright negative, though, so make sure you're strolling on the right side of that line, filling your head with positive vibes. Don't be disheartened by what you think is slow progress, and don't think that not being able to achieve the results you imagined you would get is down to a lack of inherent ability. No one takes amazing photos from the get-go, and most photographers have gone through a phase of thinking their photos suck. Criticise constructively: don't just think about how your image is lacking in quality; think about what you can add to it to make a great photo.

Take a look at your most recent photos and mull over how you can improve on the following three things:

Technical

There's no need to worry too much about images that are slightly out of focus or a little off with the exposure; they are easy and obvious fixes. You need to think about how you could do things differently with the technical side of things, to improve on what you've taken already. It could be using a longer shutter speed to blur the motion more, or using a shallow depth of field to isolate the subject more—these are the kind of technical aspects you should think about when evaluating your photos.

Subject Matter

If you start off with a boring subject, the best you can do with that is to make a pretty but boring image. The subject should be your focal point, the visual element with the most meaning. The subject matter matters the most. A blurry image of an interesting subject matter will always be preferable to a sharp image of one that is not interesting. Keep pushing yourself to look for things of interest. Continue to raise the bar of what subjects you deem worthy of a shot, and you will start off on a good foot for getting great photos.

Composition

When you're there on location, the subject keeps moving around, and the light is fading fast, it can be a challenge to fiddle with the settings and concentrate on composition at the same time.

Once you have your film scanned, you can put the files through Photoshop or Lightroom and play around with cropping it, rotating it (one easy mistake is not keeping those horizons level), and moving the framing around to try to improve the composition. You may not want to crop it that much, but at least you can get a visual idea of how your photo could be improved.

#73
LEARN TO EDIT IN CAMERA

Don't feel the need to be frugal with the film when you first start shooting. Concentrating on taking more photos, trying all the different film emulsions, and fine tuning your sense of style is more important in the early stages.

As you gain more experience and start developing your vision for a good photo, the quality of your photos will keep getting better, too. You'll get to the point where you feel more comfortable using your camera and knowing how to change settings to get what you want.

With that new-found confidence in using your camera, it's time to start editing in camera, to be more effective with your exposures. When you shoot with film, there's no turning back—what's exposed on film can't be taken back, and there's no way of previewing what it looks like. So it's good to be able to make adjustments to the look of the image before you've even taken the shot, to make sure the quality of all the frames exposed on the roll of film are of a higher quality.

Don't just look straight ahead when you're eyeballing the viewfinder. Study from edge to edge—the complete frame—to make sure you've examined all the details. There are things that you want keep out of the frame to make it look less distracting, and there are things that you want to make sure you keep in the frame. Cropping off legs below the knees always looks a little awkward, for example. It's easy to just look at the most attractive part of the subject and overlook those little, tiny details that can blemish your photo.

It's important to be as fluid as possible when composing a photo because, even though your subject might be still, and you will need to be steady when you're taking the shot, you're totally free to move your camera around before you're ready to press the shutter button. While you're studying that frame, try reframing—moving the frame up/down and left/right—and consider trying a different composition. There are many different ways to take a photo of the same subject, and the first composition you try and like is not necessarily going to be the best.

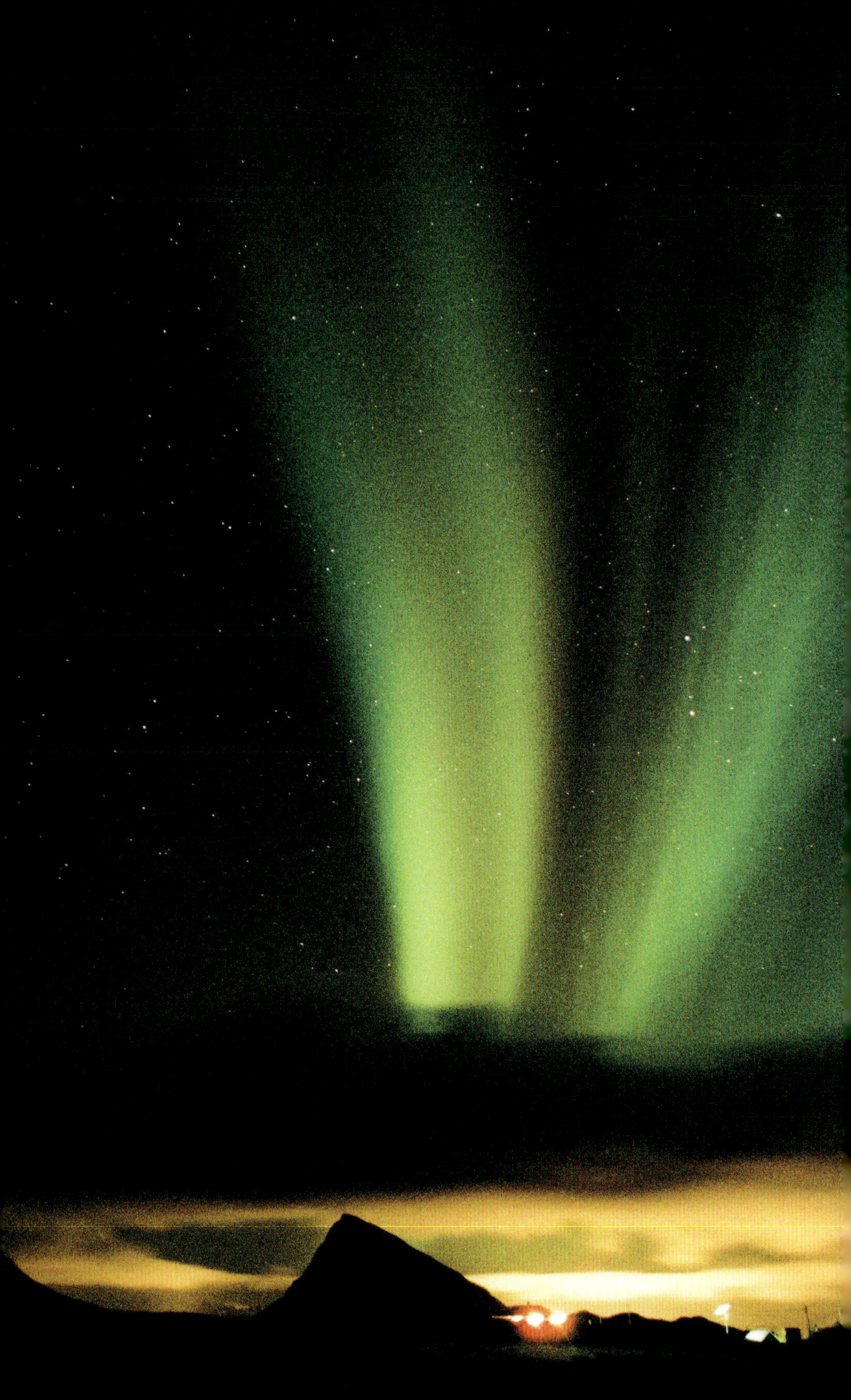

#74 PHOTOGRAPHY IS AN ILLUSION

Being a good photographer isn't all about taking impossibly perfect photos every single time. It's about showing only the impossibly perfect ones every time you update your photo stream. Photography is an illusion, kinda like magic, albeit without the creepy smooth-talking and sleight-of-hand shiz.

Your photography is your product, and every production line needs some quality control. Treat your work like a premium product and make sure you set the standards high for your output. Needless to say, the crap ones should never see the light of day, but the challenge is differentiating between a pretty decent shot and a really good one. It's easy to get attached to a photo because you took it, and making the decision not to show it can be difficult at times. But it is important that you strive to raise the standards of your photography, rather than lowering the bar. Publishing some good photos with some average ones thrown in the mix will just end up diluting the quality of your images, and wishy-washy images are not the way to go.

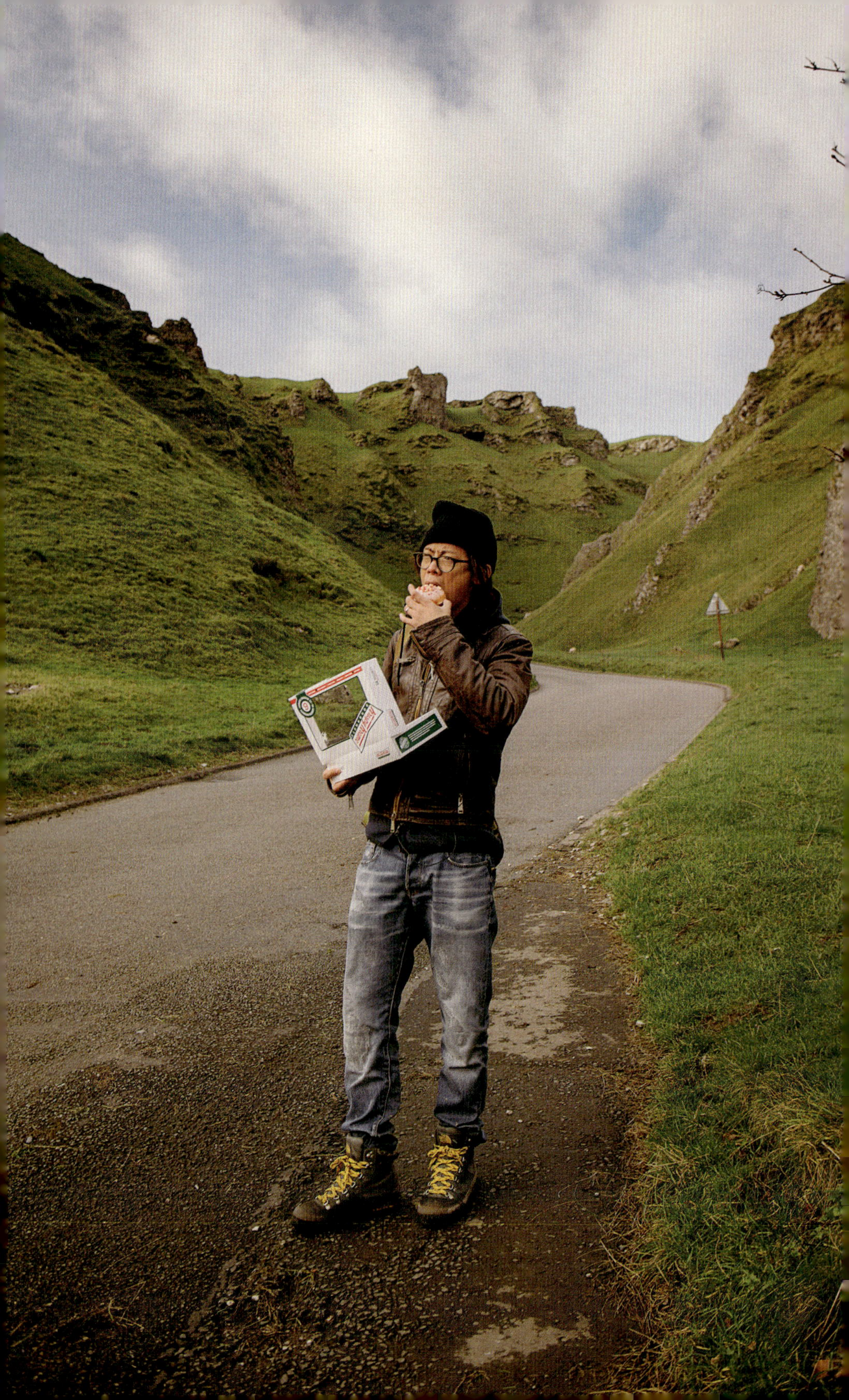

#75
KEEPING IT SIMPLE

We've come this far in the book, which means you've filled your brain with 75 percent of the information you had reserved for photography tips. That's a big chunk of information about gear, a fairly healthy dose about composition, and a good deal of other tips that don't fall into any specific category. But before we carry on, and get carried away with stuffing that grey matter with more photography advice in black and white, I want to emphasise that photography really doesn't need to be all that complex. If you want to make great photos, simplicity is the way to go.

Less Gear Is More

It doesn't matter how much gear you own (that's what I tell myself); the reason why I keep it simple with a three-lens setup is because carrying any more than that will overcomplicate things. Shooting more means higher productivity, but carrying more is most definitely not conducive to that. You might be packing some serious heat in the camera-bag department, but your back will probably need some Deep Heat spray after carrying an extra few kilos of gear for the day. Don't do it to look more pro: the professionals take more gear mainly to look good in front of clients—and because it's their assistants who have to carry it all.

If you're at a gorgeous location, with a bagful of lenses, you'll just end up spending more time looking through those expensive bits of glass in your bag, contemplating which one you should use, instead of more important things. Concentrate on looking at angles and compositions, and visually interesting stuff—you know, the stuff that actually helps to make photos interesting.

Don't get me wrong; I love gear. I really do. But you can appreciate all your cameras and lenses without taking all of them out with you.

Composition Doesn't Need to Be Complicated

There are many, many ways to make a shot, but you only need to press one button to take it. Apart from having to adjust the settings to set your exposure, there are all the rules and guidelines of composition to think about, which can not only overcomplicate the way you take photos but also overcomplicate your image. Take the photo how you want it, and put in the frame as much you feel is needed. There are lots of guides on what makes a good image, but putting all of those elements in a photo doesn't mean it'll look good.

Minimalist photography is not always easy to do because there's the danger that you'll end up making the photo look devoid of any visual interest. But if you swing it the other way, a visually complex image might make the message of your photo less obvious with all the visual clutter. Keeping it simple—not necessarily minimalist—and removing any extraneous detail is an effective way of getting straight to the point of your image.

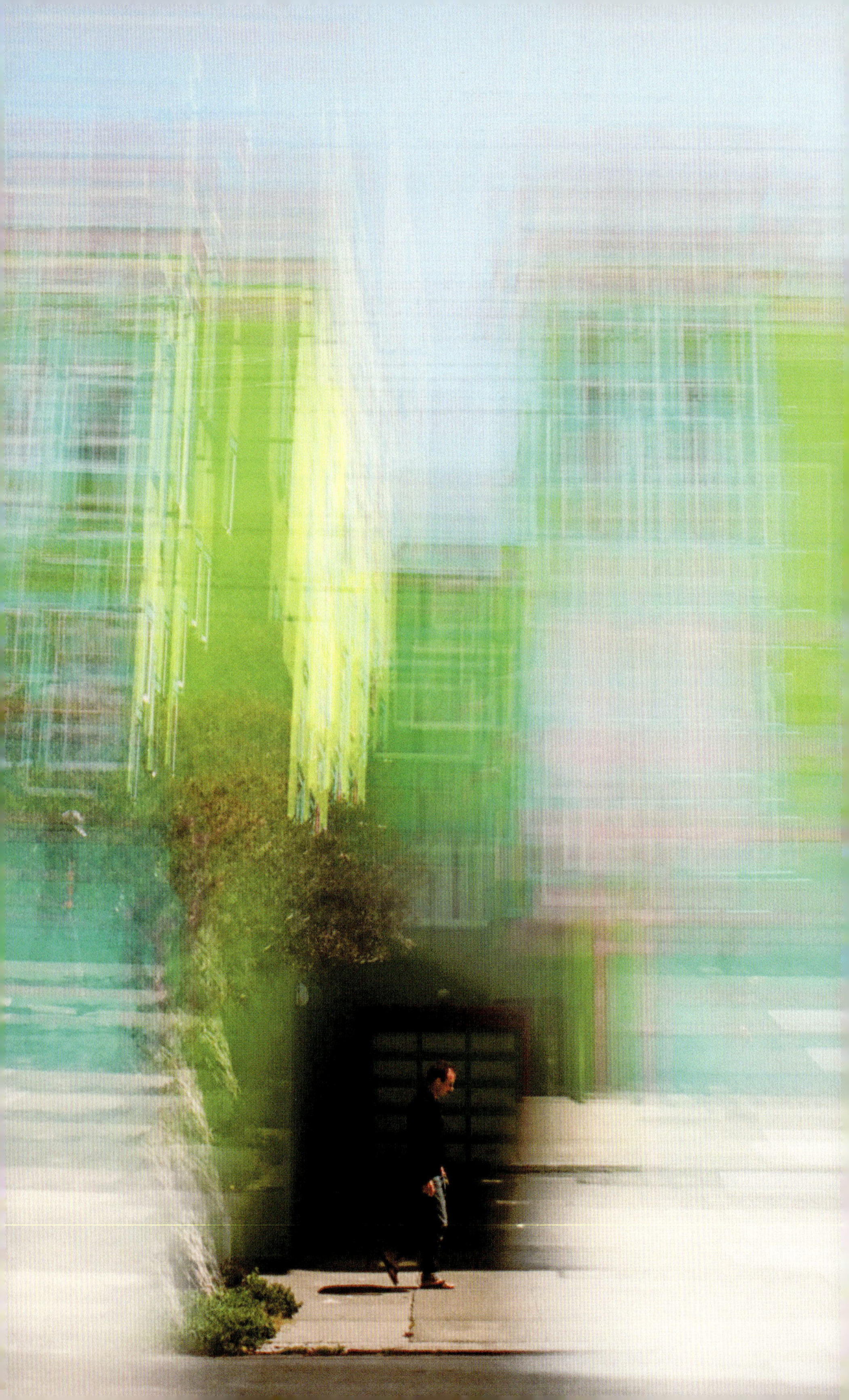

#76
UNBLOCKING THAT CREATIVE BLOCK

Sometimes the passion for photography peters out. It's happened to me on numerous occasions, and it feels like creative constipation. You want to produce something, but no matter how hard you push, nothing is willing to come out. Scat analogies aside, there are a number of ways you can try dealing with the blockage. There isn't one formula for all, but you can definitely give these a shot:

Take a Break

Don't force it. Going out to take more photos will probably just deplete what little inspiration and motivation you had left to take interesting images. Stop thinking about photography all the time, stop taking photos for a while, and the passion could come flooding back.

Find Some Inspiration

You could take a photography hiatus and lower your photo output to a big fat zero, but perhaps what your creative mind needs—rather than a holiday—is to be refreshed and revived by stimulating it with interesting visuals and images.

To keep relying on all the creativity to come from your own brain is one way of draining all the creative juices until you get to the point where you're just running on fumes. Of course, you can't ask someone else to create for you, but while you're taking a break from taking photos, you can try immersing yourself with other's images. Whether they be photography, art, or design, it could be a great way to give your creative mind a little spa break, and inspire you to get out there and start creating again.

Try Another Creative Art

I used to photograph guns. Well, toy guns. I thought it was the break a budding photographer needed. It wasn't. I got sick of it. It was so bad that I didn't even want to take photos in my spare time, either. I ended up associating using a camera with doing a menial task (it probably didn't help that my personal camera was the same as my work camera), and didn't want to use it even for a bit of casual photography.

I still wanted to do a job that was creative so I started making YouTube videos—also about airsoft guns—using a camera in a way that I felt was new and exciting. It brought back some of the enthusiasm for the job, and my passion for taking photos came back.

Buy Some New Gear

I have just mentioned in the previous chapter to keep it simple with the gear, but there are times when shelling out for a new bit of gear will give you the enthusiasm to take more photos. Buying a new lens, for example, might open up a new possibility for your photography—being able to take photos of subjects that wouldn't have been possible with the kit you had. That ability to try something a little different might just be the spark you need to keep you taking photos.

Power Through

I wouldn't recommend it, because you could make it worse, but there are times when you just need to get out there and take more photos. Make sure you visit some new and interesting places, and only then will you find out if you really do have a creative block.

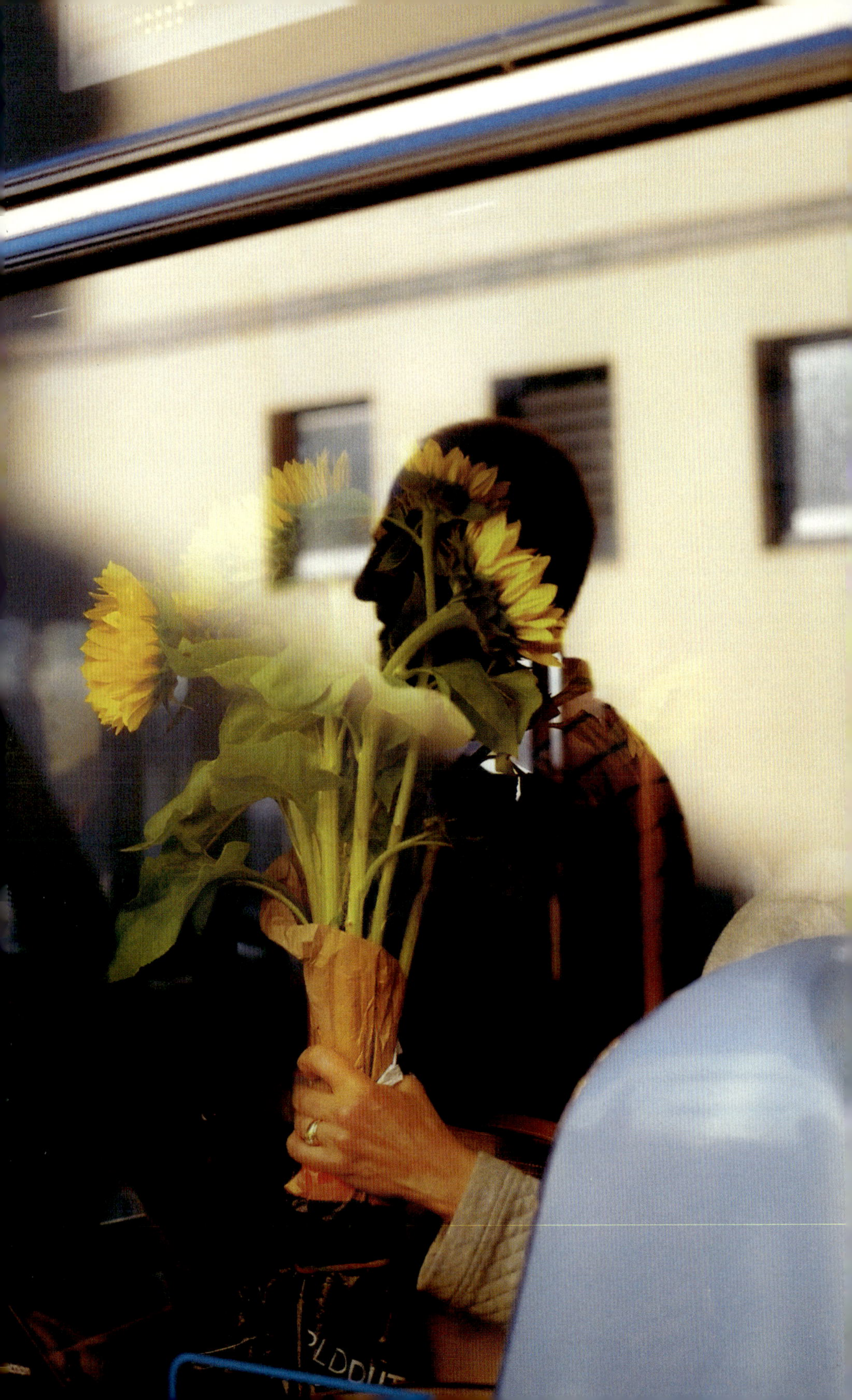

#77 ALWAYS LOOK FOR SOMETHING NEW

If I saw something in the viewfinder that looked familiar to me, I would do something to shake it up.

—Garry Winogrand

One cause for ending up in a creative cul-de-sac is getting into a routine of shooting very similar-looking images. Photography is driven by the need to see new things—new scenery, new subjects—and if you're firing off film to create a series of photos that really don't look all that different from one another, that's when the monotony might set in.

Same Subject, But Different

When you've specialised in one genre of photography, you'll most likely want to stick to that for a couple of reasons: you want to keep your style consistent, and that's what you're most comfortable taking photos of. Change is not always easy, but the good news is that you don't need to look at different subjects to take photos that feel different.

Try setting yourself some themes; focus on photographing very specific types of subject matters—e.g., taxi drivers of London, or skateboarder portraits—and stick to that until you're happy with what you have or you want to move on, at which point you move on to another theme.

Change of Scenery

Photography is a great motivator for making us explore new places. Having a change of scenery is a simple and effective way of freshening up your photography without needing to change the subject matter.

Try a New Genre

I got into landscape photography when I was in university in the UK, and was still nuts about it when I moved to Hong Kong. I soon found out, though, that Hong Kong isn't exactly full of luscious landscapes, and there aren't really four distinguishable seasons—just variations in wetness—to make taking landscape photos throughout the year particularly exciting. Landscape photography became a bit tedious.

I ended up embracing the concrete because street photography was a genre of photography that I was curious about, but it was not something that I really had any intentions to try, until I moved to Hong Kong. Taking street photos wasn't a natural progression from photographing things that don't move to unpredictable subject matters, but to me, that was what made it exciting and challenging.

Keeping yourself interested in photography is about constantly challenging yourself and stimulating yourself to new sights and sense. The camera is the tool for documenting that. The more interesting you make your life, the more interesting your photos will become.

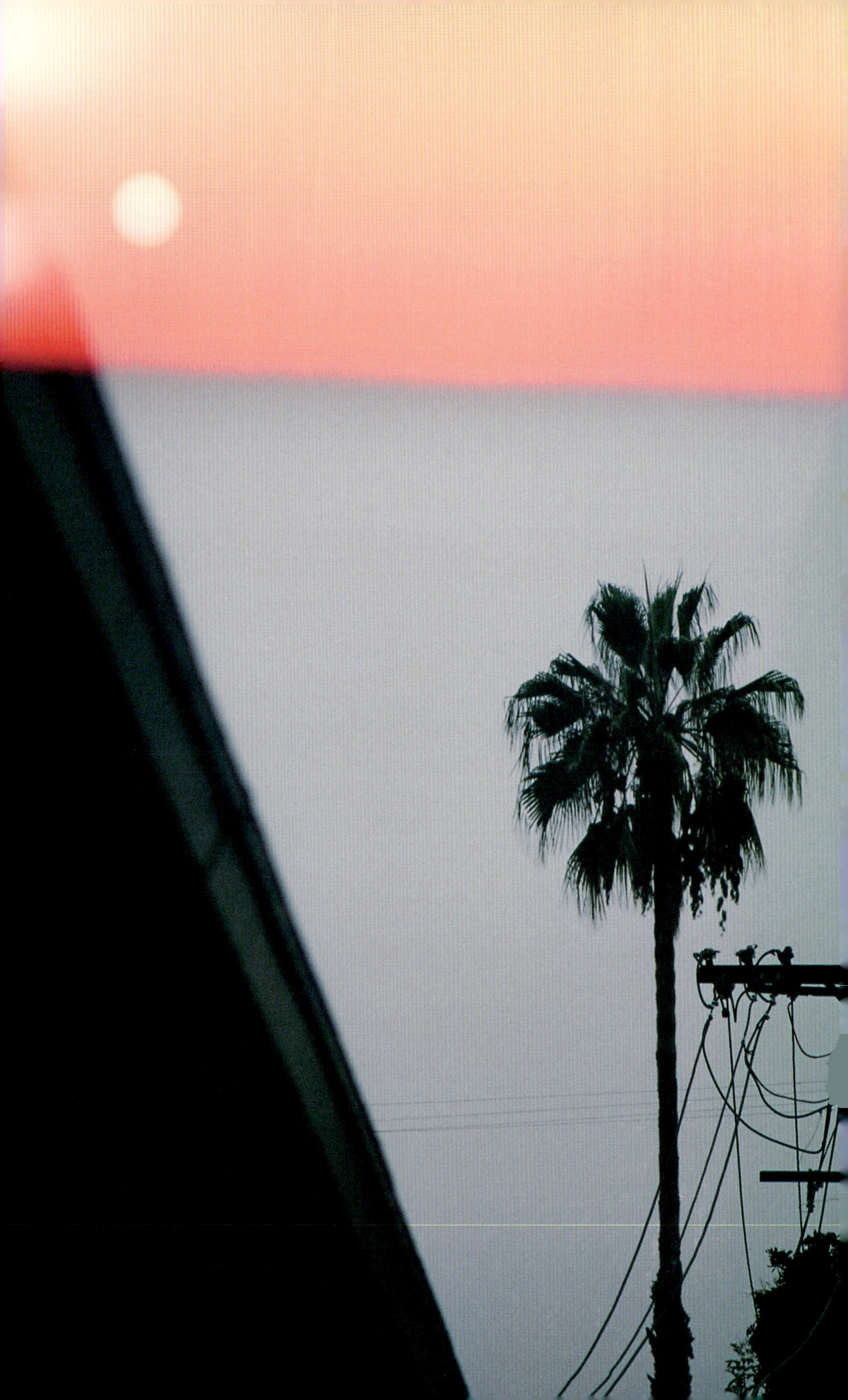

#78
DON'T THINK; JUST SHOOT

Imagine what it would be like if we had a shutter in our eyeball and a roll of film in the place where our brain usually goes; we would never need to worry about getting the right settings and focusing in time (there would be no worries without a brain). Photo-taking would become such a simple task!

The "don't think, just shoot" school of thought might sound a bit brainless, but the non-cerebral way of taking photos is what makes it so appealing. When you're so used to contemplating so many things before you even get to press the shutter button, it's actually an incredibly refreshing approach to photography. Don't worry about the settings; if you like what you see, you take a shot—a snapshot. It's a way of shooting that ditches the methodical way of making a photo and encourages you to act on your instincts.

"F/8 and Be There"

It's a quote often attributed to photographer Arthur Fellig, aka Weegee, but never confirmed. The "f/8 and be there" approach would've been right up his street if he took his street photos with a 35 mm camera, but with a large-format camera it would be more "f/16 and be there," which doesn't have quite the same ring to it.

Fellig's preferred approach was to have the aperture and shutter speed fixed—f/16 and 1/200s—with the aperture setting plenty small to give enough depth of field that focusing could be fixed at a distance of ten feet, allowing him to quickly raise his camera and take a shot. On a 35 mm film camera, f/8 should give you enough depth of field to not worry too much about focusing. If you're shooting in consistent, predictably lit environments, you can stick to the Sunny 16 rule and won't need to worry about any of the camera settings. Of course, you could just go for a fully automated camera, but with the "f/8 and be there" method, at least you know exactly what you're getting.

Whether it's with a compact camera or a manual 35 mm film SLR, this instinctive way of taking photos is something that every photographer has to give a go, if not use on a regular basis. Instead of complicating the process of taking photos by putting technical aspects in between the seeing and taking of the photo, it will show you just how simple it can be to take really interesting photos.

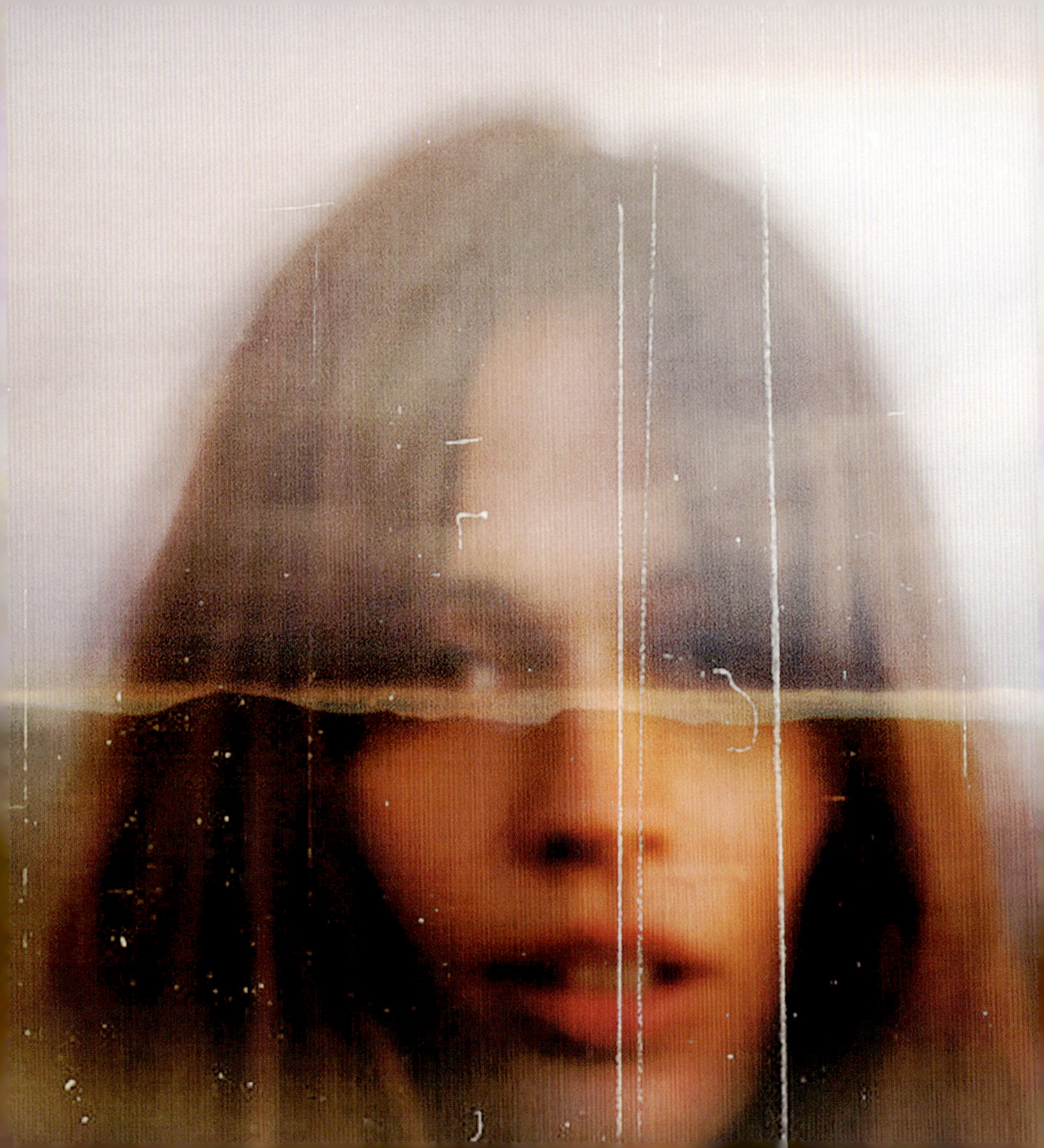

#79

LO-FI PHOTOGRAPHY FOR MAXIMUM FUN

There is nothing worse than a sharp image of a fuzzy concept.

— Ansel Adams

Photos don't always need to be sharp, especially when the photo is boring—it'll just make it crystal clear how boring the photo is. Sometimes fuzzy can be cool; lo-fi photography, when shot with the same devil-may-care style mentioned in the previous chapter, can actually be tons of fun.

Firstly, there is no such thing as hi-fi photography—it's just called photography—unless we're talking about taking pictures of the thing that plays your music at home. Lo-fi photography is a thing, though, and it's all about making the usually unwanted aesthetics that you might get from cheap, poorly made, plastic toy cameras a cool thing—think soft, distorted images characterised by light leaks and vignetting.

If you want the full lo-fi photography experience, look for a camera that has the least amount of metal and glass on it—plastic fantastic is the way to go. Unpredictable results are what it's all about, so don't keep your hopes up. Keeping your hopes low is the way to go, so you'll be pleasantly surprised when something good happens, and won't be too miffed if it all goes pear-shaped.

The lo-fi, low-expectation experience will drive you to taking photos that aren't so pre-meditated and planned—this style of shooting favours the wild and wacky subjects. Photography is a hobby that takes itself far too seriously sometimes, so it's a nice break to take photos that are so carefree.

Things You Need for Lo-Fi Photography

- A 6 x 6 medium-format toy camera. There could be nothing simpler than dealing with a square frame to compose a shot, and that's what you'll get with a 6 x 6 medium-format toy camera—silly fun photos that don't need over-thinking. There is something quite preposterous about creating lo-fi photos on a massive 6 x 6 cm film frame, but that's exactly what you should love about it.
- Use ISO 400 film. A lot of toy cameras have small, fixed aperture lenses, with a single shutter speed, so you'll need to use a film that is sensitive enough. ISO 400 should do the trick for daytime shoots.
- Buy a flash. If the camera doesn't have one built in, it would be good to have a flash to allow you to keep shooting in low light. Just make sure there's a hot shoe on the camera—the flash needs to be mounted there and is triggered via the hot shoe.

Things to Try

- Double exposures go together so well with lo-fi photography, probably because a lot of toy cameras allow you to keep taking photos on the same frame if you don't wind the film on.
- Use colour gels to put over the flash to add a colour cast to the flash. If you're taking double exposures, you can use a different colour flash for each exposure.
- Cross Processing and push processing work well with the lo-fi aesthetic, adding some crazy, funky colours from cross processing, along with the increased grain and contrast from push processing. Remember to start with slide film. It does't matter if the push processing adds a colour cast to the slide film, because that's what you want!
- Forget the rules! All that stuff about leading lines and rule of thirds—throw that out of the window, and get creative with subjects and composition.
- Shoot portraits with a toy camera—they can look quite cool and edgy, with vignetting and super-soft edges that push the attention toward the slightly less soft centre of the frame. The softness can end up looking quite flattering for portraits.
- Embrace the light leaks. You could tape up the camera to ensure you don't get any light leaks, but I say not to bother because this is lo-fi not ... erm ... hi-fi.

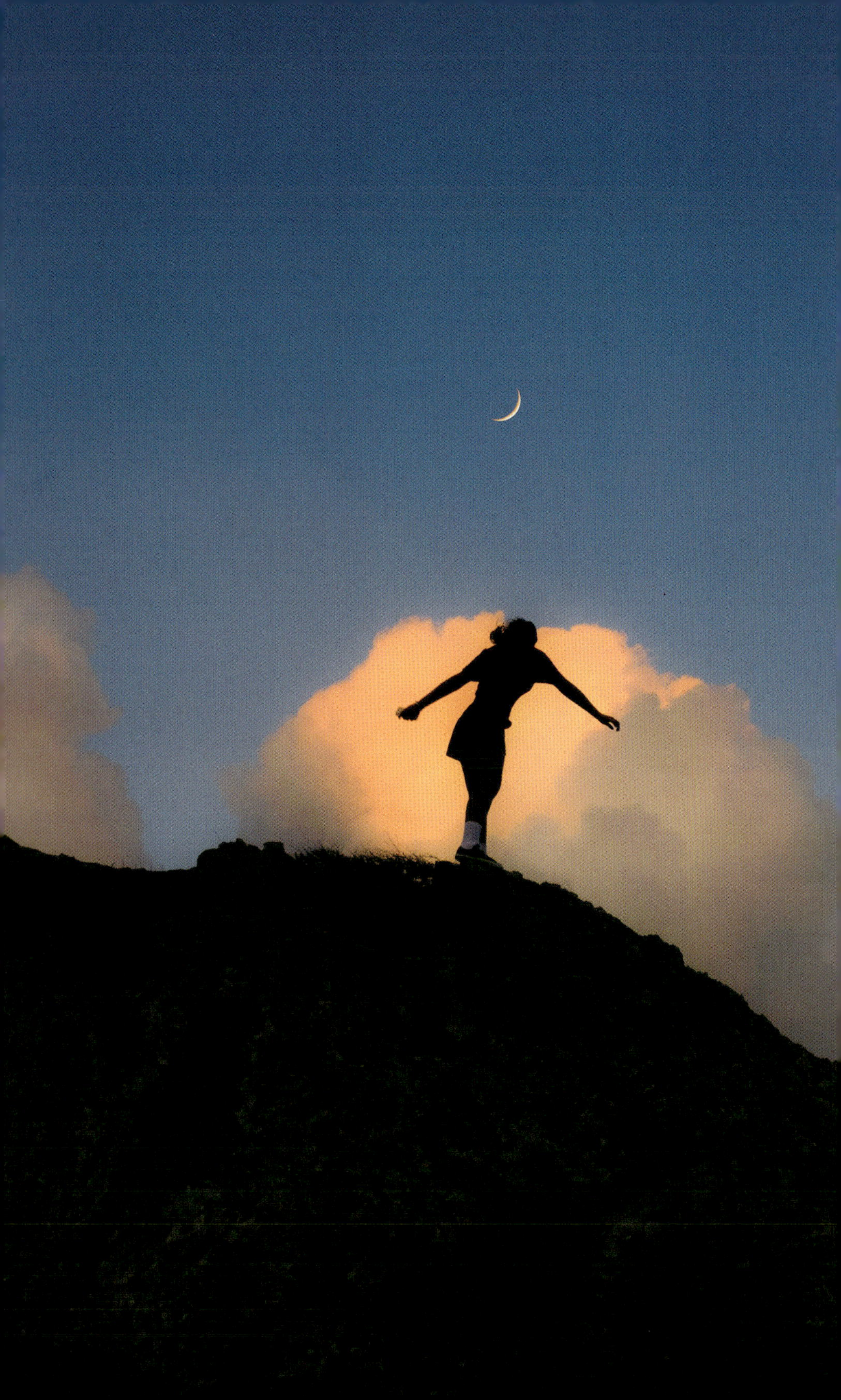

#80
MOVE YOUR FEET TO HELP YOU CREATE

Zoom with your feet, as they say. But don't slip your shoes off and wrap your feet around the barrel of your lens just yet, because (you'll get foot sweat on your lens) all that was meant is that you can do a lot with a fixed-focal-length lens by moving forward and backward with your feet.

Sure, technically, it's not exactly the same effect as zooming with a lens—taking a few steps away from your subject doesn't give exactly the same look as standing on the same spot and zooming out. But every photographer should get used to actively getting a shot, rather than letting the gear make it easier for you.

Prematurely planting your feet to one spot will commit you to taking the shot, potentially making you lose out on taking a better shot. Once you're in place and ready to press the shutter button, you're less likely to look around for a different angle or perspective.

If you're using a tripod, don't set up until you've had a good look around first. Setting the tripod down with a camera mounted on top makes your setup less mobile than if you're moving around with your feet, camera in hands. You can pull the camera up to your eye to check out how it looks through the viewfinder, bend down and get low to the ground, tilt the camera, and reposition if none of that looks any good.

Start off with a prime lens, or if you only have a zoom lens, tell yourself not to zoom. Making a composition with that limitation will force you to think, to look, and to be creative about how you frame up the photo.

The worst thing to do is to get lazy and think the camera will make it easy for you—to take a great shot, you need to work hard to make it happen.

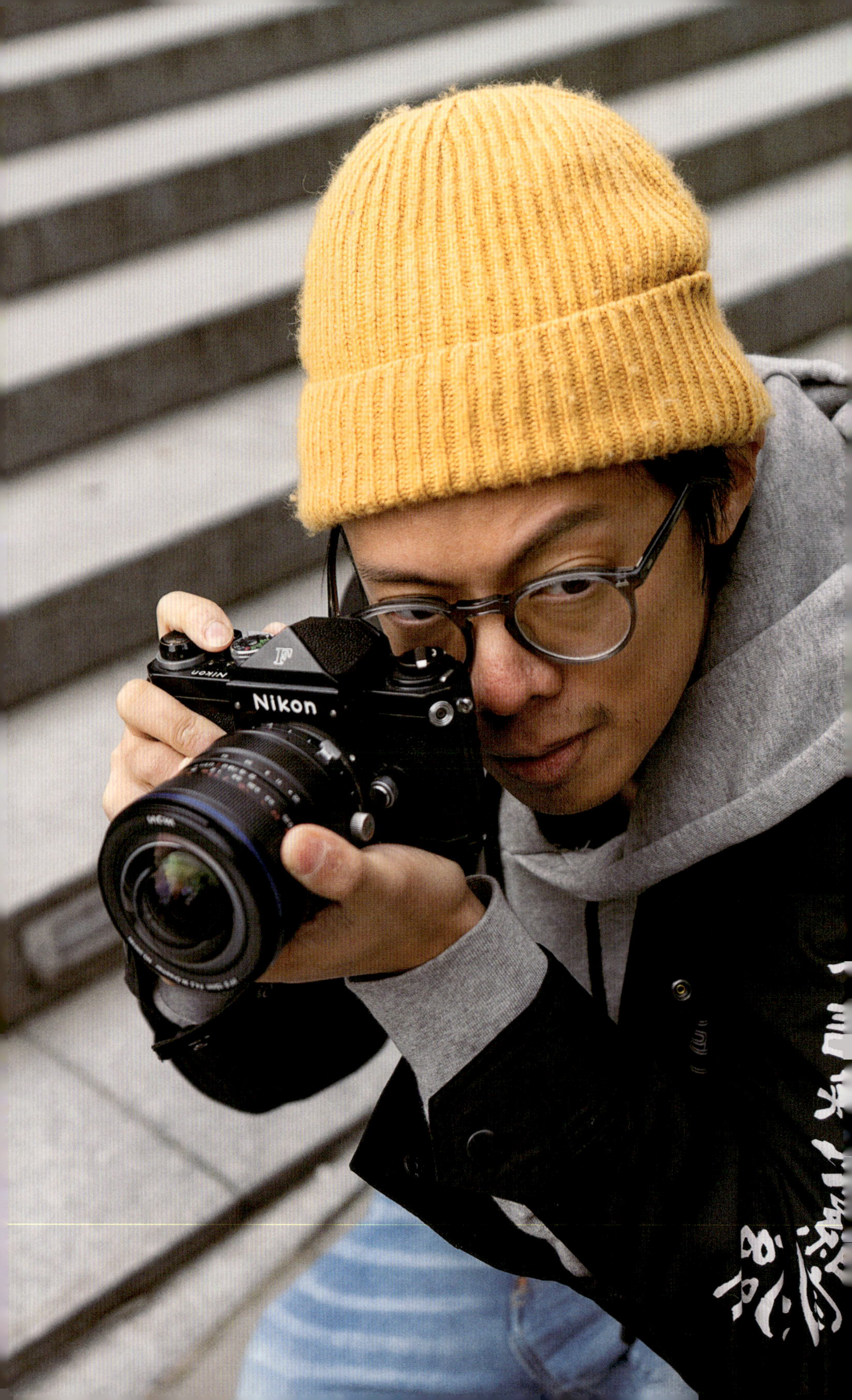
Nikon

#81 FOUR TIPS FOR ULTRAWIDE AWESOMENESS

Ultrawide angles are guaranteed to provide oodles of excitement (as much as you can get from a lens), what with their ability to suck in so much of those visual elements from viciously extreme angles. Small rooms can be made to look palatial with an ultrawide; it's a must-have for any property agent wanting to make a pokey little apartment look more appealing. For those of us who don't open doors for a living, it's the thrill of being able to pack a frame full of those intricate little visual elements.

Focal lengths wider than 18 mm are ultrawide, but I wouldn't recommend going any wider than 15 mm to start with because that wicked wideness will take some time to get used to. Fear not, though, because with these tips, you'll be mastering the UWAs in no time.

Get Close

The first thing you'll notice when you mount an ultrawide lens on your camera is that everything suddenly looks really far away, which is quite an awe-inspiring moment. You might be so smitten with getting so much more in the frame that you take the shot like that. The trouble with that, though, is that everything will be pushed so far away that any focal point seems so distant and detached. To keep the subject interesting, you need to get in close and fill more of the frame with the main focal point. The point of the ultrawide is that it will still suck in lots of the background, giving much more context to your subject.

Careful of the Wonky Lines

With a standard lens, lines and shapes will look normal—similar to what your own eyes see—but as you get to ultrawide territory, those lines will look like the wonkiest, wackiest lines you'll ever see without the use of hallucinogenic drugs. If you're thinking about using leading lines to attract the viewer's attention, an ultrawide is certainly going to make you look at those lines; that's for sure! Lines and shapes will end up elongated and exaggerated, but if you don't keep your camera completely level and/or have it tilted the wrong way, objects and lines will look unnaturally wonky.

Fill the Frame Carefully

An ultrawide-angle lens is like a visual vacuum—it's just going to suck in all manner of visual elements from crazy angles—which can make it an incredibly difficult task trying to keep out the visual detritus you don't want in your frame. Minimalist compositions are not going to be easy with ultrawides; you'll be better off with busier backgrounds. It's just that you need be extra careful to study what's in the frame so you don't realise after you've taken the shot that there was some random crap included that completely ruins the look of your image.

Forget About Focus

It can sound like hard work trying to get the best out of an ultrawide-angle lens, but at least one thing you don't have to worry about so much is focusing—because with such a wide angle, everything is in focus. If you're not using autofocus, the easiest way is to scale focus.

On the barrel of your lens is a scale of numbers in feet and metres that moves about as you move the focus ring. Adjacent to that is a load of aperture markings that have been doubled up to show the zone of focus. Refer to the aperture setting on the aperture dial, and then look at the two appropriate aperture numbers on the zone of focus markings. Anything in between those two numbers on the distance scale will be in focus. Set the focus, and boom! You're ready to go.

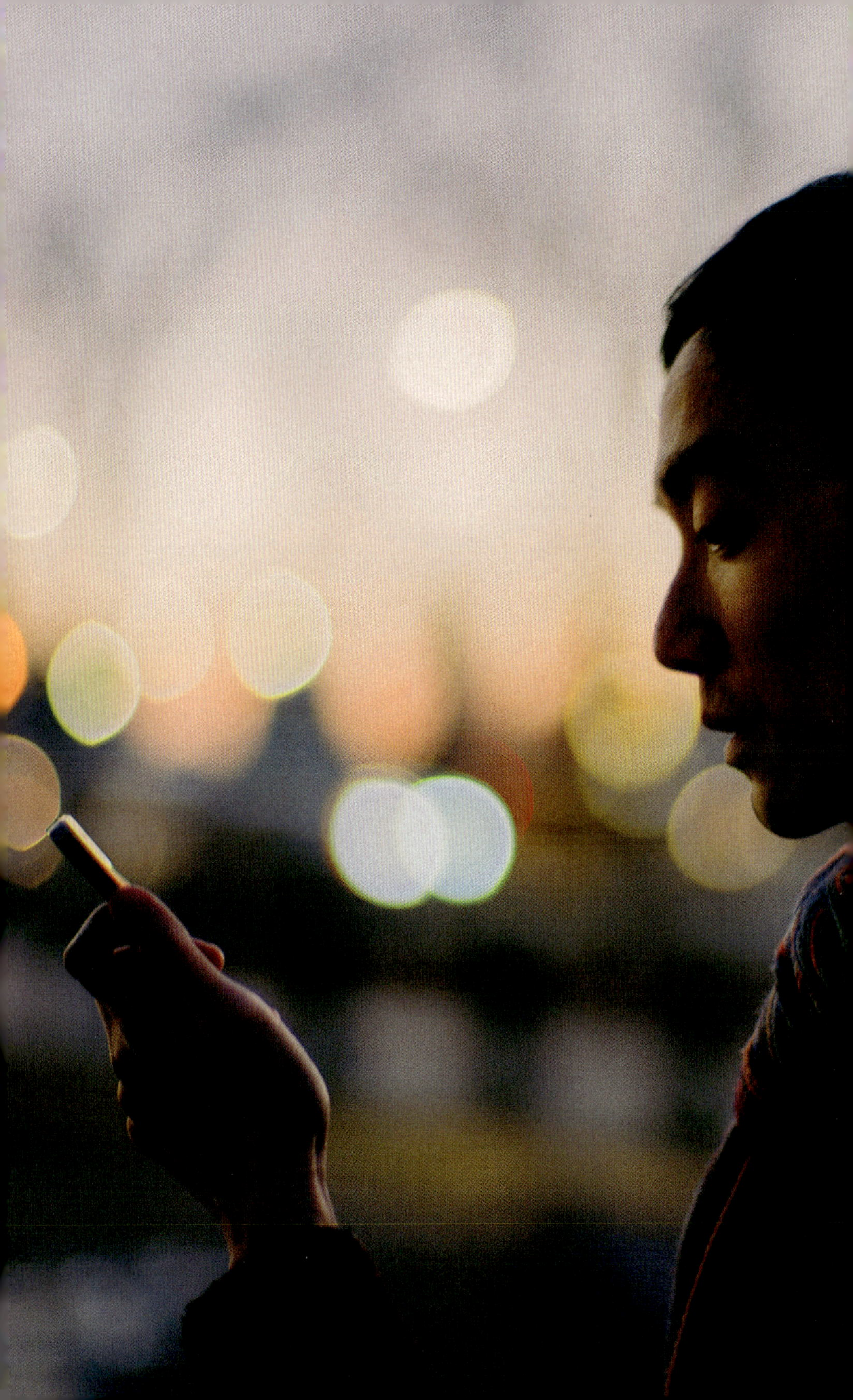

#82
HOW TO TAKE BOKEH-LICIOUS SHOTS

When you're taking a photo with shallow depth of field, throwing everything other than the subject out of focus, you're drawing attention straight to the subject. But despite the blurry bits seemingly only serving one single purpose in the image, it's just as important to get the bokeh bits right as it is the subject.

Getting good bokeh seems to be as easy as shelling out the money to buy the lens that produces the creamiest bokeh balls around. Having the right lens helps, but you'll need to put just a little more thought into it to make sure you're getting the best of your blurry backgrounds.

Study Those Backgrounds

An eye-tracking study by the University of Michigan found that, when presented with an image, participants from East Asia would focus more on the background and surroundings to figure out the context of the image, whereas the North American participants were more fixated on the main subject of the image.

Apparently, if you're American, that means you should probably look at the background more when composing a shot. Seriously though, putting the study aside, if you look at some of the shallow depth-of-field shots from photographers around the world, then I think we could conclude that photographers from all around the globe could do with looking at the background a little more when using larger apertures.

When a lens blurs a background so much, to the point where it becomes unrecognizable, it's easy to think that because it's already blurred by a lens that produces smooth-looking, out-of-focus elements, it won't be distracting anymore. But it can be.

Blurry Distraction

The trouble when you look through the viewfinder of an SLR, with the background already blurred, is that your eyes are more drawn to the subject, and it's kinda easy to overlook what's actually in the background. If you look at the scene with your naked eyes, what do you see? Are there trees in the background that look distracting? Does it look like there's a branch coming out of your subject's head? Are there lines and shapes that look distracting? If it's distracting when you look at it in focus, even with the most creamy, most bokeh-licious of lenses, it's still going to look distracting when blurred out.

A rangefinder let's you see everything as you would with your naked eye through the viewfinder, but I wouldn't recommend that you buy one just to be able to look at the backgrounds clearly (it does help, though). The cheapest, most-effective option is to just look at the scene with your own eyes before putting the viewfinder of the camera up to your eye.

More Layers for More Depth

Think about the different layers in the scene, too. If there is a large distance between background and subject, with hardly anything in between, the background is going to look incredibly disconnected from the subject. There's nothing wrong with that as such, if that's what you're aiming for, but finding some visual elements in between the subject and background will connect the subject to the background and add extra depth to the image.

As tempting as it is to use the largest aperture on your lens to get the shallowest depth of field possible, bear in mind that the blurry, bokeh-fied bits can get too overwhelming sometimes. Use the shallow DOF in moderation, whack it wide open when needed, but just make sure the blur complements the subject without taking the attention away—it's all about the balance.

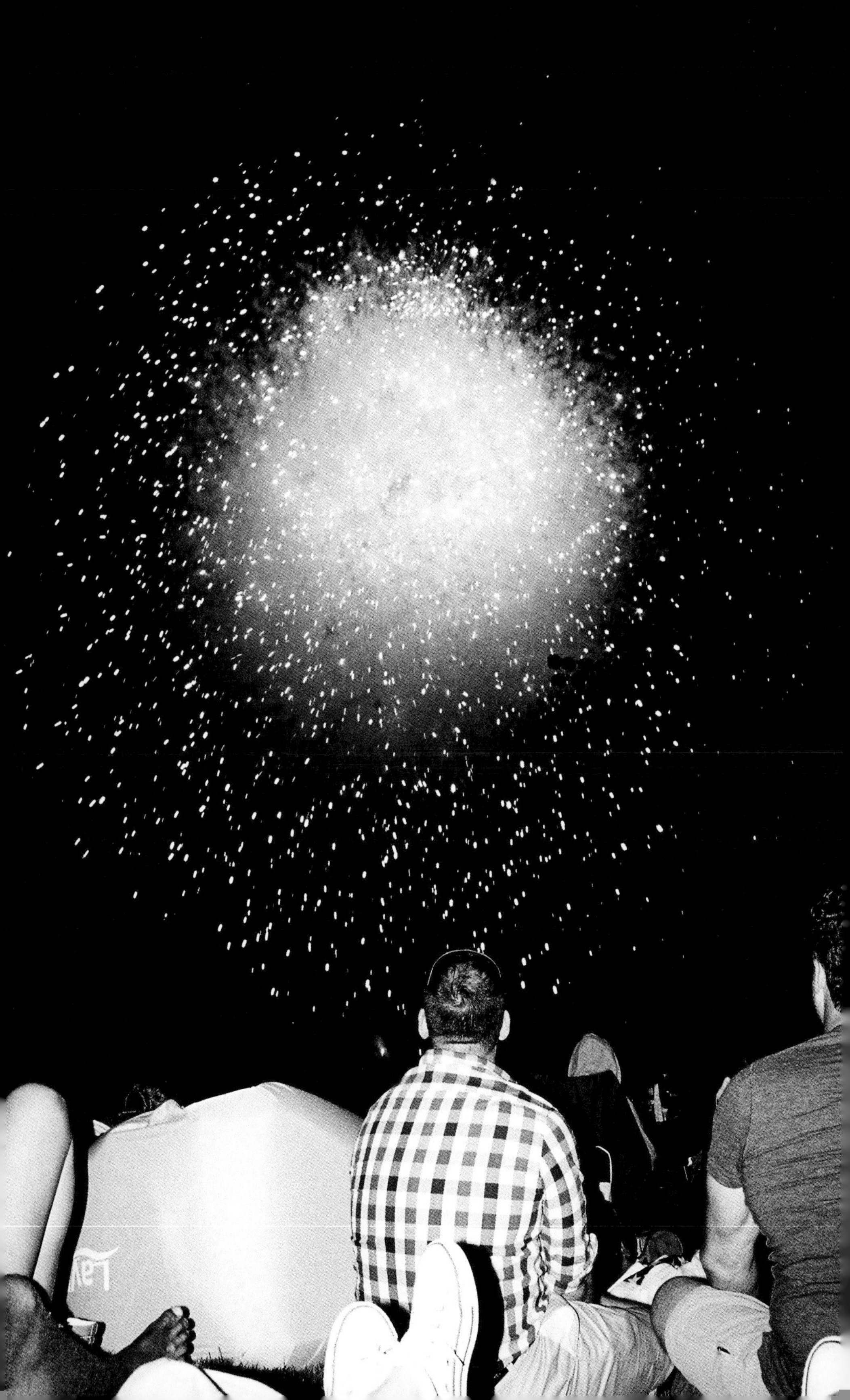

#83
ZOOM BURST FOR EXPLOSIVE EFFECT

Zoom bursts are a cheap and easy way of creating a bit of motion in your photo, even when nothing is moving in your shot. The movement comes from the zooming action (hence name), which creates streaky bits of light bursting out from the centre of the frame towards the edges, in a *Star Wars*-hyperdrive kinda way.

That makes it sound cool, but not all photographers feel that way, apparently, because it's one of the least commonly seen effects used in photography. Perhaps the biggest reason for this is that they can end up looking tacky as shit. But, you know, don't let that put you off, because if you can nail it, you'll end up with a pretty unique image.

Keep It Stable

As you'll need slower shutter speeds to make the effect more noticeable, a tripod is gonna come in handy. You still want part of your image to look still, even if it's surrounded by a load of crazy, blurry lines. A cable release is useful, but not necessary, to keep your shot looking super steady, because you're going to be twisting the zoom ring throughout the exposure anyway.

Daytime vs. Night

The effect at night is going to be in-your-face obvious, with all those artificial lights showing up like those *Star Wars* streaky things (I'm not a *Star Wars* fan). The look of a zoom-burst shot during daytime will look subtler, but that's because the scene will be more evenly lit than a nighttime shot.

During daytime, you'll need a shutter speed between 1/2s–3s, but that all depends on your film speed. I'd recommend packing some ND filters, which will help bring the exposure down to a nice, slow shutter speed.

At nighttime, you will need a longer exposure, but try to allocate half the exposure time for the zoom action; and for the rest of the time, don't move the zoom ring at all to make sure the focal point shows up nice and still on film.

Focal Point

You can get all fancy-pants and move the camera during the exposure, which is great if the subject is off-centre, but let's not get ahead of ourselves—get used to successfully racking that zoom ring through the exposure first.

Keep things simple with a clear and obvious focal point in the centre of frame. The *Star Wars* streaky things will act as a frame around the focal point, and it'll pretty much cover anything on the edges of the frame; so you don't really need to place too much interesting detail on the periphery of the image.

The subject is the deciding factor on whether a zoom-burst photo looks top or tacky; pick the wrong subject and your photo will look like a cheesy stock photo. There isn't any set formula, but you have to be extra careful with adding a bit of zoom burst to stationary objects. It might look too much like a gimmick used to make a weak shot look more edgy.

Although it's a still image, a zoom burst has the same feeling as zooming in on a subject in a video: the effect of bringing you closer to the subject—not just visually but in terms of wanting to see and understand more—even though it's just a still image. One thing you can try is to look through the viewfinder and zoom from wide to tele on your subject—does it make you more interested in the subject as you creep in through the zoom range? If it doesn't make you any more intrigued with the subject, it probably won't make for an interesting zoom-burst photo.

Lastly, don't overdo it. You don't need to go through the whole focal range to create the effect; the more you zoom, the more overwhelming those streaky things become.

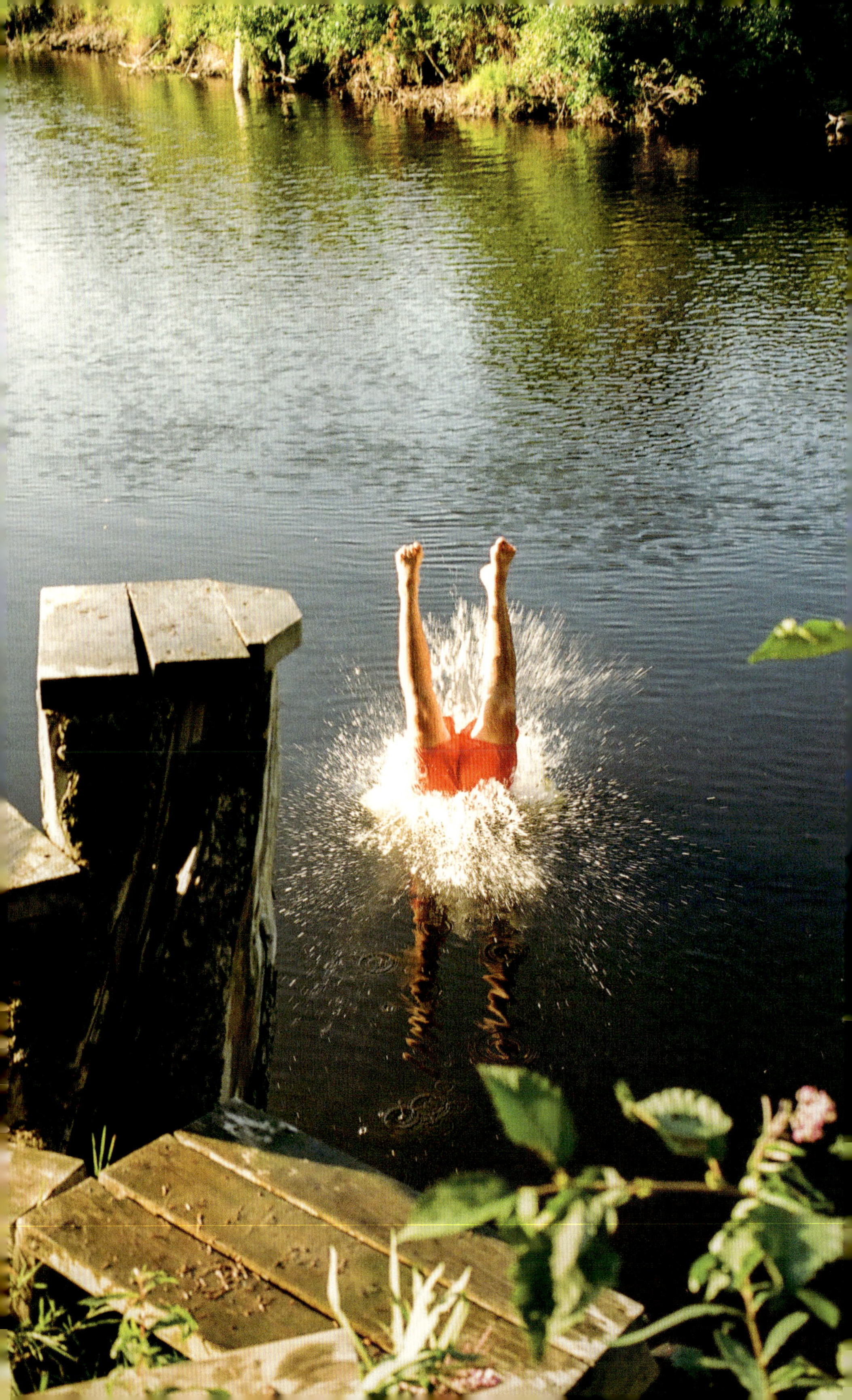

#84

MAKE MOVES TO MASTER MOTION

Mostly, using a fast-enough shutter speed is more preferable to capture a photo in perfectly fine, shake-free, sharp detail. However, there are times when you'll want to use a slower shutter speed to bring in a little bit of motion blur, which will give the sense of movement in an image that is otherwise still. Even then, you might not want to use motion blur on every type of moving subject.

Making Sports Look More Sporty

With motorsports, slower shutter speeds will bring your image to life; if you use a fast shutter speed on a moving car, they'll just end up looking like they're parked. You can only tell a car is moving if you see the wheels spinning or the background moving.

In contrast, you'll probably want to use a faster shutter speed for photos of people kicking a ball around. Anyone looking at the image can see that the subjects are in action: the ball, the tensed-up muscles, and the weird, sports-people grimaces will tell you that. So using a faster speed is preferable—1/200s to 1/1000s depending on the speed of the action—especially given that the subject's movements are less predictable than a car.

Panning: Going with the Flow

To make the cars look furiously fast, a bit of motion blur is needed. Forget the tripod and do everything handheld; you don't need to use very slow shutter speeds because the camera movement will create that blur quite easily. You will need to pan the camera with the movement of the car—pick a point in the viewfinder as a target to track the car. The shutter speed needed all depends on how fast the car is going: a shutter speed of 1/30s or 1/50s should be sufficient for a car coming into a corner but can increase if the car is pelting it along a straight. Use AF-C or AI Servo to make sure the focus follows the movement of the car. Don't bother with manual focus unless you want some arty blurred shots.

Making Moving Still Scenes

If you want to give your clouds some motion blur, you will want a really slow shutter speed because the movement isn't as obvious as a race car. I'd recommend using a tripod, cable release, and some ND filters to reduce the amount of light coming through the lens, so you can use a slower shutter speed (don't use too small of an aperture setting to keep things nice and sharp). The shutter speed you will need to use depends on how windy it is and how blurry you want those clouds. A speed of 1/10s might be enough for fast-moving clouds, but to get them looking super creamy you'll need a shutter speed that's several seconds long.

In summary, taking photos with motion blur with faster-moving subjects (or camera movement) requires a less slow shutter speed; a slower-moving subject requires a slower shutter speed. Experiment and get a feel of what shutter speed works for different types of movement. Using a slower-sensitivity film (ISO 100–400) will allow you to use a slower shutter speed; for freezing motion, a higher sensitivity film will allow you to get the faster shutter speed needed.

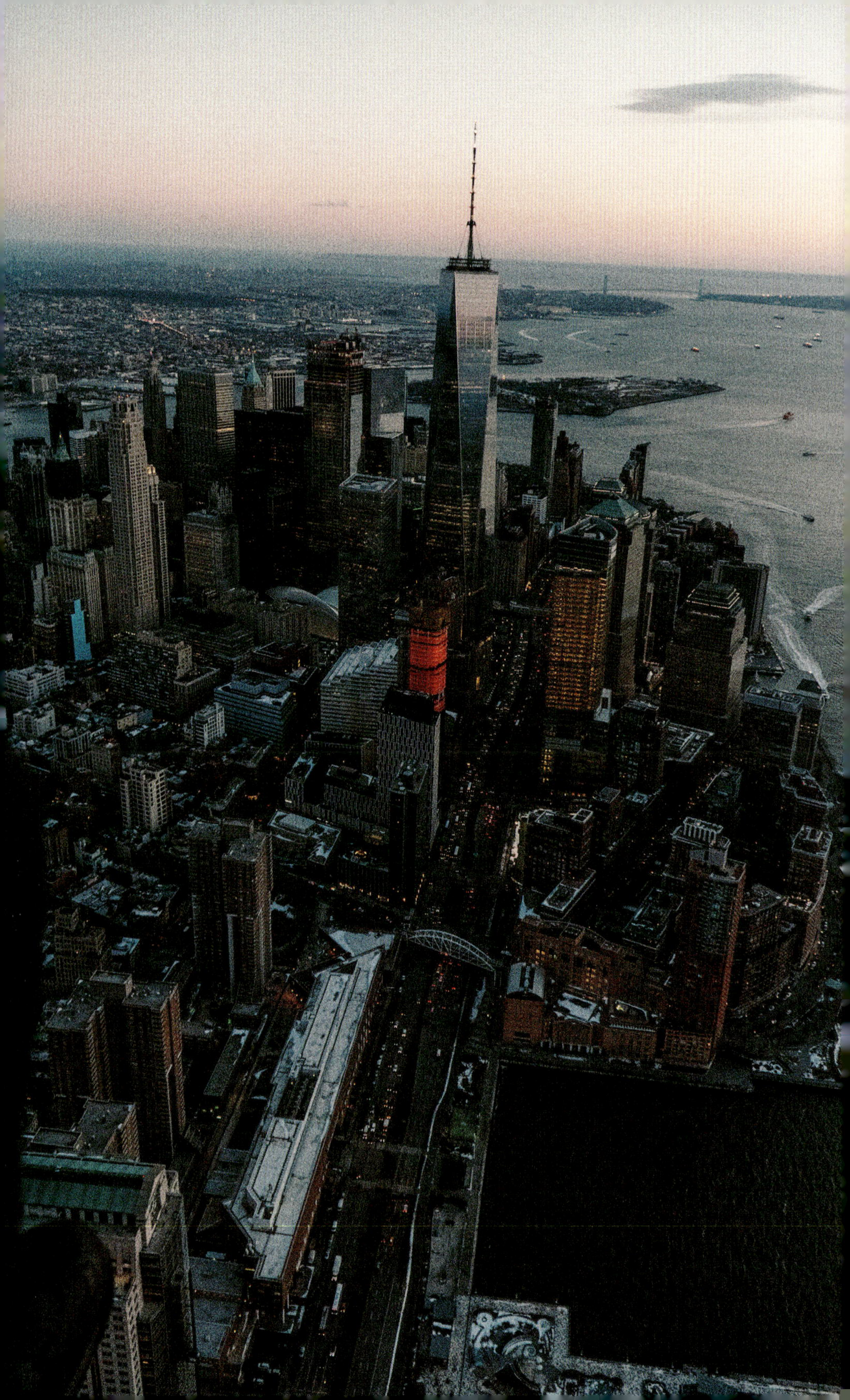

#85

FORGET GOLDEN HOUR WHEN YOU CAN HAVE BLUE HOUR

You've just bagged yourself a gorgeous golden-hour shot. The sun has finished playing peekaboo with the horizon and is heading down for the night, taking that resplendent, glowing light away with it, and you think that means home time for you. But don't pack away that camera yet because you're going to be greeted with the cool, blue tones of blue hour.

Three Things You Need to Know about Blue Hour

1. Like golden hour, blue hour is not necessarily one-hour long.
2. Blue hour happens before sunrise and after sunset, when the sun has dipped far enough below the horizon and all you're left with are bits of blue light.
3. As the sun is already way below the horizon, what light you have left is exquisitely soft.

Tips for Shooting Blue-Hour Photos

- Longer exposure times. As the sun has said sayonara already, there will be considerably less light coming through your lens. You could compensate with a larger aperture or a higher ISO, but I'd prefer to take along a tripod and use a slower shutter speed with a lower ISO film. People always rave on about golden hour, but I used to love shooting with Velvia 50 during blue hour, which would give the skies a wicked magenta cast with longer exposures.
- Be prepared and have everything in place for blue hour, because once it starts, it could be done and dusted in as little as twenty minutes.
- Look out for nice, clear-ish skies, as they can look astonishing at the start of blue hour; the remaining indirect light coming from the sun below the horizon will leave a strip of red, transitioning to orange, orangey-pink, and then the soft blue hues of that definitive blue hour.
- Blue-hour light isn't strong enough for lighting up subjects as wonderfully as golden hour, and your subjects might just end up so dark they become silhouettes. The best way is to just embrace it. You could just try overexposing colour-negative film a little, but it's still going to look all moody and stuff, and in my opinion, is what is so great about blue hour.
- Reciprocity Law Failure. Sounds like some legal terminology, but it's to do with how shooting longer exposures will result in the film becoming less sensitive to light. There might be some freaky colour shifts, too (the Velvia magenta cast). For shooting Velvia 50, I adjusted the exposure times to the following:

  4 sec. —> 5 sec.

  16 sec. —> 28 sec.

  32 sec. —> 1 min., 6 sec.

  1 min. —> 2.5 min.
- Look for artificial light. Blue hour is great for taking photos of cities; the blue look contrasts so delightfully with the orangey, sodium glow from the street lights.
- If you want to try something a little different to golden hour, I would thoroughly recommend blue hour. It's beautifully moody and it happens right after golden hour, so you can try it immediately after you've finished taking golden-hour shots!

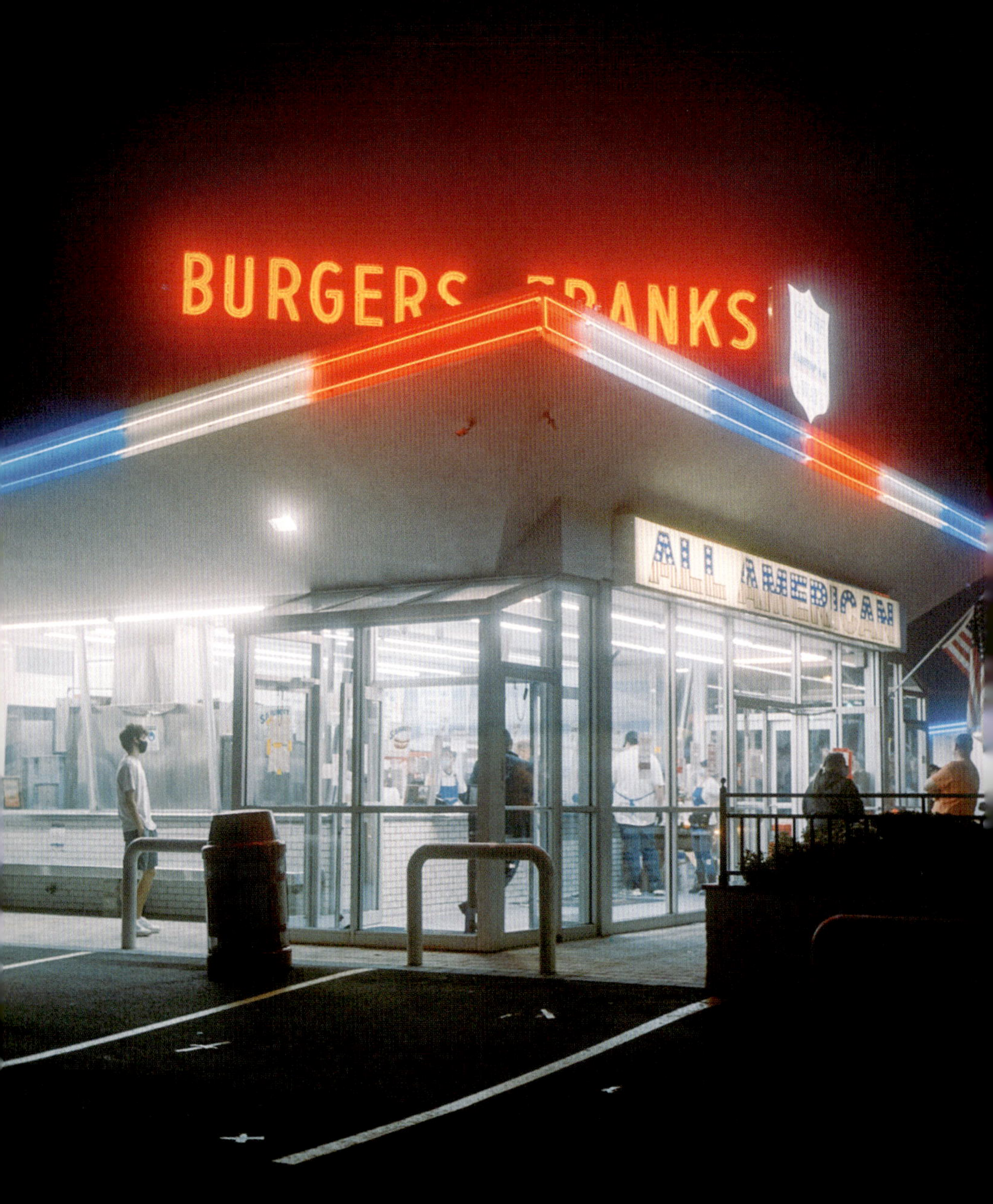
BURGERS
ALL AMERICAN

#86 A SHORT GUIDE TO LONG EXPOSURES

Long exposures take a long time. A short guide will give you more time to take more long exposures, so here we go:

Tripods Are Essential (and a Cable Release, Too)

Long exposures will show up any cheap, flimsy tripods. With exposure times that could take minutes or even hours, you better make sure the tripod isn't the weakest link in your setup. Sturdy doesn't necessarily mean heavy. If your three-legged friend has a hook coming out from its centre column (that sentence sounds wrong), hang your bag off of it (not sounding any better) to weigh it down.

You'll need a cable release, obviously. A locking mechanism to lock the shutter-release button in place is useful for when you're using Bulb mode (for exposures longer than 30 sec.), because otherwise you will need to hold that button down for the duration of the exposure, and I wouldn't wish that experience on anyone.

Low ISO Film

A low-ISO film is thoroughly recommended—the camera's on a tripod anyway, so no need to worry about camera shake— to keep the grain fine and the results looking mighty fine. If you're using slide film like Velvia, check out the bit about Reciprocity Law Failure in #85, otherwise your photo might end up underexposed.

ND Filters

Longer exposures can create some stunning dramatic looks, with wispy, candy-floss skies and creamy-licious looking water, but to make that happen you'll definitely need to own some ND filters. Something like the Lee Filters Big Stopper (props to whoever came up with this name) 10-stop filter will block out a lot of light, effectively turning daylight into night. If you want to take distinctive-looking long exposures, get a Big Stopper. The sensible option would be to get a lighter ND filter for versatility (you can't use a 10-stop for everything), or perhaps you could just get both. You can even stack them on top of each other for even longer exposures.

Take a Torch

Probably the most useful tool for photography isn't actually a tool for photography. A torch comes in handy when you're taking long exposures at night, to see what you're doing—you don't want to twiddle the wrong knob. You can also shine a light on your subject temporarily to see it more clearly through the viewfinder, to make sure it's in focus.

They can also be used creatively for painting with light or light painting. Although they sound the same, and some people mix the terms up, there is a difference:

Light Painting

With light painting, you're taking a long exposure shot and using the torch to illuminate a subject that doesn't have a strong-enough light source lighting it up. This is something you can try in a blue-hour shot or at night, when there are elements in the foreground that would just end up silhouetted due to the lack of light. All you need to do is open the shutter, and then use the touch light to paint over the object, bit by bit, as evenly as possible, before the shutter closes.

Painting with Light

This method makes use of the torch again, but instead of shining the light from behind the camera, the person holding the torch stands in front of the camera, shining the light at the lens. While the shutter is open, you use the torch to draw some shapes—it's like using sparklers to make shapes in the dark—or write your name. You could always try attaching the torch to a piece of string and swinging it around like a mentalist to create perfectly circular shapes. Just make sure it's attached to the string, otherwise you'll have to pack up and make your way home in the dark.

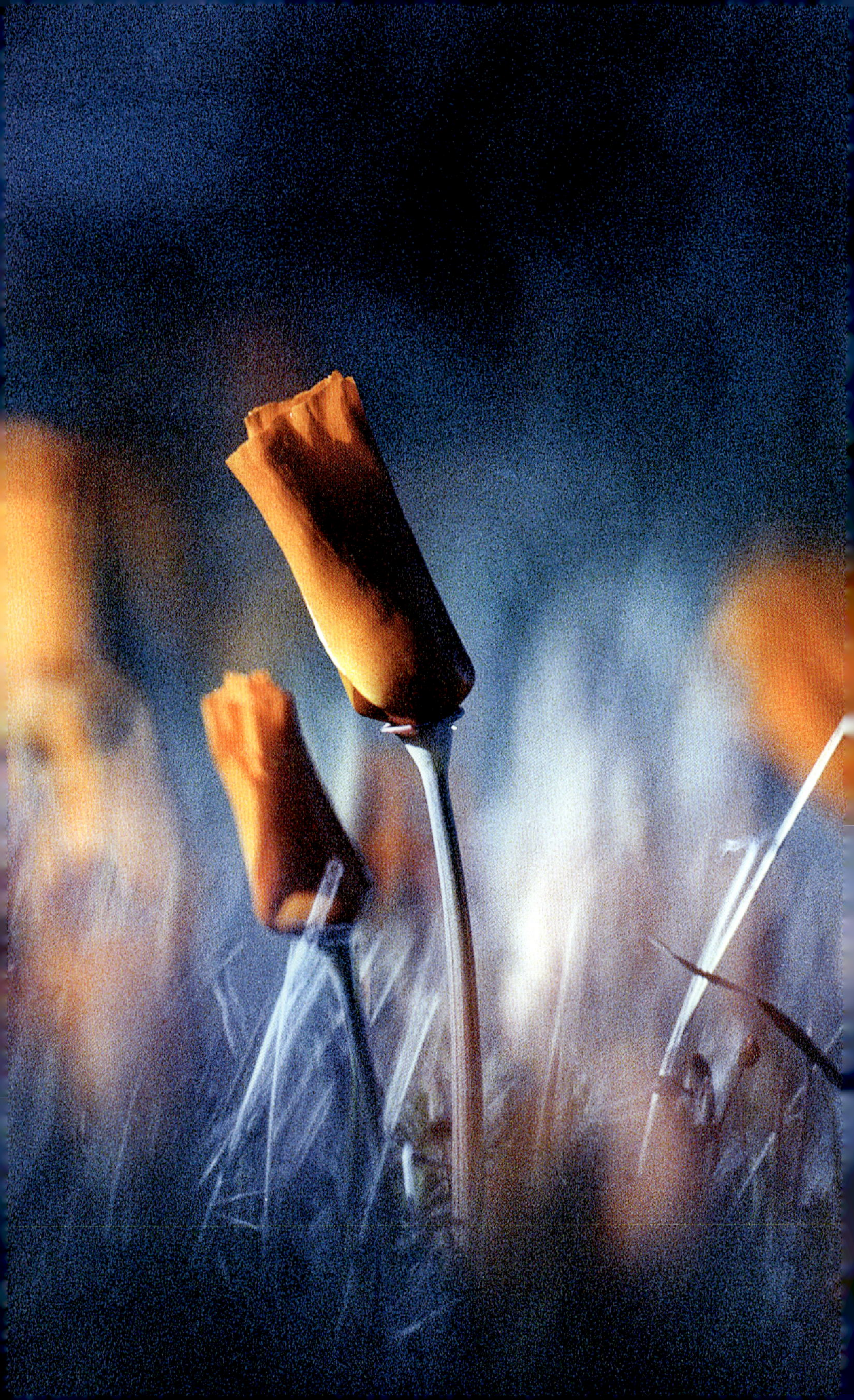

#87 GET CLOSE UP WITH MACRO

Macro photography isn't all about disgustingly detailed close-up images of insects. It's about arachnids, too. Seriously though, macro photography does get a reputation for being all about close-ups of creepy-crawlies, but there is a lot more that can be done with a macro lens. With the ability to get so much closer to a subject than one of your regular lenses, it's great for rendering all manner of different textures in super-fine crisp-o-vision.

Taking macro photos does require lots of patience, a bit of creative vision, and one macro lens. When you're shopping for one, there are two key things you need to consider:

Magnification

The first bit of info you need to know about any macro lens you're considering buying is how much it will magnify a subject.

A lens that allows you to shoot with a 1:2 magnification will magnify a subject to half its real size. In other words, if you're photographing a 10 mm long insect, it will appear 5 mm long, and will take up just 5 mm of a 35 mm film frame. In my opinion, a lens that has a maximum magnification of only 1:2 is not enough for anyone looking for some serious macro action.

Good macro detail starts at a 1:1 magnification ratio, rendering your creepy-crawly subject in life size. A 10 mm long insect will appear 10 mm long, and will take up that much space on your film. It will appear bigger in your frame, letting you see properly close-up on your diminutive little subjects.

Things start to get gross at 2:1. Twice as gross. The 10 mm insect will look twice the size it does in real life, filling a significant portion of that film frame.

Working Distance

This little bit of info may or may not be particularly useful information to know; it all depends on what you're taking photos of. The working distance (who comes up with these terms?) is the distance between the front of the lens and the subject, whereas the minimum-focus distance of a lens takes the distance from film to subject. Macro photographers need to know what the working distance of a lens is at its minimum-focus distance, because if their lens end gets close to the subject, it might scare them off. Of course, if you're into photographing oranges, then you won't need to worry too much about working distance.

What Film

Macro is all about the detail so you'll want minimum grain to make sure it's crisper than freshly deep-fried katsu. You can either go for the super-saturated look, in which case a slide film like Velvia 100 will provide some properly pumped colours, or alternatively, Kodak Ektar 100 is a super-punchy colour-negative film. If you want something a little more natural, Kodak Portra 160 is always guaranteed to deliver the goods, or if you want to use slides, Fujifilm's Provia 100F will look gorgeous with going OTT with the colours.

DOF

The closer you get to the subject, the thinner the depth of field gets. If you're photographing at the largest aperture setting on the lens, most of your little friends are going to be bokeh-fied. Only a tiny part of their bodies will be in focus, made more apparent if their bodies are not parallel to the film. The quick fix is to either position the insect (or whatever the hell it is) as parallel to the film plane as possible, and/or to make the aperture smaller to get deeper depth of field.

With a low-ISO film, you can't set the aperture too low, otherwise you'll end up with a stupidly slow shutter speed that will make your macro shots all blurry, and the little insect-y subject would've buggered off halfway through the exposure. You could use a flash to make sure the subject is well-lit (it will probably blind them)—a macro-ring flash is the best way to ensure it's evenly-lit—or just take photos outside on a sunny day. Just be careful where the light is coming from and where your camera is positioned, because with the lens being so close to the subject, it can quite easily cast a shadow over it.

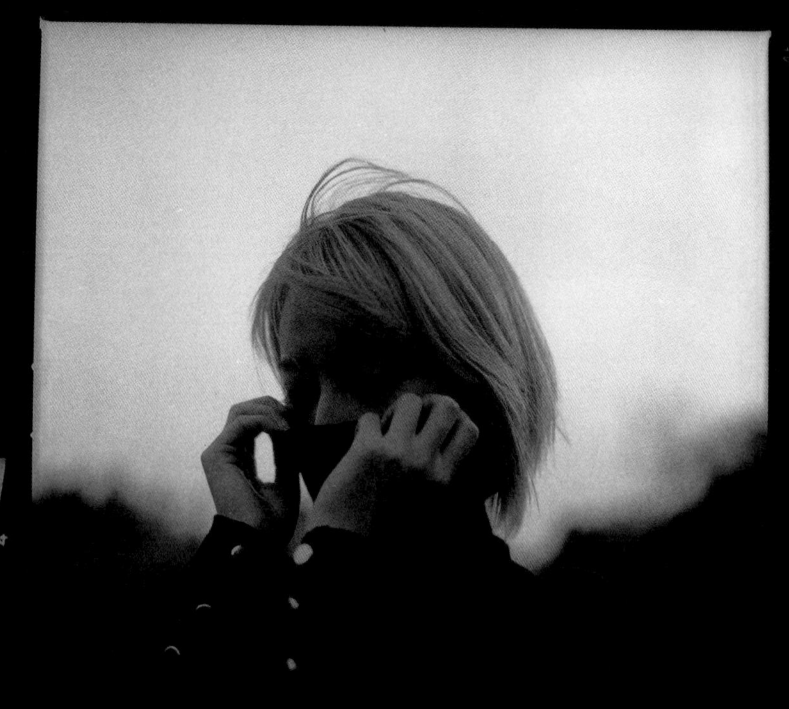

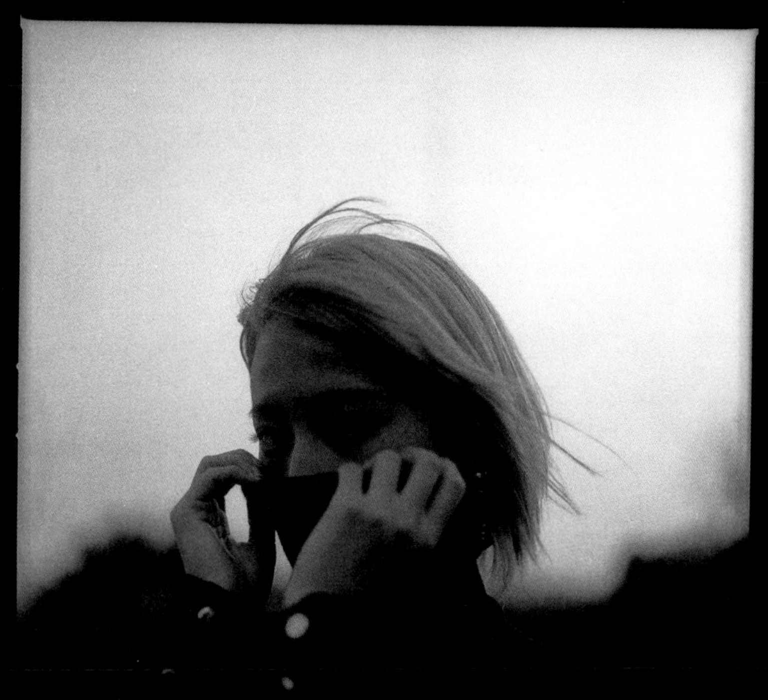

#88 QUICK START TO SHOOTING PORTRAITS

A portrait is not made in the camera but on either side of it.

—Edward Steichen

Portraits look easy—seemingly easier when the person being photographed is easy on the eye—but there is a lot more to portrait photography than just snapping pretty-looking people.

Be Human

Most people have social skills, even hardcore photo nerds. But something strange happens to some people when they peer through the little peephole of a viewfinder to look at a human subject—they just completely ignore the person right in front of them. If there is no communication, no direction, everyone is winging it through the photoshoot.

Have an idea of what photos you want before the day of the photoshoot—know your model, pick the right location, and think about poses and styles—to make sure you understand how to direct the shoot. When you meet the model, just have a regular conversation with them; the shoot will always run smoother when everyone is feeling relaxed.

When you brief the model, give them some visual examples of the look you're after. During the shoot, give clear explanations with your directions. If you need them to turn their head to catch the light in the right way, tell them exactly that; it'll keep the model motivated to be doing something for a purpose rather than just being told to move their head.

The Lens: Obvious Isn't Always Best

The most obvious lens to use for a portrait photo is a telelens—try an 85 mm—because it's flattering on faces, and it will also create more subject isolation with that compressed perspective and shallow depth of field. It is the obvious way to go, but not the only way to go.

Using a wider lens is great for making the background a more prominent part of the image. With a wide-angle, the backgrounds will be clearer than the ones shot on a telelens, which will help to give more context to your subject. If the background is interesting, then it seems a waste to use a telelens to turn that background into a big, blurry mess.

If you're going the way of wide, just be careful with anything wider than 35 mm because the lens will start to exaggerate the size of things in the frame, especially when they are put closer to the frame. Probably the widest you should go is 24 mm, but unless you want to make your subject look like a long-armed, big-nosed freak, then you shouldn't poke the lens too close to the subject, and keep most of their body as parallel to the camera as possible.

It's All About The Eyes

Focus on the eyes is important because that's what everyone looks at first in a portrait photo, so you want to check the focus on the eyes. But don't just think about the eyes without thinking if the other parts of the face are in focus. It's an odd look if the eyes are tack sharp, and the nose is all blurry, so check that your aperture setting is going to give you enough depth of field.

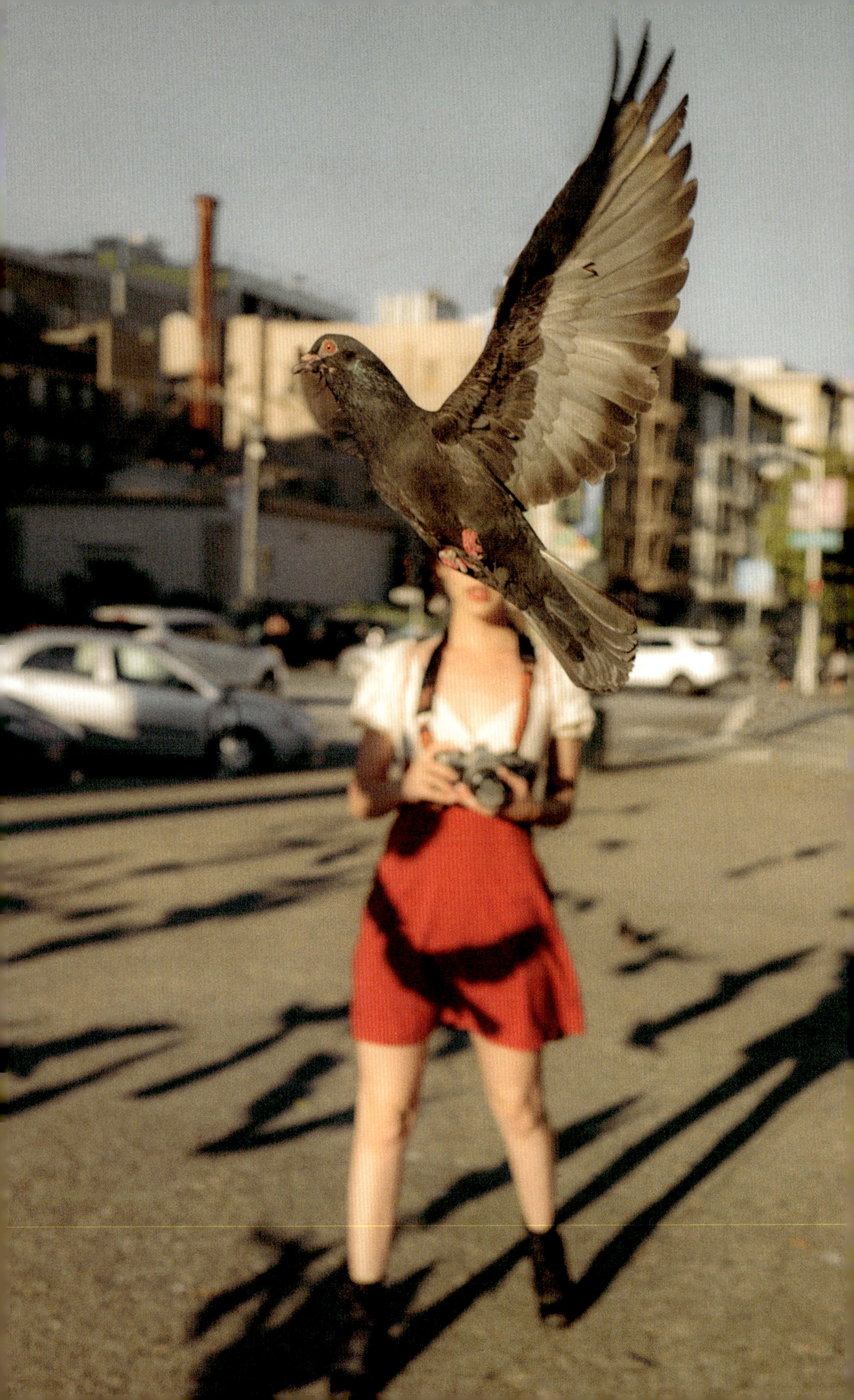

#89 NAILING THE DECISIVE MOMENT

There is a creative fraction of a second when you are taking a picture. Your eye must see a composition or an expression that life itself offers you, and you must know with intuition when to click the camera. That is the moment the photographer is creative. Oop! The Moment! Once you miss it, it is gone forever.

—Henri Cartier-Bresson

The Decisive Moment was the name of Henri Cartier-Bresson's first book: one of the most influential photo books of the twentieth century that has inspired many a modern street photographer to ingrain the ethos of capturing the decisive moment into their style of shooting.

Although the title for the French edition of Cartier-Bresson's book was *Images à la Sauvette*, which roughly translates to *Images on the Run* (according to Google translate) and kinda makes it sound like a photo book made by a fugitive, the decisive moment is one of the first things mentioned in the preface of the book:

There is nothing in this world without a decisive moment.

—Cardinal Retz

Cartier-Bresson is often wrongly attributed to this quote, but in the preface he does articulate the importance of the decisive moment in photography: "To me, photography is the simultaneous recognition, in a fraction of a second, of the significance of an event as well as of a precise organization of forms which give that event its proper expression." In other words, to take a bad-ass photo, you need to recognise when to press that button. And here's how you figure it out:

Pre-Visualise

People are quite predictable. If you start looking at a street scene, there's a pace and rhythm to it; people have things to do, places to get to, and by putting yourself right in the thick of all the action, you soon get a sense of what might happen next. Then it's a matter of putting yourself in the right place to raise your camera when the elements fall into place.

Be Prepared

The last thing you want getting in the way of capturing a fleeting moment is the gear. You can't always rely on the gear to do the clever bits quick enough, so you have to be smart about it. Giving yourself enough depth of field with a smaller aperture will make the concern about nailing focus a nonissue. Make sure you've metered and you know the exposure settings already, and ensure the film is already advanced and ready for you to press the shutter button. You could always just use an automatic camera, too.

Be Patient

There are times when you have the perfect scene, just not the subject in the right place to make it the photo you have in your mind. Spend some time to hang in there, make sure your camera is prepared and ready to shoot, because when it happens, and you're not ready, you'll rue the missed opportunity.

More Is More

Don't be afraid to take more than one shot to give you a number of options to choose from. The decisive moment doesn't just come with one single shot—take many moments, and pick the most decisive one later.

Even when you're trying to nail that decisive moment in other genres of photography, it's all about gaining experience and familiarising yourself with the subjects and the surroundings. When you understand them more, it becomes easier to pre-visualise the shot, so you can be in place to make sure you're ready to press that shutter button at the right time.

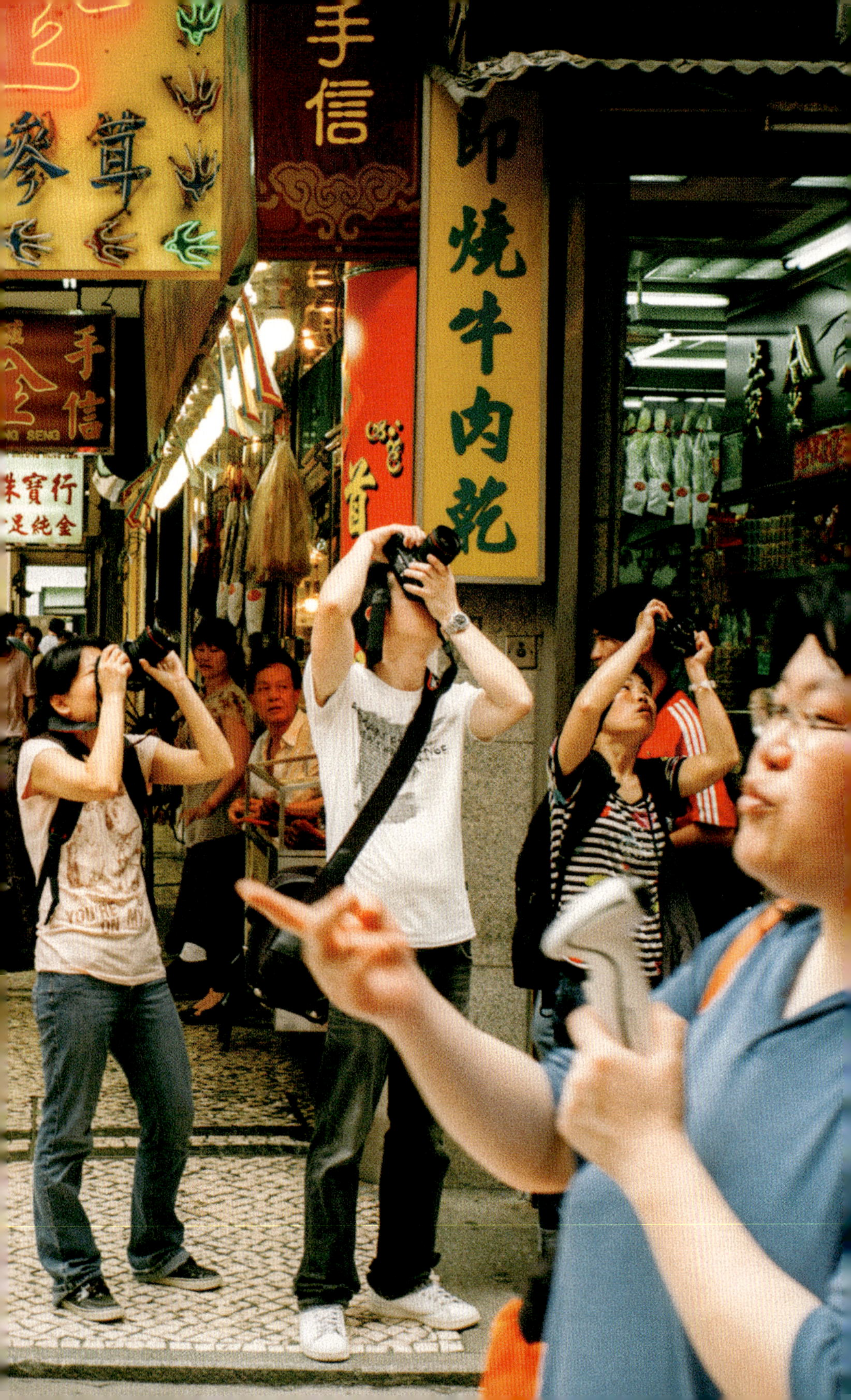
手信
即燒牛肉乾
手信

#90 MISTAKES PHOTOGRAPHERS MAKE

The biggest mistake a new photographer could make is to dwell on their mistakes. The next big mistake is thinking that they are mistakes; a real mistake is when a pro photographer messes up. For a beginner, it's all part of the learning process—they're just blips on an otherwise upward trajectory—experiences that should spur you on to make sure everything runs smoothly the next time.

There are a number of problems beginner photographers encounter—these are the most common technical blips (and how to fix them):

Photos Look Soft and Blurry

There's a difference between an image that is a little soft and one that is softer than newborn baby poo. A little lack of sharpness won't ruin every shot, but if it's prominent enough to make it a problem for you, then these are your most likely causes:

- Shutter speed is too slow. Add '1/' in front of your focal length, e.g., 50 mm = 1/50s shutter speed—that should be a guide for the slowest shutter speed you should use if you want shake-free, handheld shots. Ideally, I would double that to be doubly sure of ridding those images of shakes. If you're using Aperture Priority mode, the camera might be choosing too slow a shutter speed.
- Out of focus. If it's not the shutter speed that is too slow, it's most likely that it's not in focus. If it's an autofocus camera, make sure you get AF confirmation before pressing all the way on the shutter button. If you're manual focusing, spend some time at home to focus on things that aren't moving to get used to seeing what in-focus looks like on your focusing screen.
- Depth of field is too shallow. Shooting wide open, at the largest aperture, will make the depth of field so shallow on a subject close to you that moving just a couple of centimetres could end up putting your subject completely out of focus. Also, lenses tend to produce softer images at their largest (and smallest) apertures.

Too Dark/Too Bright

Too dark or too bright can make an image lack that fizz. The most obvious cause is that you're not getting enough light or too much light. If you've got a light meter, then these might be what is at the root of the problem:

- Metering mode not working for you. As mentioned in #26, there are different metering modes. If you're getting bad exposures, try using a spot meter and get the light meter reading from your subject. Spot metering will make it easy to get the correct exposure on your subject, and will make you understand the different levels of brightness across the scene.
- Wrong ISO setting. Some cameras require setting the ISO on the camera after you've loaded the film in; this allows the light meter to give an accurate meter reading based on the sensitivity of your film. If you've set it wrong, the exposure will be way off.

There are also creative blips, which can be impossible to remedy, because what someone might think is a major problem might seem like a nonissue to others.

Photo Too Boring

Whenever someone complains about the creative aspects of their image, essentially what they're saying is that their photo is too boring.

Boring is subjective—what is a boring photo? Is your image too flat? Is the balance of the image all wrong? Is the subject boring? The only person that can figure that out is the person that finds it boring.

The simplest thing to do is to look at super images and think about what you like about them. The best, most-constructive way to improve your photos is to understand what makes an interesting photo interesting, rather than what makes a boring photo boring.

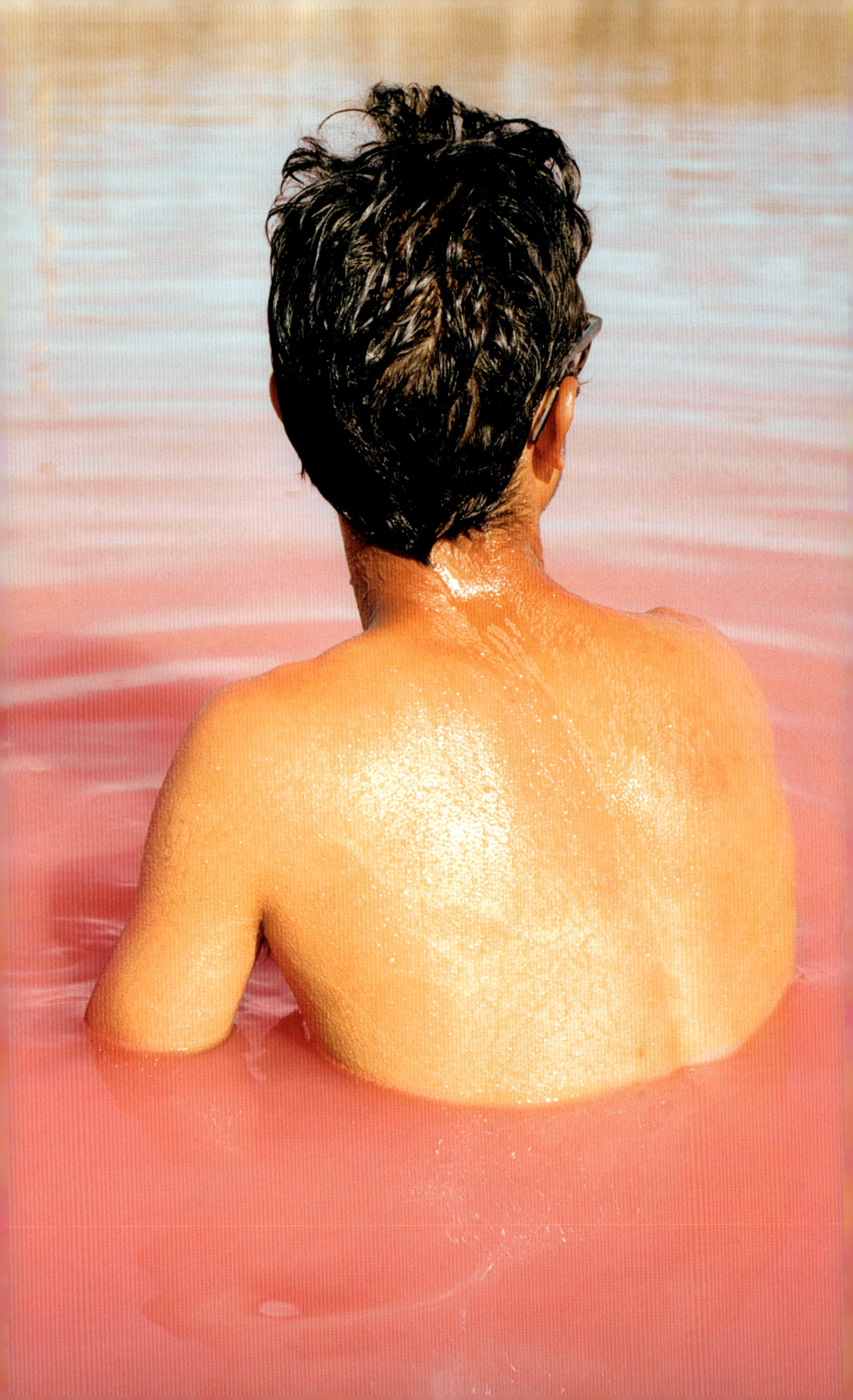

#91
SLOW DOWN YOUR PROCESS

We must avoid, however, snapping away, shooting quickly and without thought, overloading ourselves with unnecessary images that clutter our memory and diminish the clarity of the whole.

—Henri Cartier-Bresson

By choosing to shoot film, you've already decided on different. If you wanted fast and convenient, you would've bought yourself a regular, bog-standard digital camera. Modern cameras are designed to make the process as pain-free as possible—my son knew how to take photos with a Canon 5D Mark IV when he was two years old!

To master film photography you have to embrace the pace, or rather the slow pace. Shooting the spray-and-pray way might work with digital, but try that out with film and you'll just end up disappointed and out of pocket. Not knowing what you'll get will drive you to be more thoughtful about the way you take photos.

Back in university, I could've opted for an existence of living on saltine crackers and licking bar tables to get my kicks on nights out to be able to afford a DSLR, but I am glad that I started learning with a simple, manual 35 mm film SLR.

The combination of not being able to preview photos immediately and having to adjust both the aperture- and shutter-speed dials to make the correct exposure forced me to slow the process down, to think about everything carefully before committing to taking a shot.

If you just take your time to look at your surroundings, to study everything in detail, to look at what the light looks like, and to walk around to search for interesting things to take photos of, before you even get to raising the camera to your eye, you get to realise that taking good photos requires so much more than just what you do with your camera.

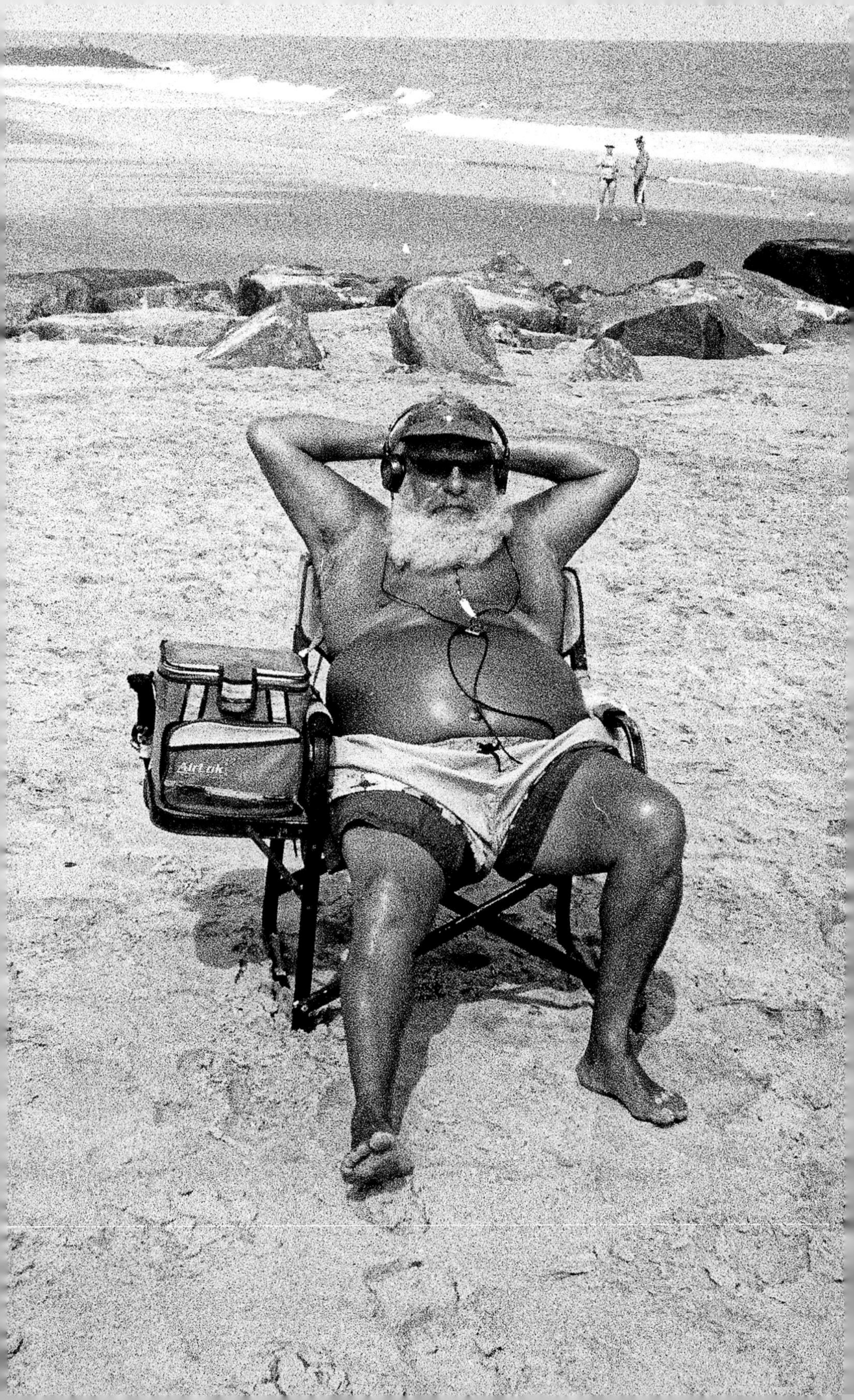

#92 IT'S NOT OVER UNTIL YOU BAG IT UP

Don't pack up your camera until you've left the location.

—Joe McNally

You've learnt a number of the rules in photography, but one thing you should definitely be made aware of is Murphy's Law: you think you've finished taking photos for the day, so you pack your camera back in your bag, only to have the most magical coming together of visual elements happening right there before your very own eyes. But you can't do anything about it because your camera is in your bag already. It's a feeling akin to being really hungry and having a load of burger-munching people parading in front of you, wafting smells of juicy, bovine goodness in your face (apologies if you're vegan).

A camera bag is supposed to carry your camera. Most of the time, my camera bag has a camera-shaped space where the camera is supposed to go. I will turn up to a shoot with my main camera in hand, with a standard lens attached—no lens cap on—and I rest my thumb on the film-advance lever and index finger on the shutter button, always ready for the unexpected. When I've finished taking photos for the day, I'll keep the camera slung on my shoulder, not looking to take photos but with the camera out; I'm ready for any eventuality (hopefully not getting mugged).

Photos don't hang around to wait for you to open up your camera bag and get everything ready. Never stop searching for things of visual interest; have a hawk-like vision for a good photo opportunity and be prepared to pounce.

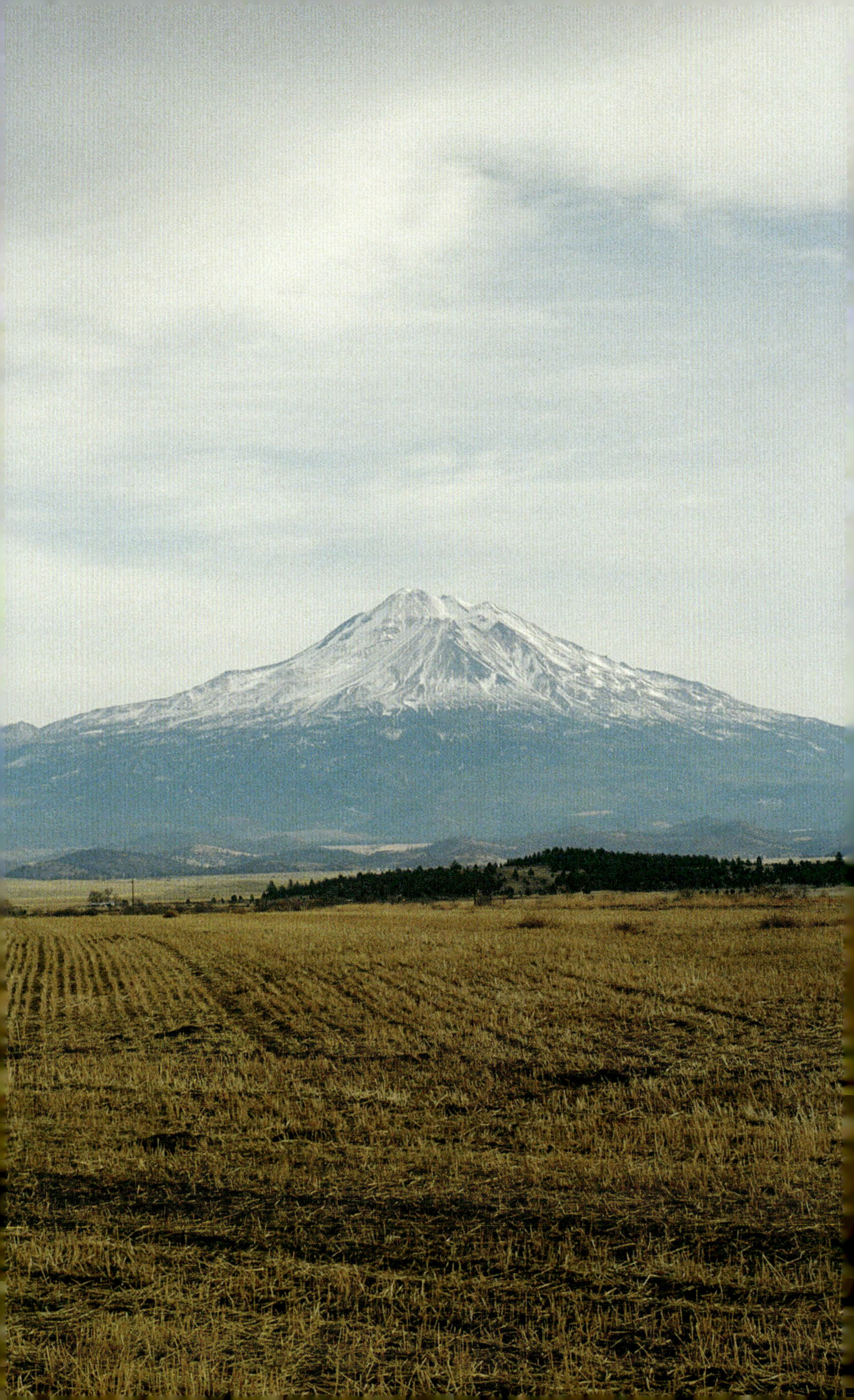

#93
TAKE YOUR CAMERA EVERYWHERE

Alright, you won't be able to take your camera everywhere. If your camera is a hefty, large-format camera, or the everywhere happens to be a doctor's appointment to get that strange itch looked at, then you're probably best leaving the camera at home. Still, as you're pumped and ready to get out there to start taking film photos, it would work to your advantage to carry your camera around with you as often as possible.

As important as it is to plan, pack, and prepare for taking those epic photos, it won't always be the case that you have a clear vision of where you want to go to take photos or even what subjects you want to see. For a new photographer, carrying a camera around with you as often as possible will give you the motivating force to actively seek things to photograph; and by taking lots of photos of a wide variety of things, you'll start getting an idea of what you actually like taking photos of.

Ever since taking up photography, I've tried as much as possible to carry a camera around with me. Whether I could be arsed to take a camera out with me or not depended greatly on the size and weight of the camera. Some people might enjoy taking a camera that weighs as much as an iron out with them all the time, but I'm not one for inflicting pain on myself unless there's a clear benefit.

The Ricoh GR is my carry-everywhere camera. It packs in a side pocket of a bag or even in the back pocket of my jeans, it's not a pain in the ass to carry around (unless I sit down with it in my back pocket), and it takes sharp photos. I mostly use it to take photos of my kids running around, sometimes for street photography, and all the time when I go travelling.

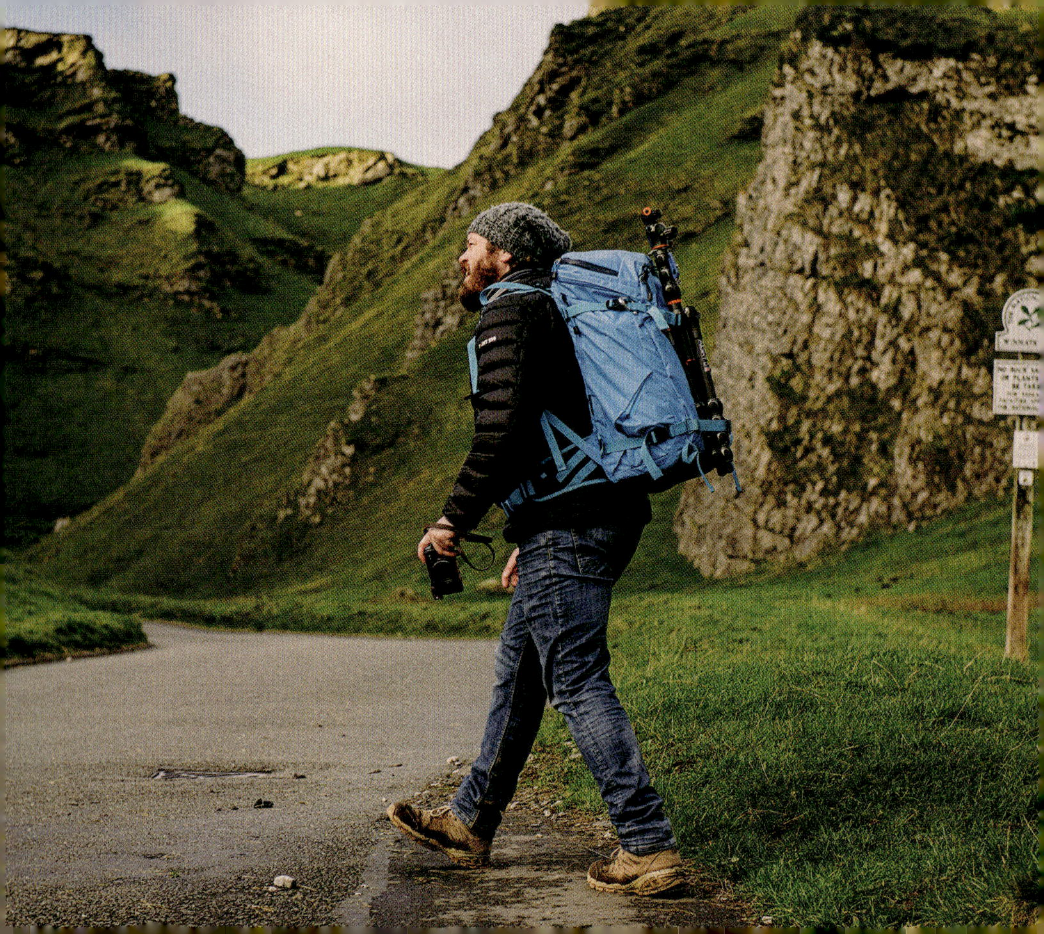

#94

BUY FLIGHT TICKETS, NOT GEAR

Whenever I'm preparing for a holiday, the thing that I put the most thought into packing is my camera gear; everything else is a bit of an afterthought (thankfully, I've never forgotten my passport or the kids, yet). If there's anything that's better than photography itself, it's the combination of travel and photography—the pair are a match made in heaven.

If you want to give yourself a little photographic treat, reconsider using the money that would've been spunked on a brand-spanking-new lens for travel instead. The initial excitement of buying a new bit of glass will wear off after a week or so, but the good times and happy travelling vibes, along with the photos to remind you of them, will last a lifetime.

Putting aside the notion of a fantastic photo as being one that is exposed perfectly and having composition that fits perfectly within the rule of thirds grid, any photo you take on your trip will be fantastic, no matter if your shots are a little blurry or a bit bright, because they'll all have stories to tell—that is the fundamental feature of an interesting photo. A photo that evokes emotion trumps any precisely shot photo of something meaningless.

Go traveling, soak up all that culture like a sponge, and fuel that fire for creativity by filling your head with all these stupendous, new sights. Don't overthink the photo-taking process, and immerse yourself in the extraordinary.

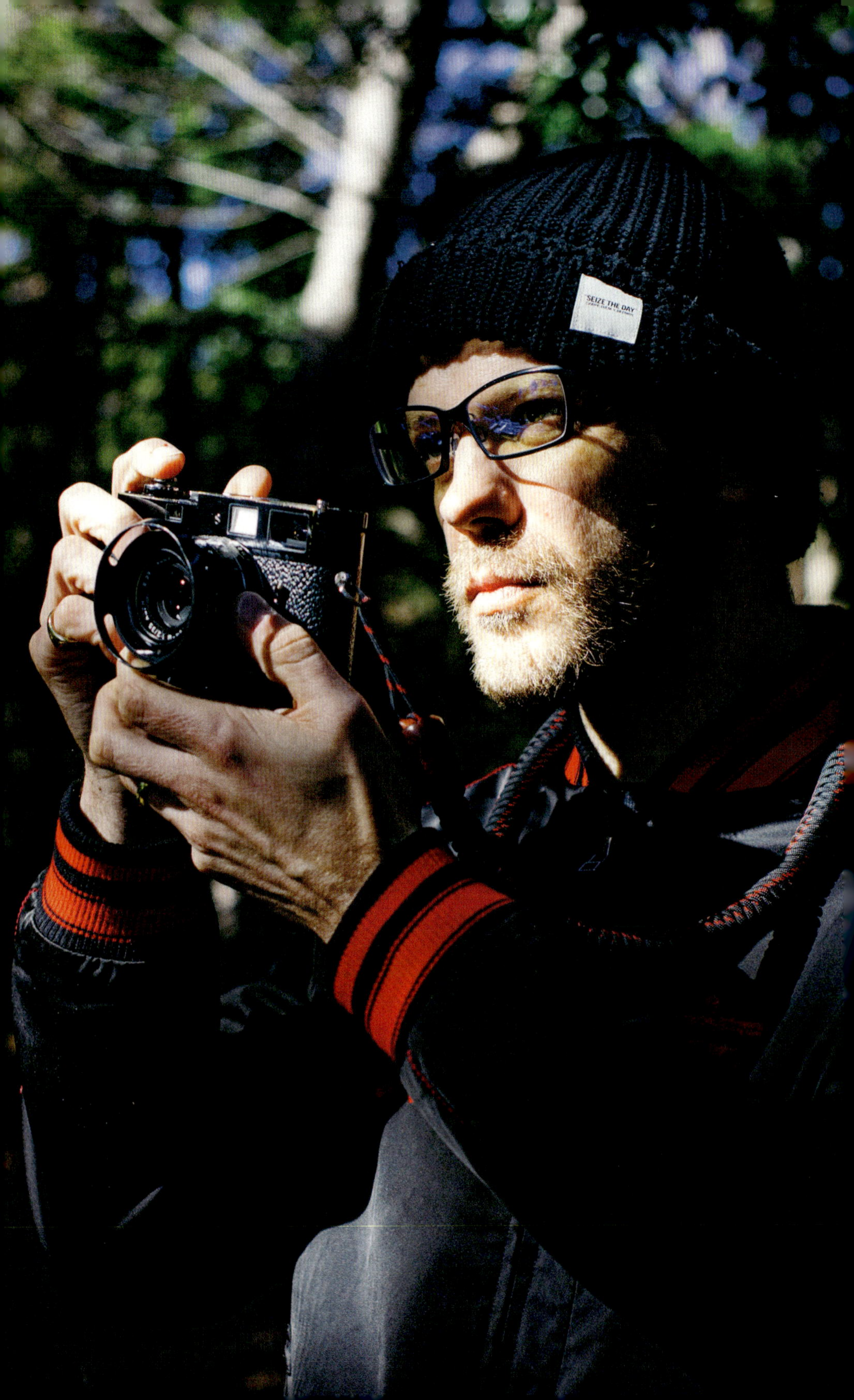
"SEIZE THE DAY"

#95

FOLLOW A FILM MAVEN

When I started learning photography, the internet was mainly emails and porn. These days it's still emails and porn, but it is also awash with a wealth of useful information that will help you to take your enthusiasm for film to a greater level of enthusiasm.

One thing you'll find is that most of the reviewers, bloggers, and retailers of all things film tend to be quite a friendly bunch. You know, actual, normal people but with a crapload of knowledge about film photography.

There's lots more that can be learnt that will turn your curiosity of film photography into a fully-fledged obsession: there's all the different kinds of wonderful film stock to explore; knowing how to develop your own film; and learning about all the different film cameras ever made. All that info is out there, it's free, and it's all written by people who really know their shiz.

Some of these film mavens are people I met through the internet (not online dating) a long time ago, like Bellamy Hunt, aka Japan Camera Hunter, who has developed his passion into a one-stop-shop/blog for everything you need for your film fun. Check out his blog, watch the gratuitous camera porn on his YouTube channel, and spunk your cash on some of the cleanest film cameras you'll find on the web in his store.

I think I have this weird gravitational pull toward stores, because I often hang out at a shop by the name of Aperture, in London, for no good reason (at least from their perspective) other than to talk about film, film cameras, and ogle over their shiny toys on display. They also repair cameras and develop film, which is handy, given that you won't always be able to easily find a place that can repair film cameras.

Although film photography is alive and well and truly thriving, it is still a bit of a niche when compared to the gargantuan digital-photography market. A lot of the experts in film photography are in this for the long run, have been doing it before digital took the reins, and are doing it because it's what they love. Following a film maven, and getting to know your local film-camera store, is one of the simplest things that you could do to enrich your knowledge of film photography, but also to support them in supporting the film-photography community and keeping film a permanent fixture in the photography landscape.

Check out the resources section in the back for a list of useful film-photography folk to know.

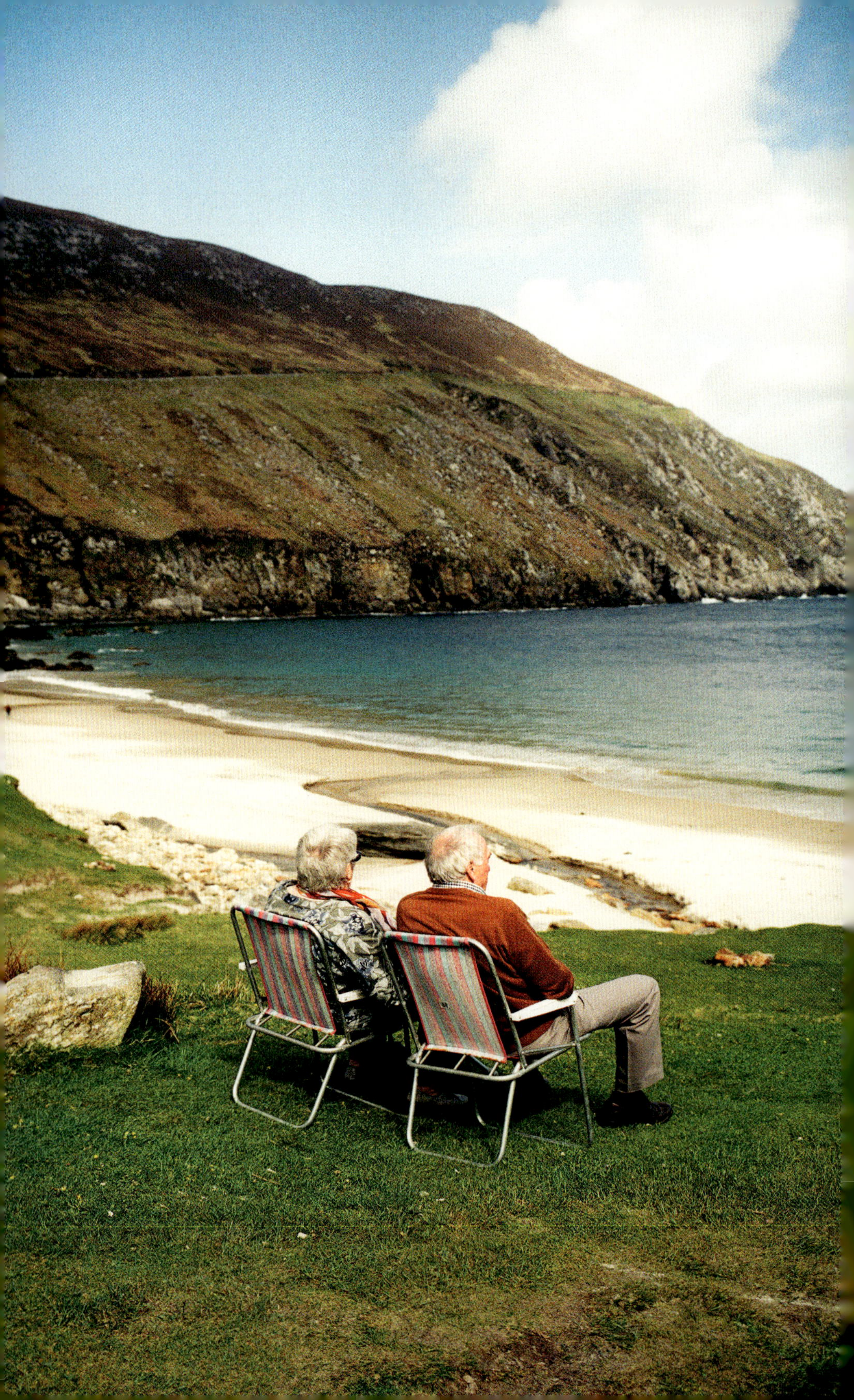

#96
TWO'S COMPANY: CREATING IMAGES TOGETHER

Photography is a lonely hobby: the photo-taking process happens by yourself; it's up to you to develop your own style; you have to be critical about your own photos; and the closest relationship you'll have with anything, when you're out taking photos, is with your camera. Although I have to admit that being able to get some alone time is one of the reasons why I love photography, there are times when it's better to create with the company of a friend.

Comprehending Together

Learning photography can be a steep learning curve—one that you will have to ascend by yourself. Going out with a photo buddy will help that learning process along because you can share experiences. If they're more experienced, you can ask them nicely for some advice; if they're at the same level as you, then you can figure things out and learn together.

Swapping Ideas

Usually, when you're out shooting, all the creative energy has to come from within. When you're with a photo buddy, taking shots of exactly the same subject and scene, it's nice to be able to see how another photographer interprets the scene. Do they see something in the subject that you didn't? How are they composing it? You will become more critical about your own composition when you see someone else trying something different than when you're on your own, with just your own compositional ideas.

Try Their Gear

Some people like taking photos in groups, mainly so they can check out another photographer's kit. That's cool if the whole group is into that, but I'm not really one for some uninvited handling of the (photo) junk in my trunk.

Share Results

Once you've both got your developed film back, you should meet up and take a look at your photos together. Looking at how the photos turned out will give you an idea of how to improve, if you can pick up on something your friend did, and you can share some opinions on each other's images.

Less Self-Conscious

Taking your first photos isn't always the straightforward task you'd expect it to be; it certainly wasn't plain sailing for me. The first few times I tried to take photos in a place where there were other humans around, I couldn't help but be overly self-conscious about being the only photo-taking geek around. Having that self-awareness could be hugely problematic if you want to take up street photography or portraiture—basically any kind of photography that involves standing in front of other human beings. Being in the company of a fellow photo-taking geek friend, and taking photos together, is guaranteed to give you a lot more confidence to start taking photos in public places.

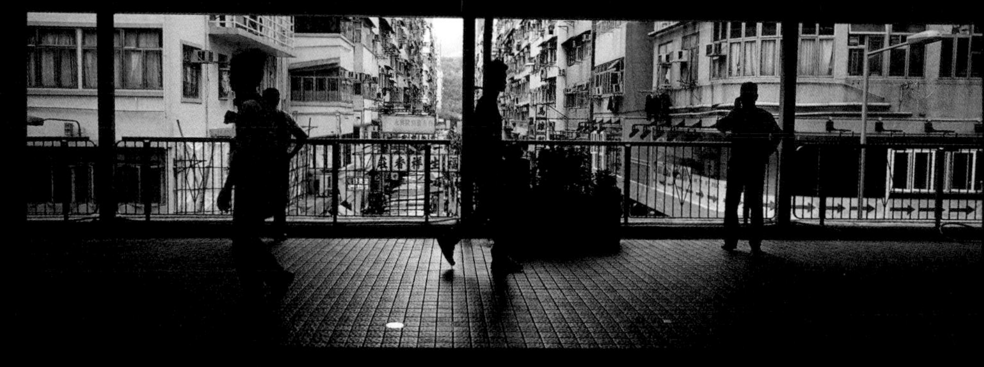

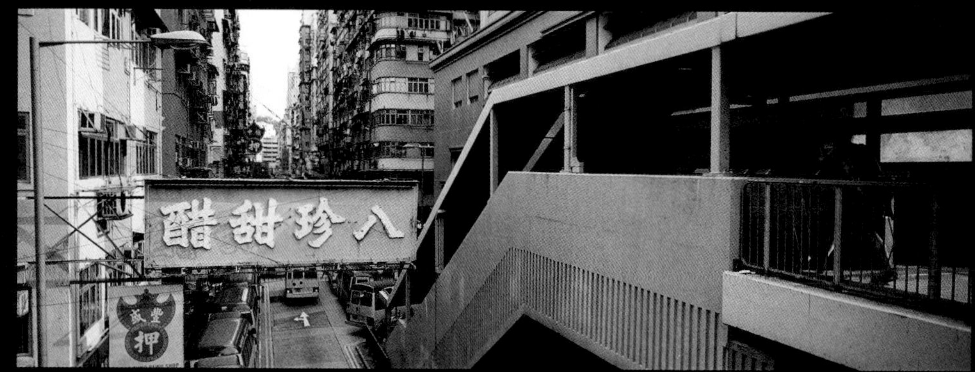
八珍甜醋
押

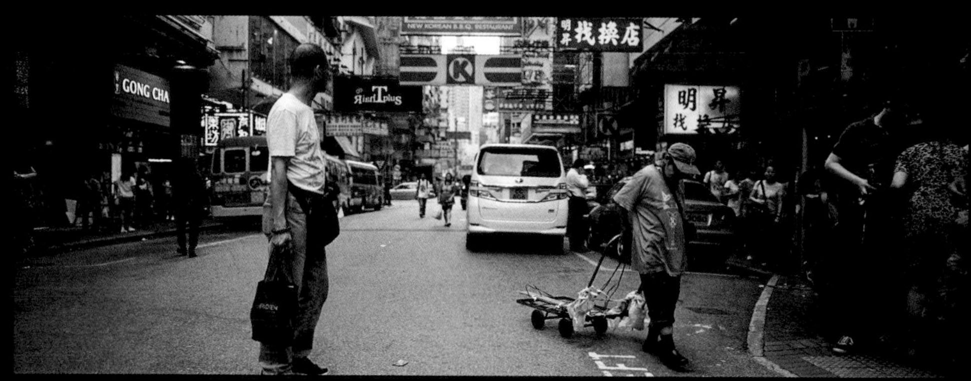
GONG CHA
找換店

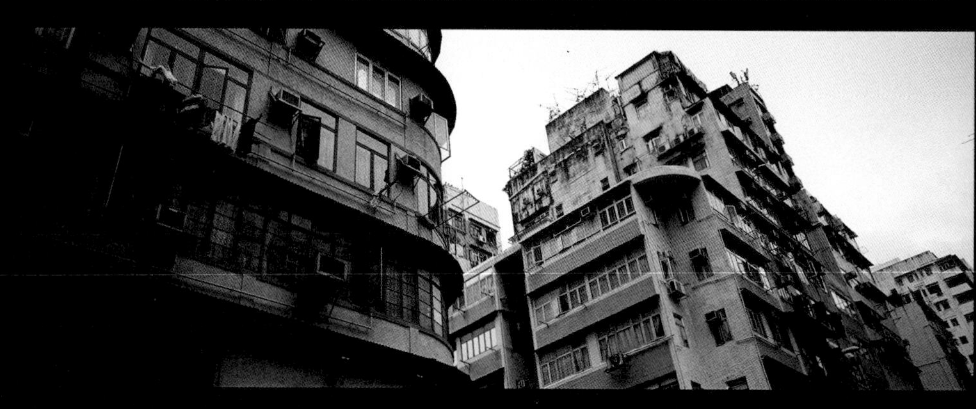

#97
TAKE PHOTOS DAILY

This could be the best thing you'll ever do ... for your photography, anyway. Taking a film photo a day sounds like a massive challenge, but chances are, you probably take at least one photo every day with your phone already. If you want to improve your photography fast, committing to taking one photo per day for the entire year is a surefire way of putting a firecracker up the backside of your photography.

That's just 365 images and ten rolls of film (£120/$120 worth of film if you're wondering). The numbers may sound a bit scary but, look, don't feel like you need to make every shot an Ansel. Just take a photo of something interesting that you've seen or done in your regular, daily activities. Although a day stuck behind a desk doesn't sound particularly inspiring, and most definitely not the ideal place to suddenly whip out a camera to start snapping away, there's still the journey to and from work, your lunch break, and the rest of the day to play with. The photo-taking will not only make you find interesting things to photograph, but will also make you seek interesting things to do; and that will inevitably make your photos much more interesting, too.

If you're happy to own two cameras (I'm happy to own more), have one camera for the serious photography, and then a compact for the daily snapshots. And I really do mean snapshots—don't overthink it. See more, be instinctive, and forget about the shot you just took. Keep notes of what frame was taken on what day, and anything else that you want to get off your chest; and then you can order all the photos you take chronologically.

It's sort of like Instagram, but done old-school style on a film camera, and with no quick way of uploading (so not like Instagram at all then). But don't feel like you need to upload your film photos to Instagram on a daily basis because that would drive you nuts. In fact, there is no need to show your photos to the people of the internet at all, because once you know your photos are going to be seen by someone else, that will start to influence the way you think about taking photos. The purpose of taking these photos is not to boost your follower count but to fuel your enthusiasm for film photography and develop your style.

If it gets too much, skip a day (nobody's watching), but once you've finished at the end of the year, and look back at all these tiny, little, physical moments caught on film, it is guaranteed to be one of the greatest gifts you can give yourself.

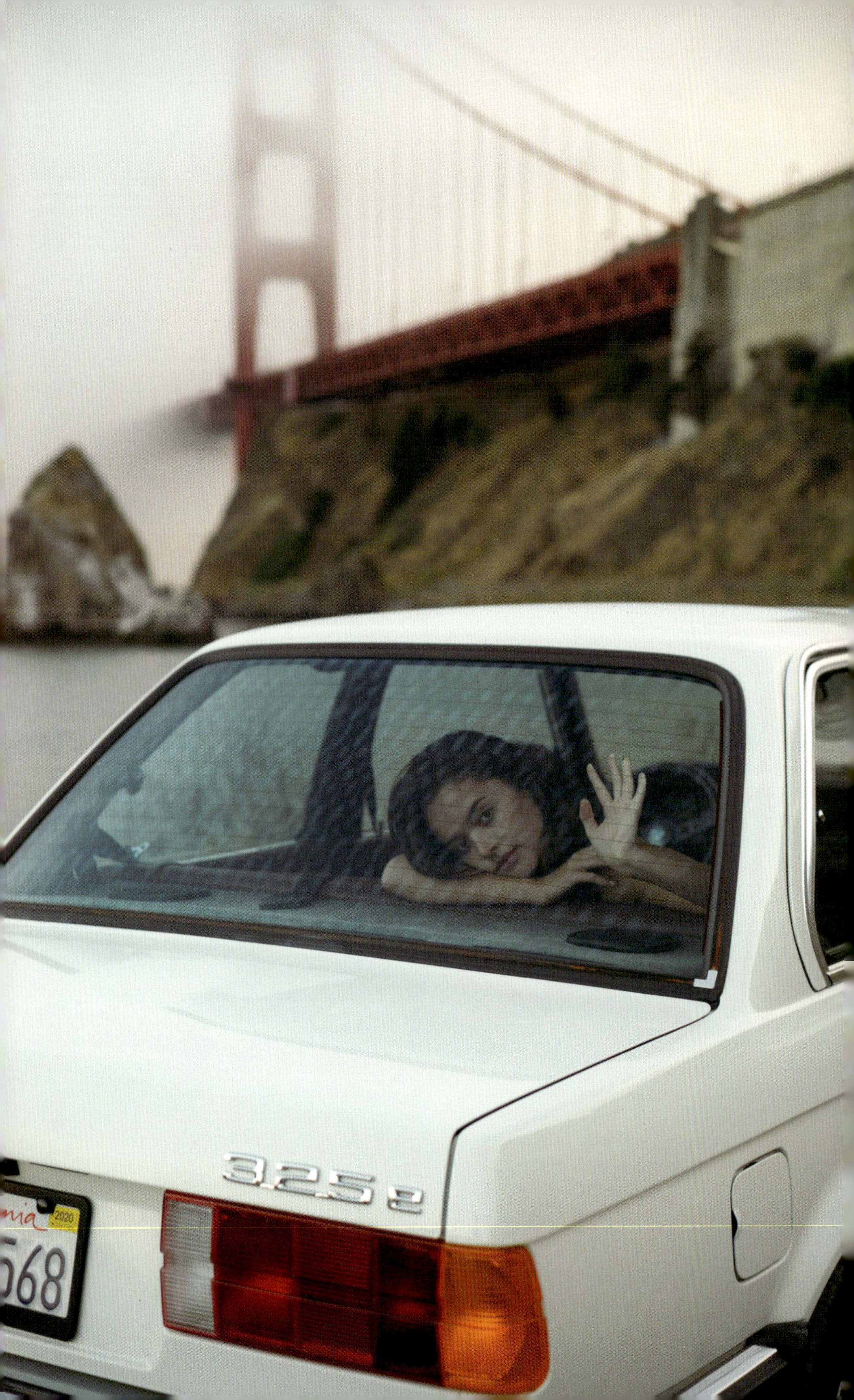
325e
2020
568

#98
LOOK BACK AT ALL YOUR WORK

Life can only be understood backwards; but it must be lived forwards.

—Soren Kierkegaard

One reason for keeping all your photos archived nicely and neatly is so that you can flick back through the archives and check out how your photography has progressed.

Sometimes I sift through my old photos to have a little spring clean. In my head, I've got Marie Kondo's voice prompting me (subtitled of course) whether the photos I have in front of me spark joy or not. If there's barely a fizz, I'll take all the offending photos out and dump them. For sure, the decluttering feels good, but even better is the feeling that progress has been made. There will be some photos that you will look back on and make you wonder, "How did I think this was a good shot?" That's the light-bulb moment when you realise that you've refined your style, improved your skills, and become an all-around better photographer.

Looking back gives you a better understanding of how your style has developed, and will make you realise what you were missing before; but it will also help you to figure out where you should be heading. It is a continuous body of work, your personal journey in photography, and looking back at where it all started will make you realise how far you've come. That is the greatest motivation to keep you going and to continue taking better photos than your last.

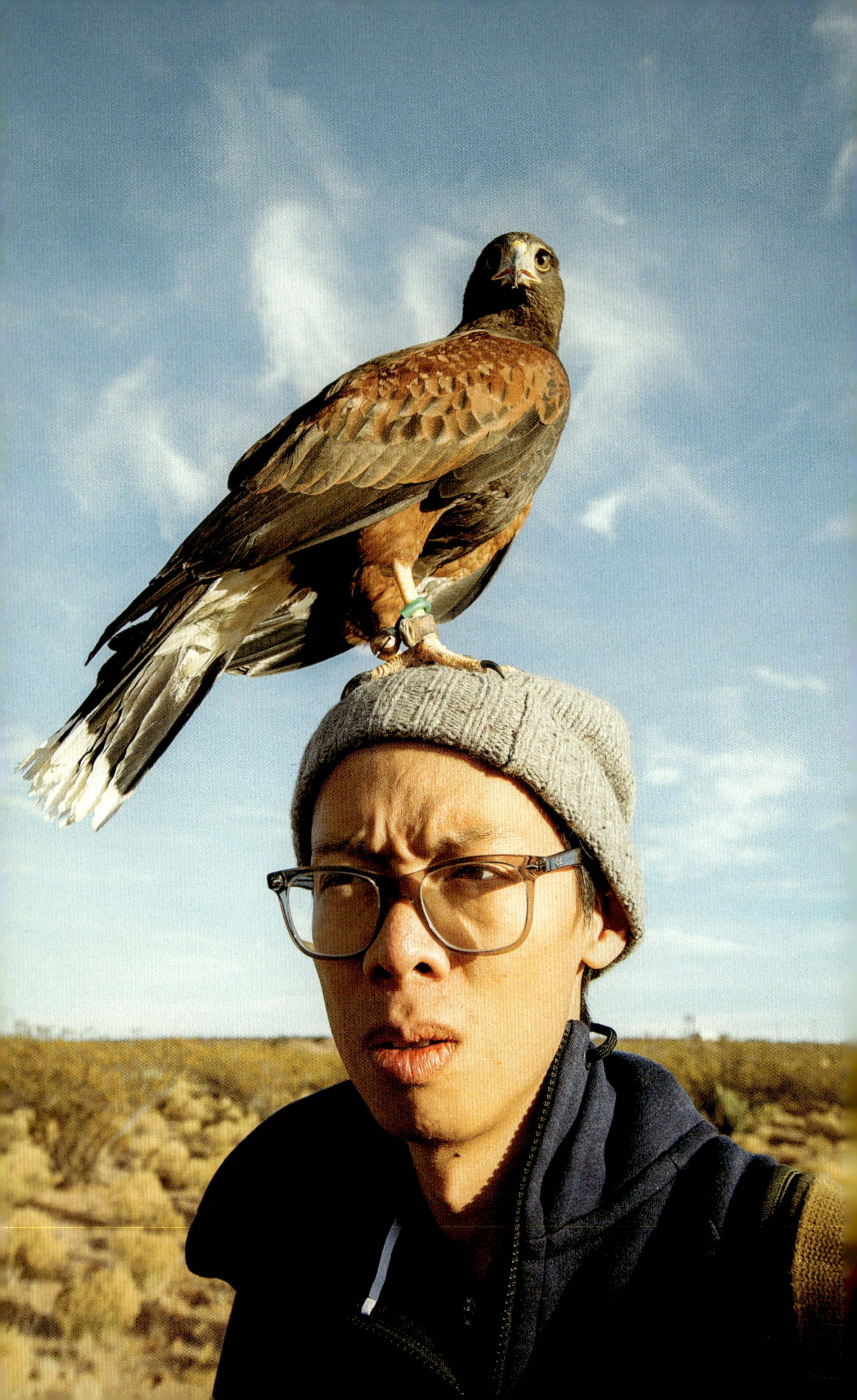

#99 WHAT YOU NEED TO MAKE A FANTASTIC PHOTO

We arrive at the penultimate point in this book, which makes this as good a time as any to neatly summarise what the key elements to making a fantastic photo are.

It goes without saying that a camera and lens are a requisite, although what you choose to use is not of importance. Paying more for a cooler camera and lens might produce a better image quality, but there is no correlation between the cost of equipment and the quality of the content of your image. What you really need to make fantastic photos has nothing to do with what's on your camera.

Love What You Shoot

When you're passionate about what you photograph, it will show in your photos. Loving what you shoot is the driving force to taking better images. If you have that desire to understand your subjects on a deeper level, you will photograph with feeling—the littlest of details can provoke an emotional response, making you react by taking a photo.

We look at a photo with our eyes but build meaning with our minds. The power of a great photo is that the photographer, through the use of subject matters and visual elements, is conveying their thoughts and feelings, and making that understood to the viewer through clever use of composition and good timing. A photo shot without feeling is just a literal representation of those visual elements—all surface but no feeling.

To me, photography is an art of observation. It's about finding something interesting in an ordinary place. ... I've found it has little to do with the things you see and everything to do with the way you see them.

—Elliott Erwitt

Vision

A photo is about what the photographer sees, so it is important to make the vision that you wish to be shown in your photos uniquely yours. It's fine to be influenced and inspired by stunning images and great photographers, but when you're out in the field, there's nothing that you can rely on other than your own vision to decide how to compose a shot.

Learning about composition techniques is cool, but keep those thoughts about rules and conventions of composition out of your mind and follow what your heart tells you to do. Develop your own style and let that dictate how you take photos.

Determination

To be a good photographer, you can't be passive; you need to actively hunt for amazing photo opportunities. Sometimes it's a matter of waiting for that elusive shot; sometimes it's about exploring and seeking stunning shots.

It is that steely determination that will keep you motivated when the results aren't quite as expected, to keep going to improve and understand what you can do to make them better.

Make sure you have all three of these sorted, and you'll be on your way to making fantastic film photos in no time.

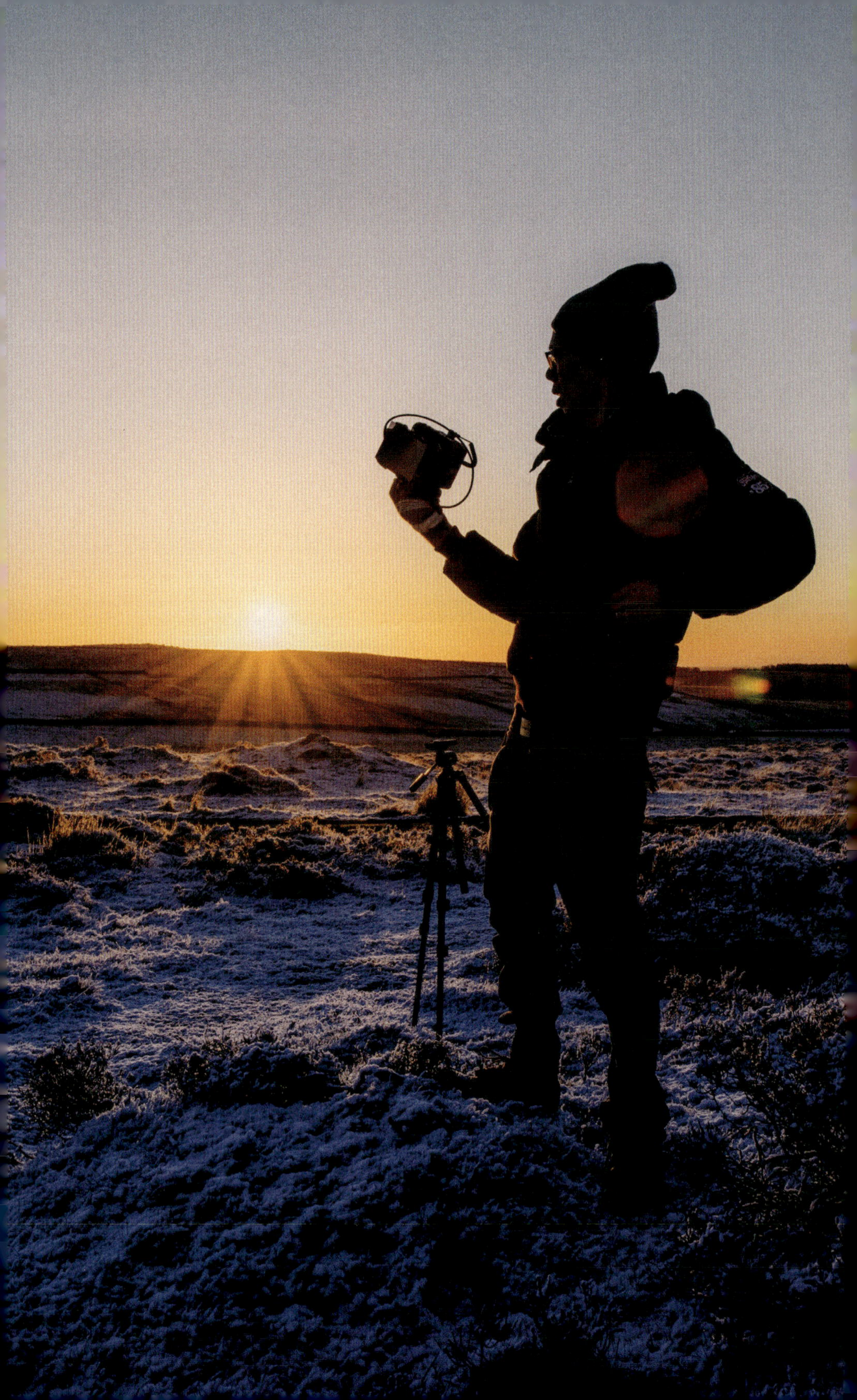

#100
STOP READING; START SHOOTING!

Learning photography can feel like a lengthy process, made more laborious by the apparent need to be fluent in the technical language of photography and knowing how to twiddle a few knobs and dials on your camera just to take a simple photo.

Photography doesn't need to be any more complex than seeing and shooting. It is a creative art that should not be bound by guidelines or rules; the very thing that makes a great photo great is you.

A book about learning photography can guide you and give you useful tips, but it can never teach you how to take a photo. That's why it's important to get out there to start shooting, and enjoy the process.

Love what you shoot; shoot what you love.

Thank you so much for reading!

Kai
YouTube: Kai W
Instagram: @kaimanwong

COOL RESOURCES

ASIA

Camera Film Photo
Hong Kong SAR, China
camerafilmphoto.com
@camerafilmphoto

Japan Camera Hunter
Japan
japancamerahunter.com
@japancamerahunter

Film Camera Tokyo
Japan
filmcameratokyo.com
@filmcameratokyo

EUROPE

Mori Film Lab
Belgium
morifilmlab.com
@morifilmlab

Camera Makers
Finland
cameramakers.com
@cameramakers

The Camera Rescue Project
Finland
camerarescue.org
@camerarescue

Kamera Store
Finland
kamerastore.com
@kamerastorecom

Nation Photo
France
nationphoto.com
@nationphoto

Mein Film Lab
Germany
meinfilmlab.de
@meinfilmlab

Safelight Berlin
Germany
safelightberlin.com
@safelightberlin

Vintage Dream Cameras
Portugal
vintagedreamcameras.store
@vintagedreamcameras

Foqus Store
Russia
linktr.ee/FOQUSSTORE
@foqusstore

AFilmCosmos Post Contemporary
Spain
afilmcosmos.com
@afilmcosmos

Boh Kay
Spain
mybohkay.com
@bohkayfilmproject

Carmencita Film Lab
Spain
carmencitafilmlab.com
@carmencitafilmlab

Film Cameras.org
Spain
filmcameras.org
@filmcameras_org

Fotografiska Museum Stockholm
Sweden
fotografiska.com
@fotografiska

Fotohaus
Switzerland
fotohaus.ch
@fotohaus_basel

305ibes
England
matthewtou.com
@305ibes

Analogue Films
England
analoguefilms.co.uk
@analoguefilmsltd

Cameras London
England
cameraslondon.com
@cameraslondon

Camera Museum UK
England
cameramuseum.uk
@cameramuseumuk

The Classic Camera
England
theclassiccamera.com
@theclassiccamera

Mr. Cad Photographic
England
mrcad.co.uk
@mrcaduk

PPP Camera
England
pppcameras.co.uk
@pppcameras

NORTH AMERICA

Reveni Labs
Canada
reveni-labs.com
@revenilabs

The Film Hound
Alabama
thefilmhound.com
@thefilmhound

The Darkroom
California
thedarkroom.com
@thedarkroomlab

film_n_cameras
California
@film_n_cameras

Film Objektiv
California
filmobjektiv.org
@filmobjektiv

Film Wholesale
California
filmwholesale.com
@filmwholesale

Glass Key Photo
California
glasskeyphoto.com
@glasskeyphoto

The Icon
California
iconla.com
@iconla

Negative Supply
California
negative.supply
@negative.supply

Photoworks San Francisco
California
photoworkssf.com
@photoworkssf

Richard Photo Lab
California
richardphotolab.com
@richardphotolab

Underdog Film Lab
California
underdogfilmlab.com
@underdogfilmlab

Englewood Camera
Colorado
englewoodcamera.com
@englewoodcamera

Treehouse Analog Selects
Hawaii
treehouse-shop.com
@treehousehawaii

Central Camera Company
Illinois
centralcamera.com
@centralcameraco

dr5
Iowa
dr5.us
@dr5chrome

Northeast Photographic
Maine
northeastphotographic.com
@northeastphotographic

The Camera Shop
Minnesota
thecamerashop.com

Old School Photo Lab
New Hampshire
oldschoolphotolab.com
@oldschoollab

Film Photography Project Store
New Jersey
filmphotographystore.com
@filmphotographyproject

Brooklyn Film Camera
New York
brooklynfilmcamera.com
@brooklynfilmcamera

Photodom
New York
photodom.nyc
@photodom.nyc

Blue Moon Camera & Machine
Oregon
bluemooncamera.com
@bluemooncamera

Camera Center of York
Pennsylvania
cameracenterofyork.com
@retro_photo_york

Indie Photo Lab
Pennsylvania
indiephotolab.com
@indiephotolab

Boutique Photo Lab
Tennessee
boutiquefilmlab.com
@boutiquefilmlab

Memphis Film Lab
Tennessee
memphisfilmlab.org
@memphis.film.lab

Third Man Photo Studio
Tennessee
thirdmanphotostudio.com
@thirdmanphotostudio

The Find Lab
Utah
thefindlab.com
@thefindlab

Shot on Film Store
Washington
shotonfilmstore.com
@shotonfilmstore

Retrospekt
Wisconsin
retrospekt.com
@retrospekt_

CREDITS

Introduction
© Dan Chung
IG @wanderingchung

#1
© John Thatcher
IG @johnrandolphhh
john-thatcher.com

#2
© Molly Steele
IG @moristeele
molly-steele.com

#3
© Michael Melwani
IG @michaelmelwani
michaelmelwani.com

#4
© John Sypal
IG @tokyocamerastyle
tokyocamerastyle.com

#5
© Kai Wong

#6
© John Thatcher
IG @johnrandolphhh
john-thatcher.com

#7
© Dan Chung
IG @wanderingchung

#8
© Amber Maalouf
IG @mountainspirit
ambermaalouf.com

#9
© Brian Cho
IG @brian.s.cho
brianchophoto.com

#10
© Stephen Sheffield
IG @stephen_
sheffield_photography
stephensheffield.com

#11
© Nathan Oliveira

#12
© John Sypal
IG @tokyocamerastyle
tokyocamerastyle.com

#13
© Christian Baba
IG @bussi_und_baba

#14
© Kai Wong

#15
© Ian Teraoka
IG @ianteraoka
ianteraoka.com

#16
© William Gilbert
IG @williamejgilbert
williamejgilbert.com

#17
© Taylor Thompson
IG @strawberry_blond_

#18
© John Sypal
IG @tokyocamerastyle
tokyocamerastyle.com

#19
© Emanuele Valenti
IG @immanu__el

#20
© Dmitry Gorochovsky
IG @dm_goro

#21
© Paul John Bayfield
IG @pauljohnbayfield

#22
© John Sypal
IG @tokyocamerastyle
tokyocamerastyle.com

#23
© Fabien Dendievel
IG @fabien_dendievel
fabiendendievel.com

#24
© Frédéric Haye Baptiste
IG @hb_fred

#25
© Laura Cogan
IG @hassywonderland

#26
© John Thatcher
IG @johnrandolphhh
john-thatcher.com

#27
© Thanapol T.
IG @thanapolt

#28
© Fabien Dendievel
IG @fabien_dendievel
fabiendendievel.com

#29
© Steven Lavery
IG @filmbysteven

#30
© Clayton Barkman
IG @claytonbarkman

#31
© James Simpson
IG @jamessimpsonphoto
jamessimpsonphoto.com

#32
© Kai Wong

#33
© Andrew Royal
IG @groovejunky
groovejunky.me

#34
© Paul John Bayfield
IG @pauljohnbayfield

#35
© Teresa McCullough
IG @tresmack
tresmack.com

#36
© Faisal Shah
IG @faisaltreshah
faisaltreshah.com

#37
© Kai Wong

#38
© Enrique Tarazona Gurrea
IG @qtarazona
enriquetarazona.com

#39
© Ben Andrewes
IG @bandrewes
benandrewes.com

#40
© Craig Whitehead
IG @sixstreetunder
sixstreetunder.com

#41
© Thibault d'Auriol
IG @tibs_eyes
thibaultdauriol.com

#42
© Joe Lamberti
IG @joe_lamb
joelamberti.com

#43
© Meg Messina
IG @megmessina
megmessina.com

#44
© Michael Weitzman
IG @mwphotographi-carts
michaelweitzman.net

#45:
© Kai Wong

#46
© Simon Gustavsson
IG @simon__gustavsson
simongustavsson.com

#47
© Sabath M. Trejo
IG @dr._tre_

#48
© Ahmed Al Shorouqi
IG @shorouqi

#49
© Colette der Kinderen
IG @coletteonfilm
coletteonfilm.com

#50
© Steven Meyer-Rassow
IG @smrphotoart
smrphotoart.com

#51
© David Teran
IG @hasselblad_ballet
davidteran.com

#52
© Kai Wong

#53
© Danny Rowton
IG @dannyrowton

#54
© Kai Wong

#55
© Kai Wong

#56
© Kamiel Scholten
IG @_crooked_teeth
kamielscholten.com

#57
© Ching Lok Cheung
IG @lokcheung
lok-cheung.com

#58
© Kai Wong

#59
© Paul John Bayfield
IG @pauljohnbayfield

#60
© Steven Lavery
IG @filmbysteven

#61
© Riley Russill
IG @rileyrussill
rileyrussill.com

#62
© Kai Wong

#63
© Paco Poyato
IG @pacopoyato
pacopoyato.com

#64
© Kai Wong

#65
© Iggy Smalls
IG @norsksalami
iggysmalls.com

#66
© Paul John Bayfield
IG @pauljohnbayfield

#67
© Kai Wong

#68:
© Kai Wong

#69
© Sarah Merker
IG @shesgotthesauce
flickr.com/sarbnb

#70
© Paco Poyato
IG @pacopoyato
pacopoyato.com

#71
© Stephen Sheffield
IG @stephen_
sheffield_photography
stephensheffield.com

#72
© Jon Pham
IG @jonpham
jonphamdp.com

#73
© Tristan Hollingsworth
IG @dreamgaia
tristanhollingsworth.com

#74
© Tiago Almança
IG @tiagoalmanca

#75
© Paul John Bayfield
IG @pauljohnbayfield

#76
© Jason Corning
IG @jcornn
jasoncorning.com

#77
© Craig Whitehead
IG @sixstreetunder
sixstreetunder.com

#78
© Carl Fieler
flickr.com/carlfieler

#79
© Tristan Hollingsworth
IG @dreamgaia
tristanhollingsworth.com

#80
© Sam Johnson
IG @samjsn
samjsn.com

#81
© Dan Chung
IG @wanderingchung

#82
© Kai Wong

#83
© Alex Colombino
IG @alexcolombino
alexcolombino.com

#84
© Wade Montpellier
IG @just.wadeing
wademontpellier.com

#85
© Kai Wong

#86
© Tim McCarthy
IG @timmccarthyphoto

#87
© Carl Fieler
flickr.com/carlfieler

#88
© Timothy Ko
IG @timothyko
timothykoportfolio.com

#89
© John Thatcher
IG @johnrandolphhh
john-thatcher.com

#90
© Kai Wong

#91
© Iggy Smalls
IG @norsksalami
iggysmalls.com

#92
© Alex Colombino
IG @alexcolombino
alexcolombino.com

#93
© Victoria Pourian
IG @filmbytory

#94
© Kai Wong

#95
© Michael Nguyen
IG @thericerocket26
michaelnguyenphoto.com

#96
© Sarah Pannell
IG @sarahpannell
sarahpannell.com

#97
© Kai Wong

#98
© John Thatcher
IG @johnrandolphhh
john-thatcher.com

#99
© Paul John Bayfield
IG @pauljohnbayfield

#100
© Paul John Bayfield
IG @pauljohnbayfield

OLD SCHOOL PHOTOGRAPHY

100 Things You Must Know to Take Fantastic Film Photos

BY KAI WONG

Edited by Steve Crist

Art Direction: Gloria Fowler
Creative Advisor: Lok Cheung
Design: Carrie Worthen and Ben Pope, Thirdthing
Production: Kayleigh Jankowski
Photo and Rights Coordinator: Alex Colombino
Copy Editor: Sara DeGonia
Illustration: Adam Rufino

Acknowledgements

I would like to give a special thanks to Steve, for reaching out and making this book happen. Big shout-out to Miles, too, for putting in a good word for me.

Thank you to Sara and Gloria for turning a load of text into a slick-looking book.

To my brother from another mother, Lok: thank you, not only for the support through the years of working together, but for this project, too.

Thank you to all the photographers who have contributed fabulous photos for this book, and a big high five to Alex for making all of that happen.

Dan, thank you for making me look alright in the photos of me in this book. And for being grumpier than me—you make me look cheerful.

Thank you to May, for the support and understanding. And doing the washing-up duties for the duration of making this book. Always grateful to my boys: Lucas, for reading my writing (he's four years old), and Nicholas, for keeping shit real with the nappy changes.

To my lovely big sis, Sophia: if you never bought me my first camera ... well, I would've bought my own anyway ... but I would've never felt as inspired to do something good with it, so thank you for that, and for all the love and support throughout the years.

Thanks to my Dad for supporting my career choice to make videos on the internet. Mum, wish you were still around to see this book.

To PJB: thank you for always having my back; for all the crazy photography-related antics and for making me look cool in photos, even when my pants were falling down—you should think about taking photos as a profession.

Last but not least, to everyone who chose to read this book: you're the ones that make this all worthwhile, so from the bottom of my heart—thank you. And for anyone who has followed my work over the years, without you, I wouldn't be here writing this, so—THANK YOU VERY MUCH!

Kai

ISBN: 978-1-7972-0944-9
Library of Congress Cataloging-in-Publication Data available.

Manufactured in China

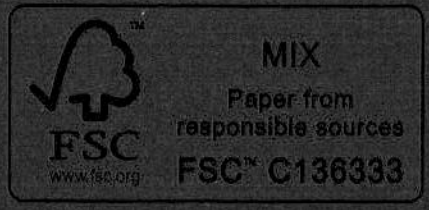

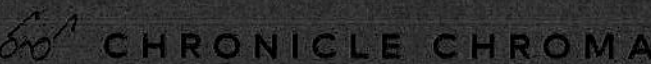

Chronicle Chroma is an imprint of Chronicle Books
Los Angeles, California

chroniclebooks.com/chroma